Praise for SUPERPREDATORS

"Peter Elikann is correct. Too many of us tend to drop-kick responsibility to political leaders more concerned with getting votes than protecting our future. The trouble with America's children is America's adults. *Superpredators* refutes the conventional wisdom by arguing that we can save thousands of children if we invest now in programs that help kids get the right start and prevent them from becoming criminals in the first place."

— From the Foreword by **Marc Klaas**, Children's and Victim's Advocate, Founder, KlaasKids Foundation, Sausalito, California

"*Superpredators* is a well-researched and compassionate book; it shows the way out of the morass of political rhetoric and fear-mongering that has dominated the juvenile justice policy debate. Essential reading for all communities who are genuinely interested in safer lives for our children."

— **Barry Krisberg,** President, National Council on Crime and Delinquency, San Francisco, California

"Peter Elikann has pulled together a vast amount of information into a provocative book that makes a powerful argument for a sensible approach to juvenile justice. He has done a tremendous job of debunking the myth that all, or even most, of the kids who churn through America's juvenile justice system are irredeemable superpredators. His ideas warrant consideration by serious policymakers and reformers."

— **Vincent Schiraldi,** Director, Justice Policy Institute, Washington, D.C.

"*Superpredators* reveals a shocking escalation of juvenile crime across the United States, including violent felonies. Elikann provides rare insights into our justice system—an education (so to speak) in the juvenile crime wave and the system's attempts to treat and punish."

— **Nancy Grace,** Court TV Network Anchor, Former Felony Prosecutor

"Law enforcement leaders today are saying that we could dramatically reduce crime by investing more in kids—from early childhood education, to after-school programs, to helping troubled kids get back on track. Elikann's book shows that these are indeed our most powerful weapons against crime, and that we pay a heavy price in money and lives when government abdicates its responsibility to make these key public safety investments."

— **Gil Kerlikowske,** Past President of the Police Executive Research Forum and Police Commissioner of Buffalo, New York

"Instead of life, liberty, and the pursuit of happiness, too many children face death, incarceration, and despair. *Superpredators* examines the causes of juvenile crime, the problem with harsh punishments that treat children as adults, and the benefits of providing young people with mentors and role models. Elikann's 15 solutions to eradicate youth crime should be memorized by pediatricians, politicians, media professionals, and everyone else who works with children."

— **Peggy Charren,** Founder, Action for Children's Television

SUPERPREDATORS
The Demonization of Our Children by the Law

SUPERPREDATORS
The Demonization of Our Children by the Law

Peter Elikann

Foreword by
Marc Klaas
Children's and Victim's Advocate
Founder, KlaasKids Foundation
Sausalito, California

PERSEUS BOOKS
Reading, Massachusetts

JAN 1 9 2000

Library of Congress Cataloging-in-Publication Data

Elikann, Peter T.
    Superpredators : the demonization of our children by the law /
Peter Elikann.
        p.   cm.
    Includes bibliographical references and index.
    ISBN 0-306-46007-6
    1. Juvenile corrections--United States. 2. Juvenile delinquency-
-United States--Prevention. 3. Problem youth--Services for--United
States. 4. Problem families--Services for--United States.
I. Title.
HV9104.E438   1999
364.36'0973--dc21   99-12713
                                                                      CIP

ISBN 0-306-46007-6

© 1999 Peter Elikann

Perseus Books is a member of the Perseus Books Group.

10 9 8 7 6 5 4 3

A C.I.P. record for this book is available from the Library of Congress

Printed in the United States of America

To my parents,
Gerald and Leonore Reiser Elikann

"Character consists of what you do on the third and fourth tries."
—James A. Michener

Contents

Foreword, by Marc Klaas ix

Preface xi

Chapter 1 • Introduction and Overview: Children as
the Enemy 1

Chapter 2 • A Coming Youth Crime Wave by a Nation
of Sociopaths 21
   Hearts Shot Full of Novocaine? 22
   Not Always Fitting the Stereotyped Profile 28
   No Longer Taken Lightly 35
   A War on Children 40
   Disintegrating Families, Growing Poverty and the Media 44
   No Communities or Role Models 60
   Blaming the Children 66
   The Dirty Little Secret of Youth Crime 69
   No Youth Crime Wave of Sociopaths 75

Chapter 3 • The Everydayness of Firearms 79
   Guns as a Way of Life 80
   Death as a Fun Game 90
   Locking Up Guns 92
   Gun Suicides 94
   You Shoot Who You Know 96
   Gangs and Guns 97
   The Effectiveness of Gun Crime Prevention 102

Chapter 4 • Adult Trials and Prisons for Juveniles 107
  Legislation by Anecdote 108
  Transfers to Adult Courts and Prisons 110
  Minorities Lead the Way 114
  Females: More Crime, Still Less Jail 116
  Nonviolent Offenders Jailed Most 120
  Abandoning the Old Way 122
  Juveniles in Adult Prisons Endanger the Public 125
  The Myth of Deterrence 130
  Juvenile Courts Are Tougher 134
  Juvenile Competency 135
  Juvenile Records 142
  Curfews 145
  Abuse of Children in Prison 148
  The Death Penalty for Children 151
  Fewer Adult Prisons, Fewer Crimes 154

Chapter 5 • Shame: The Little-Known Secret Of Crime 161
  There Are No Motiveless Crimes 161
  The Significance of Being "Dissed" 164
  Young, Urban, Violent "Suckers" 166
  The American Tradition of the "Honor Culture" 168
  Mainstream America's Pervasive Need for Respect 172
  Shame: The Deadliest of All Emotions 176
  Early Abuse and the Fear of the Death of One's Soul 178
  The Misguided Popularity of Shaming Sentences 179
  The Positive Aspects of Pride and Conscience 180

Chapter 6 • The Solution: Intervention, Families,
Role Models, the Media and Rehabilitation 183
  Resilient Kids 185
  How Youth Crime Dived in One City 189
  Community Policing and Faith-Based Programs 193
  Other Forms of Intervention 197

Chapter 7 • Conclusion: A 15-Point Plan 203

Notes 213

Index 237

Foreword

Basic American doctrine states that every generation gives the succeeding generation a better world than that which was given to them. That is, until now. Increasingly, children are being born in poverty, living in fractured families, coming home to empty houses after school, targeted by budget cuts, and are being surrounded by images of mayhem and destruction, gun and drug proliferation, and defined as second-class citizens. That we ostracize children for feeling disenfranchised is more a commentary on our refusal to accept responsibility for this sad state of affairs than on their inability to conform.

The trouble with America's children is America's adults. We are a self-indulgent society obsessed with fantasies of violence. We think nothing of waiting in line for the latest Tinseltown pyrotechnic extravaganza, or watching as television serves up a constant diet of unedited violence in both entertainment and news programs. The increasingly popular Internet makes readily available serial killer manifestos and recipes for explosive devices. Two hundred million guns adorn our walls, hide in our cupboards, and linger in personal armories as we await an Armageddon of our own creation. Misguided children have internalized the message that violence is a solution to problems of stress, anger and alienation.

The response to the current climate surrounding violent juvenile crime suggests that we are raising a generation unable to live within the moral and legal parameters of social acceptance. Politicians, radio talk show hosts and conservative pundits emphatically state that the best way to combat the violent behavior of troubled youth is through increasingly draconian measures.

There are many battles to be fought in the war to make America safe for all children. However, America's current focus on stronger sentencing is a simple solution to a much more complex problem. We are kidding ourselves if we think we can declare victory by treating youthful offenders like adults. These solutions only address a small percentage of the current generation of young criminals, and if other families are to be spared the pain that mine has endured, policymakers need to look beyond the death penalty or prison sentences. Instead, they must focus on the critical steps our communities and nation can take to protect all children. This is the battlefront that will protect future generations from an epidemic of crime.

Superpredators: The Demonization of Our Children by the Law refutes the conventional wisdom by arguing that we can save thousands of children if we invest now in programs that help kids get the right start and prevent them from becoming criminals in the first place. The plain truth is that we ignore the most powerful weapons we have against crime. Programs like Head Start, parenting education, mentoring, job training and investments in good schools and afterschool programs can dramatically reduce crime by helping kids become productive citizens instead of brutal criminals.

We do need to get dangerous criminals off the street and behind bars. However, if we do not invest in programs that help children become caring citizens instead of violent criminals, we will all pay an unfathomable cost in broken lives and broken hearts.

We will win the war on crime when we are ready to invest our time, energy and tax dollars in America's most vulnerable children, so that they never become America's most wanted adults. Suggesting that we can win the war against violent crime solely by building more prisons is like saying that we can win the war against cancer by building more cemeteries.

Peter Elikann is correct. Too many of us tend to drop-kick responsibility to political leaders more concerned with getting votes than protecting our future. These talking heads spout philosophies that deny reality. Unwilling to emulate the proactive proven solutions to youth violence, we are reassured that our children are beyond redemption, that they are a generation of superpredatory psychopaths. We must hold ourselves accountable for fostering an environment that nurtures the brooding dark side of humanity.

Marc Klaas
Children's and Victim's Advocate
Founder, KlaasKids Foundation

Preface

Childhood used to be its own built-in excuse. The line of reasoning was that, if a child was in trouble, go to the source, find out what made him or her that way and try to make changes in their lives. Children were capable of changing for the better, and it was seen as infinitely cheaper and safer to invest in and save the child. This, rather than pay for a lifetime of prison cells, detox programs, unemployment and losses due to things like theft and the hospital bills of others.

Today, one can glean a different, not-too-subtle undercurrent beginning to surface in American culture. More often, many people, particularly politicians, are fed up with that sort of pampering of children who get into trouble. Concerned about the rising rate of juvenile crime that took place between the mid-1980s and mid-1990s, when murders by juveniles actually tripled, the new slogan is "adult time for adult crime." When we vilify them with names such as "superpredators," they become less human and more like animals. It's easier and more acceptable for us to beat up on monstrous animals than on kids.

So, despite the fact that the juvenile violent crime rate dropped significantly beginning in 1995, we're starting to try 12-year-olds in adult courts and give them life sentences to serve in adult prisons. We're one of six countries in the world—along with Iran, Nigeria, Pakistan, Saudi Arabia and Yemen —who have a death penalty for children. True, there are probably a few children who, by the age at which they commit a crime, have been so brutalized and neglected that they themselves have become violent, dangerous, psychopathic killers from whom society needs protection. But few children are born evil or predisposed to violence from organic brain damage or their parents' addictions. Rather than do nothing, wait until a tragedy or grievous crime occurs, and then say, "Ha! Gotcha! Now we'll spend millions to lock you up forever after the fact because you do, quite frankly, deserve it," wouldn't it make us safer and be a lot cheaper if we intervened in children's lives at an earlier age?

It would certainly provide much more solace to victims and their families. The threat alone of severe and harsh legal punishments of children has never served as a deterrent to children who commit their crimes on impulse without doing a grown-up-like weighing of the costs and benefits of committing a particular crime. Also, significantly, as I discovered during my research for this book, youths who are sent to serve their incarceration in adult prison rather than juvenile facilities for the same crimes, tend to endanger the public and get rearrested far more often, once released.

In an attempt to find out if anything could be done before a child gets into trouble, I wanted to examine how a child may come out of the womb pure and innocent and become a vicious killer. Are we raising a nation of sociopaths—unfeeling and remorseless—who will kill for a pair of sneakers or a little girl's bicycle or for nothing at all? Are we raising a generation where the Ten Commandments have come to be regarded, if at all, as the Ten Suggestions? Is there in this country, as noted criminologist James Wilson states, a growing "hopeless struggle of lonely souls against impulses they can neither understand nor control"?[1]

Are some kids different today from kids years ago, and if so, why? The answer, as this book will argue, is no. But there still are too many children in trouble due to a combination of factors including fewer intact families, increasing childhood poverty, pervasive guns and an increasing bombardment of graphic violence by the media.

Clearly, the disintegration of the American family is to blame for much of it, but from time to time don't we hear about kids from fine, loving homes who turn out extraordinarily violent? And why did the other members of earlier generations raised in poverty and, perhaps, in broken homes seem to have a better moral compass? Was it that if they didn't have an intact family, they at least had an intact community filled with tight-knit neighbors and role models? Despite all the activities and programs you can throw at a kid, are there people to look up to who'll show them the way?

Because the dirty little secret is that, as this book will show, while young people killed others in much greater numbers between the mid-1980s and the mid-1990s, increasingly, they also killed themselves. The child suicide rate soared. What has caused this despair where life, including one's own, seems to mean so little?

"[T]he truth is," says Jack Levin, who runs the Program for the Study of Violence at Northeastern University, "when we ask our children to raise themselves, we are not doing a very good job raising them."[2]

I repeat: Are there people to look up to who'll show them the way?

Harvard psychiatrist and Pulitzer Prize-winning author Robert Coles asked that very question in his 1997 book, *The Moral Intelligence of Children*:

> [T]here are those endless hours that await our children—and their questions ought to be ours: Where are the grown-ups in our life upon whom we can really rely, whom we can trust, whose values are believable, desirable, because they have been given us out of the shared experience, moment to moment of a life together?[3]

It reminds me of a televised story journalist Bill Moyers did years ago as a camera followed him returning to his boyhood home of Marshall, Texas. Standing on the main street, he recalled a day at that same location when, as a young schoolboy, he accidentally broke a shopkeeper's expensive neon outdoor sign with a ball. As I vaguely recall, since I watched this program years ago, Moyers said the shopkeeper came out and told him something to the effect of, "You're going to pay for that sign. I know your father." Moyers said that looking back at it over the years, he realized that the shopkeeper could have called the cops or grabbed him by the scruff of the neck. Instead, he uttered the single, powerful, "I know your father."

And, years later, Moyers found great comfort and warmth in those simple words that made him part of a community: "I know your father."

Moyers' father did pay the shopkeeper. Half a week's salary.

Contrast Moyers' experience with that of a 15-year-old girl I'll call Ineka who lives in a violent inner-city neighborhood in Hartford, Connecticut. I spoke to Ineka, who, at the time, was successfully participating in an alternative to incarceration program where seven days a week she would go to a day reporting center to take classes and participate in life skills programs. She told me she was sent there because "I was out of control . . . selling drugs." Ineka had about the worst family history. She said:

> I seen my mother . . . she was a drug addict before she died of AIDS last year. . . . My aunt was raped and killed, cut into a million pieces. My uncle was shot in the head two times and they cut his eye out. My sister was 14 when she got 50 years for killing a cab driver. Only she didn't do it. She stole the taxi guy's wallet from the boy who killed him. The last time I seen her was just before my mother's funeral. They brought her in in shackles. I can't visit her now for another three years because I have to be 18 to visit her at the prison. . . .

Ineka told me she had had a baby daughter when she was 13, but reluctantly had to give her over to foster care. In telling me about her daughter, she said, "I was mad 'cause I have a daughter and I had nobody to help me raise my daughter. I had nobody to ask questions of. I always think of it as me against the world because you can't really call nobody a friend." Ineka was clearly calling out for help, guidance and a mentor in an echo of Robert Coles' question, "Where are the adults in my life?" She was desperate for "somebody to ask questions of"—someone like Bill Moyers had.

Her eyes lit up when she told me that recently she had made a connection with her father's girlfriend, who had become her confidante. Watching Ineka as she described her new mentor reminded me of a person dying of thirst who had just been given water.

> It's easy to talk to her because she knows the right answers . . . been there, done that. I wish she was around when I had my daughter. . . . She tell me so many things . . . I don't want to go down the path my mother went down. I want to provide a mother and father for my kids. Otherwise, if I go down that path, I will die early, too. She was only 39.

The frustrating thing is that we really do know the solution to juvenile crime. Rather than investing all our money in prisons—though they're absolutely still necessary but to a much lesser extent—we should be using some of our resources to shore up the American family. If that first best option just isn't possible, then we still should be doing the second best thing—intervening in the lives of young people with mentors and role models to develop a sense of conscience in young people.

SUPERPREDATORS
The Demonization of Our Children by the Law

Chapter 1

Introduction and Overview

Children as the Enemy

When I was about eight years old, I lived with my family in a small village on the Saint Lawrence Seaway outside of Montreal, Canada, for two and a half years. My father's job had transferred him there and it was the only time we lived outside the United States. It was an almost magical time and place. We had a lot of friends and were very much entrenched in the community there.

One Saturday, a friend and I went door to door in a nearby neighborhood selling candy for a kids' group to which we belonged. In later years, I would have been too shy to do such a thing. I've never really had a salesman-type personality. But on this day, it was a wonderful adventure. Everywhere we went, people seemed friendly and welcomed us. When the door to one home opened, we recognized a classmate. Her parents, whom we had never met, invited us hard workers in and made us each a sandwich. As the day wore on, our sales were high.

Then it happened. At one house, a girl, not much older than us, answered the door and, although her parents weren't home, told us she wanted to buy the candy. Unfortunately, she didn't have the full 25 cents to pay us. She only had 23 cents.

But we were filled with a generosity of spirit and quite magnanimous. Sure, we'd give her the candy for 23 cents. We were no penny-pinching, miserly, green-eyeshade-type businessmen solely fixated on the bottom line.

As we walked away from her home, though, after having completed the sale, it suddenly dawned on us that we had our first business dilemma on our hands. Suddenly, we were operating at a deficit. We realized that when it would come time to hand in our money, we would be 2 cents short. We were now in the red. What to do?

But we were sharp, cunning businessmen, and like a bolt of lightening it suddenly hit us. We'd make up the difference by charging the next person an extra 2 cents.

Twenty-seven cents must have seemed like an oddly priced amount, but the elderly man who fell for our con job paid it readily. Once again, our books were balanced and we were in the black. Then our customer did a curious thing. He handed the candy back to us.

"No, you paid for it," I said. "It's yours."

"No, it's for you," he replied. "I don't really eat candy. But it seemed like you boys are out here working so hard selling this that you should be able to have some, too. I bought it for you."

It was a truly elegant gesture.

Yet, though were only eight years old, we were two young men upon whom the irony was not lost. The one person that day who we had conned and cheated was the one person who, with great generosity of spirit—a total stranger, mind you—spent money to buy us a gift. We walked away from his door, awash in guilt. We were destroyed. We talked about it between us, and although we gave the candy away to some kid on the street who was even younger than us in an attempt to assuage our temporary self-loathing, we were moved by the concluding events of the day.

The reason I bring up this story from the 1960s is because, ultimately, it raises a much larger question for me. As I began to hear reports in the late 1990s of a coming youth crime wave—of a new generation of increasingly violent young people without remorse or conscience—I wondered if it was really true. Are there any differences between my generation of young people and today's generation? To be sure, as my story indicates, we were eminently capable of behaving badly and doing the wrong thing, even participating in criminal behavior, minor though this 2-cent crime may be. But, on the plus side, we did have a conscience. We did know the difference between right and wrong. Upon reflection, we were able to acknowledge the wrongfulness of our conduct, feel badly about it and even be disappointed in ourselves. In other words, we certainly had the ability to mess up as much as the next guy, but we weren't entirely lost causes because, at the very least, we were aware our behavior was bad. That's a starting point.

But what of this generation? Anecdotally, at least, reports of brazen cruelty by young people with seemingly few regrets appear increasingly across the radar screen of our public consciousness. In one month alone—June 1997—it seemed like incidents of youth crime without a sense of right and wrong had reached a crescendo:

- A New Jersey teenager, Melissa Drexler, stepped into the bathroom during the high school prom and delivered her baby by herself which she left for dead in a trash bin. She then went back to her table, ate a salad and then returned to the dance floor. After the bloody stall and dead baby were discovered, she was approached while in the process of making a song request to the disc jockey. She later pleaded guilty.

- Malcolm X's 12-year-old grandson set fire to the Yonkers, New York, apartment of his distinguished grandmother, Betty Shabazz, where she was burned over 80 percent of her body. She lingered for days until she died. It was believed that his only intent was to create a situation where his grandmother would be so upset with him that she would let him move back with his mother, from whose home he'd been removed for neglect. He eventually pleaded guilty.

- Jonathan Levin, a very popular young New York City public school teacher and son of Time Warner CEO Gerald Levin, was allegedly tortured and then shot fatally in the head by a teenage former student who wanted Levin's ATM card and password. The former student was found guilty.

- A 15-year-old daughter of a millionaire businessman and her friend sat drinking one night in Central Park in New York City. In the evening, it's a secluded, dangerous area of paths and clearings where frequently estranged youths are curiously drawn to the shadowy world of drunks and vagrants who congregate there. The girl and her friend shared some beers with an older man, then slit his throat, stabbed him fifty times, hacked off parts and tried to gut him before cleaning out his wallet and dumping him in the lake. She pleaded guilty and her accomplice was found guilty after trial.

Then, in an astounding six-month period between late 1997 and early 1998, Americans were rocked by the series of five electrifying school shooting sprees where students ranging in age from 11 to 16 killed and wounded classmates and teachers in the rural small towns of Pearl, Mississippi; Paducah, Kentucky; Jonesboro, Arkansas; Edinboro, Pennsylvania; and Springfield, Oregon.

Violent crime is still the almost exclusive domain of young men, but, as this book will explore, young females are beginning to make inroads here.

The question invariably arises—are we raising a nation of increasingly sociopathic children without feeling, repentance or empathy?

An attorney I know who represents many juveniles accused of crimes told me:

> Let me give you my take on this thing. When I represent an adult ac-
> cused of a crime, they'll usually do one of two things. They'll either
> admit that they did the crime or they'll deny it to me. But they'll never
> tell me that the crime itself wasn't a bad thing. I represent these young
> kids and many of them don't even get that what they did was wrong.

Only the week before, a young client, whom I had represented previously on a very minor offense, called to inform me that he had once again
been arrested. This time a relative of his had been involved in an incident
where someone had cut someone else off in their car and angry words had
been exchanged. He told me that, after learning of the event, he had gone
to the place of work of the person who had cut his relative off, bringing
along some of his friends. He and his friends were arrested after being accused of threatening the person and coaxing him to fight.

Although he denied making the threats, he still asked me, "Is that really a crime? Can they arrest you for that?"

In an article appearing in the March 25, 1996, issue of *U.S. News and
World Report* entitled "Crime Time Bomb," Florida psychotherapist and
criminologist Kathleen Heide tells the story of a teenager who shot and
paralyzed a jogger who wouldn't give up his gold chain. When asked
what would have been a better outcome of the encounter, the teen shooter
replied, "He could have given me his rope (chain). I asked him twice."[1]

Heide commented that many juvenile killers are, "incapable of empathy."

Are we really entering a new world without a moral or ethical center?
No.

This, despite the fact that some of the emerging statistics, at first
glance, misguidedly seem to point to the fact that there might be something to these stories. For instance, homicides by American youth tripled
between 1984 and 1994, according to the Justice Department.[2]

I wasn't alone in my initial questioning doubts about the future generation—though some appeared to have no doubts and had already ar-
rived at strong conclusions. In their book *Body Count,* authors John J.
DiIulio, Jr., William Bennett and John P. Waters, write that:

> America is now home to thickening ranks of juvenile "super-preda-
> tors"—radically impulsive, brutally remorseless youngsters, including
> ever more pre-teenage boys, who murder, assault, rape, rob, burglar-
> ize, deal deadly drugs, join gun-toting gangs and create serious com-
> munal disorders. They do not fear the stigma of arrest, the pains of
> imprisonment or the pangs of conscience.[3]

A 1997 poll found that most adults believe that "today's adolescents face a crisis—not in their economic or physical well-being but in their values and morals."[4]

But the week after these polls were released, writer Walter Kirn, in a tongue-in-cheek but sharply written piece in the July 2, 1997, issue of the *New York Times*, commented on the polls :

> Excuse me, but I see a pattern here. First, the members of the 60's generation hated their parents. Now they hate their kids. The generation that gave us instant divorce, pot, speed and insider trading is worried about the moral failings of the young? Please. If I were 15 now and thus charged with moral corruption, I'd take a long hard look at my prosecutors. . . .[5]

I dispute the view of today's youth as an incorrigible ethical wasteland. Many of the young people I spoke with always had a solid core of morality. But I was also fascinated with stories told to me by children who had done very bad things in the past, yet were somehow able to be turned around through remorse and a sense of conscience and shame.

One 16-year-old I'll call Joe told me of an incident that happened three years earlier:

> I robbed somebody once. I couldn't do it any more. I needed cigarettes, marijuana, beer. So, at nighttime, I saw some lady walking. I just stuck a knife in her back and said, "Give me your purse." So, she gave it to me and left. After that, the next day, I was thinking about it and said to myself, "If I do that to people—old ladies and guys—how would they survive if they're not working?" Say if I put myself in their position, how would I feel? I imagine myself in their position. I picture myself old and someone sticking a knife in my back.

Joe's horrible act was never repeated due to his sense of real empathy and he now works as a community youth organizer and still attends school.

Yet the wrongheaded perception that today's younger generation is more amoral and dangerous than ever is coupled with a widely held belief by a great number of criminologists that "you ain't seen nothin' yet." That's because it's long been generally acknowledged that the peak crime-committing years are ages 14 through 24 with some residual up until about the age of 40. Crime in this country went down beginning in 1992 at, coincidentally, the same time that the population-dense baby boomers started to age out of this crime-prone age. This was no surprise to criminologists, since historically, crime in the United States has gone up every time there's a large population of 14- through 24-year-olds. Conversely, it goes down every time that age group dwindles. So it is believed by many that this current respite may be short-lived. That's because the bulk of the children of the baby boomers—the baby boomerangs—already feared to be more dangerous and with less conscience, will soon be hitting those teen years. The logical, but erroneous, conclusion to this line of reasoning is that this will result in the long feared coming youth crime wave.

Perhaps that's why one California police chief in the late 1990s quipped that he was not taking credit for the drop in crime because he did not want to be blamed for an increase if and when it comes.

Calling juvenile crime the "demographic crime bomb," John J. DiIulio, Jr. predicts that, by 2010, there could be three times the current number of juveniles incarcerated.[6]

Yet this increasing belief that today's young people are more immoral and dangerous and can't be reached on our ethical plain has now led to a profound and defective alignment in the way many politicians want to treat children headed on the wrong path. Harsh and severe punishments are now in vogue, including eliminating juvenile courts and many juvenile facilities in favor of trying children as adults before sentencing them to lengthy incarceration in adult facilities. The United States is already one of six countries in the world that sentence minors to the death penalty along with Iran, Pakistan, Nigeria, Saudi Arabia and Yemen. A centurylong tradition of treating youthful offenders differently from adults—of trying to turn their lives around through rehabilitation and education—is being abandoned.

Kent Scheidegger, legal director of the Criminal Justice Legal Foundation, echoed that opinion by saying, "You have a system that was designed for shoplifters, truants and joyriders that is now filled with rapists and murderers and people shooting each other with guns."[7]

When in 1997 the United States Congress passed a law requiring that juveniles aged 14 or older charged with federal crimes be tried as adults and incarcerated in adult prisons, they were following the lead of every state in the country.

But despite the tremendous popularity in lowering the age of adulthood by the criminal justice system, there's no evidence that it works to lower crime. In fact, ironically, the evidence shows the opposite.

Certainly there are juvenile psychopathic murderers from whom, if released, the public could never be assured of protection. But as nightmarish as are those headline cases of brutal murders by juveniles, they make up an infinitesimal fraction of serious youth crimes. Most juveniles who are tried in adult courts and sent to adult prisons are sent there for lesser crimes than homicide and will be released someday.

Every study available so far, as this book will reveal in greater detail, shows that those juveniles who are sent to adult prison have higher recidivism rates than those who remain in juvenile facilities. That means that juveniles sent to adult prison tend to endanger the public and get re-arrested at much higher rates once they've been released.

The reason youths who have served time in adult prison are so much more dangerous when released than their counterparts who have served time in juvenile facilities is that, for those who are capable of having their lives turned around, they stand the best chance of picking up the life skills they need in juvenile facilities. For most—but not all—education and treatment in youth facilities that are set up to try to save kids really does work.

Certainly, rehabilitation doesn't have a 100 percent success rate, particularly in those rare instances when the youngster either is incapable of or not open to it. One teenager I spoke with whom I'll call Jesse had abandoned a fine family with seemingly caring working-class immigrant parents and successful siblings for an essentially homeless life of no school, fighting and crime. He couldn't articulate to me why he preferred his rootless life and in a rambling interview he continually answered with "I just don't know." He told me:

> Maybe I'm the black sheep. All my brothers and sisters are doing good in school. Me . . . I got kicked out of school. From the time I was five years old, I was stealing . . . food, candy. Fighting, too. The cops would take me to the station and then my parents would sit and have a talk with me. Sometimes they'd hit me and tell me I couldn't go outside and play. Didn't have any effect. I was fighting all the time. Because I was in a gang. I don't know why. . . . I've been surviving by myself for years now. I don't have a home. I bounce to friends' homes . . . sleep here or there. I got no job. Sometimes, I can't find a place to stay and stay up all night. Just try to stay up and walk around. Sometimes I stay on one corner or sit on someone's porch. I just can't stay out of trouble. I have no clue why. I go to a party and get into a fight. I want to stop. Can't. Right now I'm too lazy to do something. Too lazy to go out and get a job. I don't even have a dollar in my wallet. My parents didn't do anything. I'm the stupid one. I just go day by day.

Jesse's story is the rare one. In the following chapters are studies showing the phenomenal success rates of intervention programs and, in the case where someone is sent to a youth facility, remarkable statistics of youths having their lives turned around. In contrast, adult prisons today have largely abandoned trying to prepare young inmates for life on the outside world, once released.

This is primarily because, according to Mark Soler of the Youth Law Center, "Sending kids into the adult system sends them into schools for crime."[8]

It's not surprising that hanging out for years with older, more violent, hardened criminals while doing absolutely nothing to prepare yourself to cope better with the outside world once released, is a prescription for disaster.

An older prisoner with whom I have had a longtime correspondence and who spends much of his time counseling the young inmates who serve time with him, agrees on this point:

> I don't claim to know what the answer is, but I'll tell you what the answer is not—putting them side by side with hardened convicts whose sense of morality is long since gone. They become better thieves and harder thugs. They become repeat offenders.

Many police and corrections officials feel the same way.

"Sure, some kids are dangerous and should be locked up in secure juvenile facilities," said former San Jose police chief Joseph McNamara, a police officer for 35 years and now with the conservative Hoover Institution in a June 11, 1997 interview on MSNBC News. "But this doesn't make any sense to put them in with hardened adult criminals. We know that they'll be brutalized and we know that when they come out, they'll be worse than when they went in. They really will be violent people."[9]

But the alarmists are wrong. There will not be a coming youth crime wave.

In 1995, juvenile crime stunned most criminal justice experts by actually moving downward, although it was a dip in a high plateau. Overall violent crime arrests for youths dropped 2.9 percent. The following year confirmed it wasn't just a temporary aberration, with an even more significant drop of 9.2 percent. "This drop, I think, is real now," said Attorney General Janet Reno in 1997. "I don't think we can talk about it as a blip."[10] Then, for the third year in a row, in 1997, it dropped again, this time by 4 percent. That's more than 16 percent in three years. Minority arrests had fueled much of this rise in great disproportion to their actual numbers for reasons this book explores.

In fact, despite the hysteria over the highly publicized school shootings that took place over the 1997–98 school year, the number of violent school deaths has actually declined since 1992. While even one school death is too many, school is still the safest place for a young person to be since more than 99 percent of all violent youth deaths take place outside of school.[11]

Besides, even during its worst period between the mid-80s and mid-90s, it was very geographically concentrated, with a third of the nation's killings by youth taking place in just 10 counties. It rarely happened anywhere else, so perhaps the concept of an overall American youth crime wave was misleading.[12]

So, the explanation for the turning around of the rising youth crime rate beginning in 1995 appears to be that serious efforts were made to attack youth crime in just a handful of cities. For example, when the youth crime rate was significantly lowered in just one city, New York, that was enough to help send downward what were once rising youth crime statistics for the entire nation.

Contributing to the lowering of the youth crime rate were a diminished access to guns, less childhood poverty due to an improving economy, the beginning of a turnaround in the vanishing American family, and community policing. Still, the fact that youth crime may actually be declining is no excuse for us to rest on our laurels. It is down from an almost unprecedented level and is still way too high.

But the point which needs the most serious debate is whether individual young people commit a much greater number of acts of violence than ever before, or their violence is just more lethal. The often cited example is that the old schoolyard shoving match or fist fight of yesteryear has given way to just shooting a classmate, as kids are entering school buildings with handguns in absolutely unprecedented numbers. This book will argue in detail that today's child isn't a great deal more violent; he's just better armed.

This is borne out by statistics. The walloping increase in homicides by youth from the mid-80s to the mid-90s was solely the result of guns. The fact that murders by juveniles tripled during that period is interesting when you realize that gun murders quadrupled during that period while juvenile murders by all other weapons did not increase one iota.[13] If America's youth were more predisposed to kill than ever before during that period, we would have seen a rise in every kind of murder, not just gun murders.

Youth crime rates for nonviolent crimes didn't go up either. It's guns, guns, guns. . . . Guns are the sole area of youth crime that has shown a marked and significant increase.

"Academics and politicians . . . need to go to the president, congress, the media and say, 'It's the guns, stupid!,' " echoed Vincent Schiraldi, director of the Justice Policy Institute in Washington, D.C., and attorney Mark Kappelhoff.[14]

But rather than intervene and attack the problem of youth crime at an early stage—keeping in mind that no child is born evil (though there may be an almost microscopic number who are born with congenital mental health problems)—politicians, for the most part, seem to have come up with only a short-sighted two-part approach: (1) adult trials and adult prison, and (2) a wholesale disinvestment in youth. Year by year, they've chipped away at after school programs, education, mentoring and recreation, decrying them as "pork," "big spending," "coddling," "pampering," and the deadly conversation-stopper "liberal." Deep funding cuts in areas that could be used to prevent crime in the first place by bolstering up and supporting families are abandoned in favor of doing nothing and just waiting for tragedies to occur. Then a greater amount of money is spent, after the fact, to process and warehouse people in prison, where they learn to be better criminals from the older, more violent ones.

There is a real and reprehensible beat-up-on-children mood pouring across the political landscape. Children are the scapegoats of this generation. To be a child today is to be suspect. There does appear to be a sad combination of both abandoning them and then meting out severe and Draconian punishments once they falter. Several people have suggested that since we no longer have the specter of Communism hanging over our heads as our main threat and nemesis in the world, we've replaced Communists with children. Children are now, for our intents and purposes, the new Communists. "What we are really frightened about is guns, but instead of launching a war against guns, we are launching a war against kids," says Barry Krisberg, head of the National Council on Crime and Delinquency.[15]

Even the way we speak about children makes it easier for us to go after them. The now popular term "superpredator" is the ultimate example. You wouldn't want to squash and brutalize a "child" would you? But squashing and brutalizing a "superpredator" wouldn't generate too much sympathy, would it? These terms help distance us from children. After all, you're attacking a "thing" or a "beast," not a person.

When Representative Bill McCollum introduced the 1997 federal bill to try to incarcerate more children as adults, he cynically first named it the "Violent Youth Predator Act." It was as if he was preparing us for a social

Jurassic Park. Eventually, he was forced to change it to the "Juvenile Crime Control Act."

Rebecca Young, director of Citizens for Juvenile Justice, says:

> Well, we don't even talk about adult offenders as superpredators. I personally think part of what's scary about using that kind of language is that the sort of thinking that goes behind that language is the sort of thinking that led to the Holocaust. It's this sense that these people, well, they aren't people. And you'll hear people say that. You'll hear people say that about people who have committed certain offenses. They'll say, "He's not a human being. He's an animal. He should be in a cage."
>
> As soon as you start drawing that kind of a line, you say, "Based on this act you committed, you're not human anymore." Well, as soon as you're not human anymore, boy, we can do anything to you, and we can feel like we're morally superior. And that's pretty frightening. Now I'm not saying that the people who coined that term and the people who continue to use it are thinking, are actually aware of thinking, "I'm trying to dehumanize this group of people," but I personally think that's, in fact, what's going on.

Young is correct when she points out the hypocrisy that we don't even refer to adults as superpredators. This, in light of the fact that 90 percent of all children under 12 and 75 percent between the ages of 12 and 17 who are homicide victims are killed by adults.[16]

In some highly publicized cases during the past several years, there's been an increasing use of the law to get at children for things that one never dreamed would merit such overreactive revenge through the legal process.

- A seven-year-old girl in Rhode Island brings a three-inch pink squirtgun to school and is suspended and ordered to participate in psychological counseling. A school official says, "It may be a toy gun today, but it could be a real gun tomorrow."

- A 14-year-old boy in Texas calls a classmate a "fat cow" and uses a profanity and, instead of his school taking its own disciplinary action, they call in the police and have him charged with misdemeanor disorderly conduct.

- A six-year-old boy in Florida kisses a female classmate and is charged with sexual assault.

Meg Greenfield, in her October 7, 1998, column in *Newsweek*, commented that she wanted to write the story of this six-year-old Romeo while there was still time and before:

> ... one of the two fates common to such startling stories overtakes it: either it turns out to have been a hoax or a misunderstanding of some kind or, and this is the really depressing alternative, everyone starts taking it seriously and saying things like, "Well . . . you know it may sound crazy at first . . . but when you really think about it. . . ." In the tiny window of time available to me before one or both of these things come to pass, I'd like to say that the story seems to me to sum up more about American life today than, say, a careful reading of the United States Statistical Abstract from cover to cover would.[17]

All of the above may, indeed, be various forms of unacceptable misbehavior or violation of the rules, but there is a more efficient and cheaper method of correction than bringing the courts and the lawyers into what always was the traditional province of parents and teachers.

More subject to debate was the 1997 Florida case, for which I did live commentary on the Court TV network, in which three teenagers from the Tampa area, with no prior history of legal trouble, were alleged to have vandalized or stolen some street signs as a prank. A knocked-down stop sign at one intersection resulted in the deaths of three other people.

"I don't believe for one minute that you or the other two defendants pulled these signs up with the intent of causing the death of anyone," said Circuit Court Judge Robert "Maximum Bob" Mitchum.

But despite the plea for leniency from the mother of one of the deceased who believed the teenagers' story that they hadn't pulled up the particular sign and after denying a request for a new trial based on the claim by one witness who stated the prosecutor forced him to lie, he sentenced the teens to 30 years in prison, but suspended half of that sentence. They'll be eligible for parole after 13 years. Despite serious questions about their innocence including more evidence concerning prosecutorial and police misconduct in intentionally ignoring and not disclosing evidence that would point to their innocence, the case raised compelling issues. In this instance, there at least were good arguments to be made for either side. Some felt that since there was no intent to do more than a prank, three youngsters didn't need to have millions of dollars spent on them to imprison them for so long in order for them to learn a lesson or for society to be protected from them. Others felt that a message must be sent that though you may feel it's only a foolish prank made without intent to endanger anyone, juveniles have to be made to understand the severe, deadly consequences of their silly actions. These three were old enough to understand the consequences of what might result from their act.

It is so very popular for so many politicians to join in on the war against kids, in spite of the fact that a survey of police chiefs across the country conducted by Northeastern University found that charging youthful offenders as adults was their least favorite option. The police said that intervening in young people's lives at an early age with crime prevention programs is the best way to reduce crime.[18]

But perhaps, as David Broder, the dean of American political journalists, wrote in his syndicated column, "It is a fascinating paradox of current politics that the further removed an official is from the front lines of the war on crime, the tougher he is likely to talk. That is particularly the case when it comes to violence by juveniles."[19]

Robert G. Schwartz, the executive director of the Juvenile Law Center, says the reason politicians don't hesitate to vilify youth is "a no-brainer. . . . Kids don't vote."[20]

It's this political feeding frenzy that is behind the great rush to pass new laws to try children as adults. Again and again the same pattern is followed. A state will have juvenile laws in place that may have worked well for years. Then a single horrific crime will be committed by one juvenile in that state, and legislators will fall all over themselves rushing to the media to announce a new proposed "get-tough" law. They never show research or evidence on how the new law will be more effective against youth crime. They simply call for more prison time and leave it at that.

Take, for example, the state of Massachusetts. For years, it had one of the most progressive and effective sets of juvenile crime laws. Prosecutors and defense counsel alike praised the results of the Massachusetts laws and they served as a model for the rest of the country on how to reduce youth crime. At the same time, by the mid-1990s, a number of cities, particularly Boston, were putting together remarkable coalitions of local clergy, the police and youth workers to set up a variety of youth projects of mentoring, counseling and jobs programs. Again, Boston lowered its juvenile crime rate so dramatically, without incarcerating more young people than the other states, that the eyes of the rest of the nation focused upon it. Crime in Boston had dropped to a 30-year low. Overall gun homicides were down 80 percent, and there were no youth murders in that city for a record two and a half years.

Unfortunately, it was during this period that the Eddie O'Brien case happened.

Eddie O'Brien was a 15-year-old, seemingly happy-go-lucky kid living in the middle of a very cohesive working-class neighborhood of

Somerville, Massachusetts. His grandfather had been the long-term police chief of Somerville, and his large family was well entrenched there. He had lots of friends and his crowd wasn't known for using drugs or alcohol. He had never been in trouble with the law, never got into fights or showed any aggressive behavior.

Then, as it was alleged, on the night of July 23, 1995, he gave out some popsicles to the neighborhood kids on his front porch, put a tape of *Sleeping Beauty* into the VCR for his little sister and walked across the street to his best friend's house. There, it was said, he encountered his best friend's 42-year-old mother, Janet Downing, and for reasons never known, murdered her by stabbing and slashing her 98 times.

Under the Massachusetts law, at that time, youths between the ages of 14 and 17 who were charged with murder would undergo a hearing before a judge to determine whether they should be tried as an adult or juvenile. The key question was whether they were deemed capable of rehabilitation. In this case, the judge determined that O'Brien was capable of rehabilitation and should be tried as a juvenile. There was an ensuing political uproar led by an extremely political district attorney who had ambitions of running for attorney general.

After a successful appeal by the D.A., O'Brien was later tried and convicted as an adult. But the district attorney and other politicians never wanted to take that chance again. They rapidly pushed through a law making it mandatory without a hearing that all juveniles charged with murder would be tried and sentenced as adults. Furthermore, the new law gave the prosecutor discretion to try juveniles as adults for a variety of other, less serious crimes. So, although the juvenile law was remarkably effective in reducing youth crime for years, and there were very, very few juvenile murders in the state, one solitary case that made the headlines encouraged the politicians to rewrite the law without any assurances that it would make the public safer.

"It was certainly appalling and extremely frustrating . . . to watch the abdication of a system that was going in the right direction," said former juvenile prosecutor Sarah Buel.[21]

Buel wasn't alone.

"We're letting 5 percent of the cases govern how we treat 95 percent of the cases," remarked noted Massachusetts Juvenile Court Judge Jay Blitzman. "Everybody legislates anecdotally."[22]

In other words, an almost infinitesimally small number of children are letting the grown-ups off the hook in really having to face and take on the very real and serious problems of youth today. It's an easy out for adults and permits them to ignore the more complex quandaries of childhood. Just throwing away every single child without exception is much easier than examining each case and each young person in their entirety.

The single most regrettable thing about this debate is that we're distracted from what we should be doing. We should be intervening in the lives of young people before they get into trouble rather than doing nothing, waiting until they get into trouble and a tragedy occurs and then saying, "Ha! Gotcha! Now we'll spend money on putting you away forever!"

This was put more eloquently by Marc Klaas, the father of 12-year-old Polly Klaas who was so brutally abducted from their Petaluma, California, home in 1993 and murdered. Just before the sentencing of her convicted murderer, her father said:

> Polly's killer may soon be sentenced to death. Neither that penalty nor anything else can bring Polly back. But we can save thousands of children and adults—and spare their families unimaginable heartbreak—if we invest now in the proven programs that help kids get the right start. Anything else will always be too little, too late.[23]

There does exist, though, a single, most powerful argument on why juvenile crime can be prevented rather than just attacked after the fact. This lies in the now-recognized statistic that most juvenile crime occurs not late at night during midnight basketball time or the hours when politicians want to impose youth curfews. Most juvenile crime occurs after 3 in the afternoon and before 8 in the evening. It's immediately obvious to everyone that this is the period after school, but before parents come home.

"It used to be 'It's 10 p.m. Do you know where your children are?,'" says former New York Youth Commissioner Richard Murphy. "Now the line should be, 'It's 4 p.m. Do you know where your children are?'"[24]

Having parents around is the No. 1 crime prevention tool, bar none. One teenager, whom I'll call Charlie, told me the reason he left a gang was because:

> Like when you're in a situation and your mom's worried about you. That's what made me change. Without my parents, I wouldn't be here talking to you, Mr. Elikann. I would be out chilling . . . doing stuff. . . . Family is important. You can't trust nobody else besides your family.

Ideally, it would be more beneficial to children if one parent was home during this time. "Because about 40 percent of juvenile crime occurs after school closes and before parents come home, so much for the argument that parents don't make any difference," spoke President Bill Clinton.[25]

In his book *The Moral Intelligence of Children,* Robert Coles acknowledges the sanctity of parenthood as the very best factor in creating an ethical child of conscience and feelings: "The conscience does not ascend upon us from on high. We learn a convincing sense of right and wrong from . . . parents who are persuasively ready to impart to their children through words and daily example what they hope to hand on to them. . . ."[26]

But the reality of the situation is that today a majority (57 percent) of homes are either headed by a single parent or by two parents who must both work outside the home.[27]

Sometimes that's enough, as in the case of a 14-year-old Cambodian immigrant whom I'll call Lin Chorn, who lived in a tough urban neighborhood in New England. His single mother worked in a vegetable market from 2 in the morning till noon. When he was 11, he did something bad, and both his mother and the conscience she gave him stepped in. Lin told me:

> I once stole money from my own relative but I don't do that any more. I gave it back. It was my grandmother. In the nighttime I stole it and in the morning, she was looking for it. I just gave it back. I was 11. I felt it was the wrong thing and she was crying. I knew it was the wrong thing. . . . My mother she helped me a lot. She works hard, but when she came in, she had me sit down, gave me a pen and piece of paper and had me write a story about my future.

So while it's clear that intact, loving families are the best weapon in fighting crime, if they don't always exist, is it worthwhile to try for some kind of second-best?

The answer is yes to the question of whether, in the absence of family, we should be looking for ways to bring other adults into the lives of children. The reason for that lies in the responses I received from many elderly people who lived through the Great Depression when I'd ask them if they blamed poverty and the lack of intact families for youngsters turning to crime. They'd tell me no and explain that they'd grown up in dire poverty, possibly on relief, as welfare was called in those days, and one of their parents had died and still they'd all stuck together and not turned to crime. Why? What was the difference between then and today?

The difference was that, more often then than today, even if one's family was in shambles, it was more likely that you lived in much more of a real functioning community. People looked out for each other, knew each other and knew each other's business. If a kid got in trouble and his parents didn't see it, the neighbors would and they'd tell his parents. You may have known all the neighborhood shopkeepers and cops on the beat.

You also had role models and people in the community who served as mentors. Maybe your father had died, but there were plenty of surrogate fathers around—a neighborhood priest who'd play ball with you, a coach or the next-door kid's dad. It would never quite replace the excellence of having one's own family up and functioning, but at the very least, you had a general model of the kind of person whose values you should aspire to have. Sure, it was merely a second-best replacement, but plenty of kids were saved.

Today, you not only have latchkey kids—kids who let themselves in to an empty home in the afternoon. You have latchkey neighborhoods. Your parents may not be home, but neither are the neighbors . . . if you even know them.

Typical of this kind of youth is Eric Rodriguez, now a remarkable youth leader in his early 20s planning to enter college, who grew up without parental supervision or adults in his early life. It is compelling to see how, without guidance or direction, he led a childhood in the economically depressed city of Chelsea, Massachusetts, of crime, drug dealing and violence:

> My dad was around till I was about eight years old, then he went to prison for six years, then he came out, left my mother and moved to Florida, went to jail again. My mother had mental health issues throughout my life, so a lot of times I found myself either in foster homes or out on the streets or at home by myself.
>
> Well, I was involved with DSS [Department of Social Services], but in the mix there I would fall through the cracks. So if she was hospitalized, there would be no caseworker saying this is what you have to do. So my brother and I would stay home by ourselves. It started when I was eight, probably pretty much until I was eighteen. . . . We didn't do the cleaning part so well, and as far as cooking went, we'd get food from our friends, and literally out on the streets. There's a little store on Broadway and we'd literally go in there and just steal food every day. . . .
>
> Didn't know to expect anything else, so just kind of rolling with it, saying, yes, this is what happens when you grow up, but pretty much understood that I had to fend for myself, and my brother, too. No adults in my life. Missed 53 consecutive days of school in fifth grade, and nobody even noticed. So the sister of a friend of mine called the

principal and said, "Hey, they're hanging out in the basement every day by themselves." Didn't really click with school. Didn't understand what school was. Why school when I could be out? So I didn't exactly have the resources to make decisions that important in my life. I just didn't understand school, so I didn't go to school. . . .

I would have to say that having my mother hospitalized was hard. Yeah, just to know that you couldn't really help and not being in the loop. Because you're so young, you don't really talk to doctors and they don't really inform you of what's going on and how long do you think she's going to be there, etc. You just kind of have no expectations. You say, all right, whatever happens, happens. And that was tough. That was tough to cope with.

Started hanging out with my brother's friends, who were older, and they started selling drugs and making good money. I was 11, too young to work, and they said, "Well, if you keep a lookout for us and just tell us when the cops come, we'll give you all the singles that we get at the end of the night." So at the end of each night, they gave me like 30 bucks, 40 bucks, just to stand there and say, "Oh, cop's coming." Didn't necessarily understand it. I knew I needed money. I knew I was hungry and I knew it wasn't a good thing, but all that's irrelevant when you're hungry. . . . You hear people talk about drugs when you're a little kid, and say drugs are bad, drugs are bad. Didn't understand it in the greater context of how it messes up the community and how it impacts people's lives, etc. But knew that it's something I'm not supposed to be doing. But that wasn't compelling enough not to eat. . . .

Well, it went from being kind of the lookout to being one of the players and really being taught the ropes by a lot of the older guys. Started making money for myself as opposed to waiting to get the ones from the older guys. . . . So there were a lot of violent episodes as you can imagine. And people try to take your stuff and then you get a group of people and you literally go get your stuff back. Oh yeah, access to weapons nowadays in unbelievable. You get a gun for $40, less than that if you know the right people. And considering that they make a gun every second, they're everywhere. They really are. And they were always around. My father had a gun, my friends had a gun. Twelve-, thirteen-year-old kids . . . they had guns. In fact, I bought my first gun off of a friend of mine who was 13 years old. I was also thirteen. . . .

What is interesting about Eric Rodriguez's story above is that it is so very clear how he drifted into the world of youthful crime. It also gives the clues on how it could be avoided despite the fact that the best method—a supportive family—was nowhere in sight.

Again, instead of intervening with communities and young people before the tragic crimes occur, some politicians insist that we do nothing, wait for the tally of victims to increase and then step in and angrily call for us to spend money on adult trials and adult prisons. This, especially in light of the earlier-mentioned research that young people in adult prisons are more likely to be arrested again once released. These politicians aren't being tough on crime. They may be tough on a few individuals, but in the final analysis, they're preventing the crime rate from being lowered.

Because even if you start incarcerating children in numbers like we've never even dreamed of before, there'll always be an endless, limitless new crop of children coming over the horizon and approaching those peek crime-committing years. This is because the greatest myth of all which politicians campaign on is that if you give out enough severe, Draconian punishments to children, you'll "send a message" to the other youths that this is what will happen if you commit bad acts.

Typical of politicians is Los Angeles District Attorney Gil Garcetti who, on the May 9, 1997, *NBC Nightly News*, declared, "The point is that juveniles do know what the law is and if they know they're going to be treated as an adult with adult sanctions, there, indeed, will be some deterrent effect."[28]

This is dead wrong. Most crimes of violence, particularly those committed by young people, are acts of impulse. They don't sit down and rationally and logically do a cost/benefit analysis on the pros and cons of what will happen if they get caught. They don't even think about it and, if they do, they don't assume they'll get caught. They don't ludicrously say to themselves, "I'm going to do this crime. I know I'll get caught, but I'll do it anyway because I'll only have to spend a few years incarcerated in a youth facility. If I was going to have to go to an adult facility, then I'd change my mind and I wouldn't do it." Of course, it would be ridiculous to think that any of these sometimes heartless, impulsive, violent people are doing some logical information processing before they commit their acts.

The proof that simply "sending a message" doesn't work is found merely by looking at the now quarter-century-long war on drugs where today more people are in for drugs and for longer sentences than ever, and it still hasn't made a dent. Today in the United States, drugs are more available, cheaper and purer than at any time. A whopping 70 percent of all people entering federal prison today are going in for drug offenses, and about 35 percent of all people entering state prisons and jails.[29] It hasn't made a dent, and yet still politicians stand in front of the scene of a major drug arrest and say things like, "This will send a message to drug dealers." It's just so much hype. Drugs and crime are such serious problems that they need to be dealt with less cynically.

The young person we'll call Jimmy who enters his classroom with a gun and starts shooting and killing the people inside, already knows his life will now be grievously ruined and damned forever if he has any ability to think at all, and yet he still does it. So, threatening him with a longer sentence or one in another type of facility won't stop him. Sure, you may have to lock Jimmy up forever to protect people in the future from him. But if you want to prevent other younger people from doing such acts, don't count on the younger kids' learning of the Jimmy's fate and then calmly and rationally reevaluating and reconsidering the act they might have done.

If we want to protect the future of the public's safety, we've got to intervene in young people's lives before they get into trouble. We can't just hope and count on all the trouble-bound children hearing about the penalties and immediately straightening out their behavior on their own.

Former Republican U.S. Attorney General Elliot Richardson, who earlier had served as a state and federal prosecutor, called on politicians in 1996 to "skip the soundbites and slogans and focus on serious solutions. . . . Locking up serious criminals is a necessary defense, but you can never win a war if you're only fighting defense. When we take the offensive by investing in early-childhood and youth development, we can win the war against crime, and make our communities safe for our families."[30]

It's very little solace to victims and their families to just spend money to punish after the fact. Sure, we may need to do it. But better to avoid the whole thing by intervening in the lives of children at very young ages. We can do this the first-best way—shoring up disintegrating American families—or reluctantly, the still effective, albeit second-best way—providing role models and mentors in the lives of young people in order to save them. This is, in fact, the chief premise of this book. The best way of fighting juvenile crime is to interfere with, intervene, bother and love children before they get into trouble. This will be cheaper and make us safer than spending money on courts and jails and victim compensation after the child has committed a crime and a tragedy has occurred.

Chapter 2

A Coming Youth Crime Wave
by a Nation of Sociopaths

When I was a 23-year-old newspaper reporter, I remember one day finishing up an interview with a public official in a small country town. After we had concluded whatever matters of consequence we had originally set out to discuss, we digressed into a long, rambling, but fascinating discussion about his childhood and the way he perceived people back then. He told me what was perhaps his most cogent childhood memory.

His father had been in a minor automobile accident where his car's rear bumper received a small dent. It was agreed by all, it had not been his fault. Several weeks later, the insurance agent drove up the small country road where they lived and got out of his car at their house. The agent walked over to the child and his father in the front yard and handed him a check for $200 for the repair of the bumper.

The father then surprised the agent with his next move. He handed the check back to the agent.

"Here, I don't need it," he said. "The dent's so small, I just wasn't planning on getting it repaired anyway."

"But the check's yours," replied the agent. "You can keep it, anyway, and do with it whatever you like."

"No," said the father. "If I'm not going to get the fender repaired, it just wouldn't be right."

The agent drove away probably trying to figure out administratively what in the world to do with that check.

Looking back on it decades later, the public official shook his head in awe at the memory of his father's towering sense of ethics and remarked, "Now where

21

*would you see something like that nowadays? It's that old-fashioned morality.
People just don't do that sort of thing anymore."*

The man I was interviewing isn't alone now in his perception. A majority of Americans today cite the declining lack of morality, not only among their older peers but, much more sharply, in young people. One poll noted that 61 percent of adult Americans think the lack of values among young people is a serious problem.[1] In fact, it's moved from a general disgust with cavalier and insensitive youths to a real fear that young people are so lacking in remorse, conscience and feeling that they've become a dangerous and lethal menace.

It was as a bit of tongue-in-cheek humor when the essayist and critic Logan Pearsall Smith (1865–1946) wrote, "The denunciation of the young is a necessary part of the hygiene of older people and greatly assists in the circulation of the blood."[2]

HEARTS SHOT FULL OF NOVOCAINE?

But today, the topic does not lend itself to humor. At least anecdotally, we're bombarded on an almost daily basis with news stories of acts of violence by youth that, on the surface, appear to be committed for almost no reason at all. The motives appear so petty that they appear to be the acts of youngsters with calluses on their souls, with hearts shot full of Novocaine.

"The young people involved in some of these violent acts are without the capacity to make the connection with another life," states Dr. David Hartman of the Isaac Ray Center for Psychiatry and Law in Chicago. "They need have no more reason for hurting another human being than they have for peeling an orange."[3]

This point couldn't have been made better than through the story of the arrest of a 14-year-old boy whom I'll call Tyrone. He lives in a tough, violent, inner-city neighborhood of Hartford, Connecticut. He told me:

> My friend and I were in the library playing chess. My friend used profanity. They kicked us out. My friend Lamont dared me to point it at the library guy. So I tapped on the window and pointed the gun at him and dared him to come out. They called the cops on me and they searched me. I felt stupid pointing it at one of the staff of the library. I wasn't thinking.

A 15-year-old boy called Ronny from the same urban environment as Tyrone told me about some of the other local youngsters. "That's the way it is right now," he admitted. "They don't care about others no more. Like, if they kill someone, they don't think about how the family might feel."

"They only think about theyselves," says Tyrell. "You have some people who just don't care. They was probably raised up in the wrong house where theys' moms and theys' dads wasn't there to guide them."

As I write these words, I have just looked at the daily newspaper and saw two articles all too typical of incidents which suggest a moral wasteland. It's not just the two terrible crimes that were depicted, but the rationale behind their having been committed. A 15-year-old, Richard Rivera, was convicted of shooting and killing 16-year-old Emir Quintana, a high school basketball standout who dreamed of playing for the NBA, becoming a businessman and a father. Rivera shot Quintana as he played on a basketball court because he had "heard" Quintana had called him a "punk." That's it. A friend had handed Rivera a pistol and told him to "do what you have to do."[4]

A few pages later in the same newspaper is the story of Levar Leggett, a teenager who just received a 32-year prison sentence for randomly picking out and shooting a 46-year-old man in the back as he walked down the street. The victim got up, tried to run, and was shot again. Leggett walked up to him, put the gun to the victim's head and was about to "blow his brains out" when a friend knocked the gun out of his hand to prevent the murder. It was reported that Leggett committed the deed solely to "earn his stripes" as a criminal.

At the sentencing, Judge Thomas E. Connolly said, "There is absolutely no reason for this attack and the viciousness of this attack—except violence for violence's sake."

Connolly referred to such incidents as "killing for the sake of killing without regard to who was being killed." He added, "Mothers and fathers in this city have had it. We are not going to stand for it any more."

This seemingly new callousness appeared to foreshadow a fearsome world to come when combined with the sheer skyrocketing numbers of youth crimes occurring from the mid-1980s to the mid-1990s. The following statistics show the huge leap in youth crime during that very time. By the end of that 10-year period:

- Homicides by juveniles tripled.
- An American 17-year-old was 10 times more likely to commit murder than his Canadian counterpart.

- The percentage increases in arrests were greater for juveniles than adults.
- Juvenile arrests for aggravated assault went up 78 percent.
- Juvenile arrests for robbery went up 63 percent.
- Law enforcement officials identified 14 percent of violent crimes in America as having been committed by a juvenile.
- Juveniles themselves were victims of crimes twice as often as those in the 25- to 35-year-old age group and five times as often as persons 35 and over.
- It was estimated that more than 30 percent of child sex abuse crimes are actually committed by other juveniles.
- In 1995, juveniles in the United States accounted for

  - 15 percent of all murders
  - 19 percent of all violent crimes
  - 35 percent of all property crimes.[5]

The United States has the highest rates of childhood homicide and suicide among the 26 most industrialized countries, according to a study released in 1997 by the Centers for Disease Control and Prevention in Atlanta.[6]

But perhaps the key statistic, to be discussed later in this chapter, is that the rise in the homicide rates correlates to a rise in the rate of child suicide. It's as if all life, even one's own, had little value. It is no surprise that after Kip Kinkel shot up his Springfield, Oregon, high school in May 1998, police found his previous writings that read, "Killers start sad" and, "Love sucks." As will be discussed later, herein could lie the key to youth crime.

As recounted in the previous chapter, America's crime rate began to decline in the early 1990s due in large part to the huge number of baby boomers who began to "age out" of the traditional peak crime-committing years of the teens through the mid-20s with some residual up until around the age of 40. Perhaps we just can't run as fast or jump those fences like we used to.

But look what's coming up on the horizon. The vast bulk of children of the baby boomers are expected to reach the peak crime-committing years shortly after the turn of the century with a 23 percent increase in 14- to 17-year-old males by the year 2005.

This population growth, along with the increasing arrest rates between 1985 and 1994, led the Justice Department itself to project that (1) the number of juvenile Violent Crime Index arrests would double between 1992 and 2010, with projected growth varying depending on the offense; and (2) by 2010, murder arrests of juveniles would increase by 145 percent, forcible rape arrests by 66 percent, robbery arrests by 58 percent, and aggravated assault arrests by 129 percent.[7]

Many at the time warned, in near Armageddon-like terms, that we should, at least, brace ourselves for the worst when the crime rate would go back up.

"It's time—we must prepare for the onslaught of juvenile violence," said Peter Reinharz, a counsel for New York City, in 1996.[8] The rhetoric was strong and alarming and, at the time, appeared to be supported by hard data.

"We have an army forming on the horizon," wrote Pulitzer Prize-winning journalist Edward Humes in his 1996 book about the juvenile justice system, *No Matter How Loud I Shout*. "It's going to invade in the next 10 or 15 years, and we're not doing anything to defend ourselves."

Noted criminologist James Alan Fox used these data only as a warning for the possibilities of what might happen if preventive steps weren't taken.

"We are facing a potential bloodbath of teenage violence in years ahead that will be so bad, we'll look back at the 1990s and say those were the good old days," he said in the June/July 1996 issue of *George* magazine.[9]

The author Bret Easton Ellis, in that same issue, seemed more certain when he wrote:

> [T]here's something far more insidious infesting America: Kids are ruining all our lives. . . . [T]hings have changed drastically in the last 20 years to the point where one can only chuckle in grim disbelief. Cheating on exams? Smoking cigarettes? Shoplifting? You wish. Murder, rape, robbery, vandalism: the overwhelming majority of these crimes are committed by people under 25, and the rate is escalating rapidly.[10]

But Fox shared the view of President Clinton, who at a Justice Department symposium on youth violence on June 11, 1997, argued that the crime wave caused by the youthful population bulge could be avoided:

> Keep in mind, this year, when school started, we had the largest class of children starting school and the largest number of people in school in the history of America. This year is the first year that the number of school children exceeded the high water mark of the baby boomers which means that, demographically, we have just a few years to deal with our young people and give them a future and something to say yes to and deal with this gang and drug and gun problem before the sheer change in population will begin to overwhelm our efforts.[11]

However, recent reports have surprised many by showing that youth violent crime started to nose-dive from such heights in about 1995. It dropped more than 16 percent in 1995, 1996 and 1997. Significantly, it's the youngest juveniles who are credited with the greatest decline in violent crimes. From 1994 to 1995, violent crime arrests declined 2 percent for juveniles ages 15–17 and 5 percent for those 14 and under.

Even the rash of schoolyard killings which galvanized the fears of the nation in the roughly six-month period between late 1997 and early 1998 was statistically misleading. Actually, school killings had gone down 45 percent since 1992. They were headline-grabbing, heart-wrenching tragedies, but they really were not indicative of any escalating trend. Perhaps it was the fact that these more recent murders took place in middle class or rural areas that caught the notice of the public. Previously, the plethora of school killings had taken place in inner-city schools and had not garnered as much publicity.[12]

It is also significant to note that the soaring of the American youth homicide rate from the mid-80s through 1995 was, in reality, not a nationwide phenomenon. It was very highly concentrated:

- It is significant that, in 1995, a third of those killings took place in just 10 counties in the United States, according to the Bureau of Justice Statistics. In fact, 84 percent of the nation's counties had no juvenile homicides whatsoever.
- Half the juvenile homicides took place in just the six states of California, New York, Texas, Florida, Michigan and Illinois. According to the FBI, about a third of all juvenile homicide arrests took place in just the four cities of Detroit, Los Angeles, New York and Chicago, alone.[13]

So, the explanation for the turning around of the rising youth crime rate beginning in 1995 appears to be that serious efforts were made to attack youth crime in just a handful of cities. For example, when you significantly lower the youth crime rate in just one city, say New York, that is enough to help send downward the rising youth crime statistics for the entire nation.

"It doesn't take success in many of the major cities to bring the juvenile homicide rate down appreciably," says one of the most highly esteemed crime experts in the country, Alfred Blumstein of Carnegie Mellon University, "because seven or eight cities account for 25 percent of all the homicides in the country."[14]

This is, in fact, what happened. The murder rate in New York City plunged 69.3 percent during the five-year period between 1993 and 1998 due to crime-fighting efforts, particularly community policing, which did not include locking up more people. Amazingly, New York's prison population had the slowest growth in the Northeast and the fifth slowest in the nation. While the average state's prison population rose 5 percent across the United States between 1996 and 1997, New York's rose a mere 0.5 percent.[15] This sole statistic is the greatest single argument for why fighting crime simply with more and more jails is the least effective way to fight crime—and anyone who advocates it is a big spender who will ultimately endanger us all.

So, the coming youth crime wave, long anticipated with dread, may not come after all. Yet, all agree that youth crime is still unacceptably high.

Are young people really different today than, let's say, 30 years ago?

At first blush, it might feel that way to you if you had spoken to 14-year-old Tyrone mentioned earlier in this chapter. He told me:

> I see a lot of guns. I've seen a lot of kids die. . . . If we heard a gunshot, we wouldn't get all scared. Not like you probably would. It's natural to us. . . . People have guns to protect themselves and protect their neighborhood. To show off. It's really cool. If you walk up the street and see a gang of kids, and they try to cause trouble, you can scare them off and they won't mess with you. . . . I got friends who got some guns and they ran into some kids who disrespected them. My friends didn't try to kill them, but they were shooting at them.

Or you might feel that way when you look at the case of 11-year-old Nathaniel Jamar Abraham, arrested for shooting his rifle without apparent motive from a nearby hill and killing a stranger walking out of a convenience store. When Nathaniel was arrested, on Halloween, he was wearing face paint just like any other playful kid in the neighborhood. But, though not yet out of elementary school, he had already managed to amass a lengthy record of violence and gun charges. Now, he faced trial as an adult in a Pontiac, Michigan, courtroom and a possible life sentence.

Another 11-year-old was convicted in 1998 of fatally stabbing a 71-year-old woman 18 times with two large kitchen knives in Norfolk, Virginia. He did this while he was helping deliver food to the needy just before Christmas for a subsidized food program operated by his mother.

Or take the case of Nushawn Williams, who at the age of 19, after a lengthy criminal career, was diagnosed as HIV-positive. In what seemed like incomprehensible cold-heartedness, he was said to have infected a mind-boggling number of girls as young as 13—possibly more than 100 of them—with HIV, usually trading drugs for sex. In effect, he may have knowingly given them all a potential death sentence. If the allegations are true, it would be attempted murder on a mass scale.

NOT ALWAYS FITTING THE STEREOTYPED PROFILE

But Nathaniel Jamar Abraham and Nushawn Williams are urban minority youths. Many middle-class Americans have long been fearful of this category. Yet the thing that's beginning to frighten many Americans is their perception that there is an increasing number of violent youths who are middle-class, white, apparently mainstream and often female. This fear is visceral because if you can, at least by appearances, relate to your assailant—he looks like you, comes from your neighborhood and has no outward appearance of being dangerous—how do you know to protect yourself from him? Sure, a person may be xenophobic about minority youth—particularly African-Americans and Latinos—but believes that he or she has some control and can take some steps to avoid them. They convince themselves that if only they stay out of the urban neighborhoods of these young, dangerous-looking types or give them a wide berth on the street, they might be able to keep themselves safe. But how can you tell if the fresh-faced, sweet honor student who lives next door is someone who would do you harm?

That's one of the reasons why the case of Louise Woodward—the 18-year-old British au pair accused of killing the infant Matthew Eappen whom she cared for in his home in Newton, Massachusetts—may have received such worldwide fascination. For a few weeks in the fall of 1997, the world media seemed transfixed by this case as the trial was telecast live and talk shows covered every nuance. The death of this infant—if, in fact, it was a homicide—seemed to attract more media attention than numerous other similar infant homicides. One of the theories on this widespread publicity was that the public found the incident so compelling and frightening primarily because there was absolutely nothing about Louise Woodward that would have tipped the parents off to any potential danger. She came from a nice family in a small town in England to work as an au pair in the United States where she hoped to learn about American culture. Though later reported by the Eappens to be a slightly immature and self-centered teenager more interested in hanging out at night with a host of new friends or getting discount theater tickets, she was sweet without any appearance of trouble.

"She didn't look scary," said the mother, Deborah Eappen. "She didn't look like a monster."[16]

Essentially, many Americans asked themselves as they watched the drama unfolding on TV, "If she did, in fact, do it, how can I protect myself or my own children from such danger since there were no warning signs? We may all be in danger if we have no way of knowing to protect ourselves."

That was the same feeling that many experienced in Paducah, Kentucky, a small town of 27,000 people and 100 churches when, in December 1997, 14-year-old Michael Carneal walked into the hallway of Heath High School and fired off 12 shots from a semiautomatic .22 killing three female students and wounding five others. Michael wasn't into drugs, had never been charged with a crime, was a band member, a B student, was the son of a prominent lawyer and had no connection with any cult.

"His father's a deacon and his sister's the valedictorian," remarked school principal Bill Bond. "Michael never dressed in black or wore upside-down crosses. He does not fit the mold of what our society says an angry person should be like."[17]

The town of Paducah wasn't much different from Pearl, Mississippi, where 16-year-old Luke Woodham shot and murdered his classmates only weeks earlier. Or, Jonesboro, Arkansas, where, in perhaps the incident which most shocked the nation, 13-year-old Mitchell Johnson and 11-year-old Andrew Golden pulled the fire alarm at their school, then sprinted about 100 yards away to wait for their prey. As the other students exited the schoolhouse, Johnson and Mitchell commenced firing their rifles, killing four little girls and a teacher and wounding 11 others.

Or the small hamlet of Edinboro, Pennsylvania, population 5,000, in the northwest corner of the state, where 14-year-old Andrew Wurth shot up his middle school dance, killing a popular teacher and wounding three others.

Or Springfield, Oregon, a mostly white, blue-collar and middle-class bedroom community of bicycle paths, neat homes and flowering shrubs in the foothills of the Cascade Range. It's an old timber community now giving way somewhat to high-tech businesses. Here people spend their time hunting, fishing and rafting. But on May 21, 1998, 15-year-old Kipland Kinkel walked into his high school cafeteria, pulled out and fired a semiautomatic, killing two students and wounding 22 others. Shortly before, he had shot his two parents to death.

All five towns—Pearl, Mississippi; Paducah, Kentucky; Jonesboro, Arkansas; Edinboro, Pennsylvania; and Springfield, Oregon—were relatively crime-free, rural, lower-income to middle-class, 85 to 98 percent white and most were in the "Bible Belt." Their residents thought it "just couldn't happen here." But small-town life was apparently no shield. Barbara Robbins, who had just moved from Memphis to Jonesboro because she thought it would be safer for her children, lamented:

> Now I'm just lost. You can't run from it. I mean, you can't get smaller than Jonesboro. I can't understand how a child my son's age could have a state of mind to do that. He'd have to be dead inside.

Robbins, unfortunately, was under the same misunderstanding held by most Americans. This is that, somehow, impersonal cities are more dangerous than the country or suburbs—that cities are breeding grounds of poor values, decay and violence as opposed to the finer virtues of the nonurban areas. In fact, violence in cities has long been in decline, beginning as far back as the mid-19th century until the rise again in the 1960s. For example, New York City averaged three to seven homicides per 100,000 citizens through the 19th century while some rural Southern states averaged as high as 28 murders per 100,000.[18] It is believed that part of the reason for this is that, as cities became industrialized, they required workers to work long hours in very regimented, disciplined factories and places of business with little leisure time. There was the advent of public schools in the cities which also taught obedience and self-control. Additionally, as will be discussed in depth in Chapter 5, many rural areas, particularly the South, operated on a traditional "honor culture" where slights, insults and signs of disrespect always had to be answered, all too often with violence. It has long been a myth that cities are more violent.

This caused a lot of soul searching in the sparse, rustic area near Gloversville, in upstate New York. Around that village in a three-month period in 1997, there were an unprecedented four separate murders. Three were said to be committed by teens. The first was when a 19-year-old boy got into a taxi with a shotgun and said he wanted to be taken to a particular place to go rabbit hunting. When they got there, he shot the cab driver twice in the face. Three weeks later, three teenagers including one female, kidnapped her 19-year-old boyfriend who apparently owed her money. They tortured him and strangled him. Two months later, the end came for a 77-year-old retiree who had complained for months that youths continually broke into his home and also harassed him. When police eventually got around to his house to check on one of the complaints, they found his deteriorating body tied to a chair which had been tipped over. It had pushed his face into the floor, asphyxiating him. Two 16-year-olds were eventually arrested for his murder. They had been riding around in the old man's car for days bragging about the murder so much that as many as 30 kids knew about the slaying days before the discovery of the body.

As usual, everyone tried to weigh in with a theory on what was going on with the youngsters in their unsophisticated area far from the big city. The head of the new town committee on youth violence, Warren Greene, said, ". . . [I]t took us seven seconds to agree that it's the parents, stupid."[19]

Other Gloversville residents blame television and the values of "ghetto chic." But Rosalie Sweet, a parent who grew up in the town, said there is just no longer any place for kids to go in town. She explained, "When I was a kid they had the Glove Theater and the Civic Center and the Littauer Playground and lots of places you could go. Kids don't have any of those things anymore."

It is interesting that these reasons—lack of parenting, a violent media and a great undirected idleness—are the same reasons often attributed for youth violence in the country's urban areas. In farmlands or cities, the causes of youth violence are similar. But again, the lessons learned by the folks in Gloversville are the same as those learned by the people of Jonesboro: that it is clear that bucolic areas in the country are no safe haven from violence.

Adding to the fear in Jonesboro was that, at first glance, the two child killers in Jonesboro didn't fit the profile of killers. They were not drug users or drinkers, and they had not been in any previous trouble with the law.

"Everyone's looking for an answer," said one parent, whose children are also in the Jonesboro school system, shortly after the killings, "But I don't think anyone believes you can raise two bad seeds around here. They want to know what went wrong but I don't think anyone really believes that an 11-year-old understood what he was doing."[20]

Scott Johnson, the father of one of the killers, said, "I don't have an explanation for any of this. Nobody does. It's not something you would expect out of your child or anybody else's child."

Friends of the parents of the Jonesboro slayers rushed to the parents' defense. Pam Crider, a friend of 11-year-old Andrew Golden's parents, who are both postmasters in nearby towns, said, "I'm so afraid that Dennis and Pat (Andrew's father and mother) are going to be portrayed as these horrible people who beat their kid up or something. I'm telling you that's not it. It's just not true. There may be some other way to explain this, but that's not it."

With every incident, commentators and experts always rush to find a trend. But, after the Jonesboro massacre, one might doubt whether there always has to be an explanation. One is tempted to suspect that sometimes they're just bizarre, terrible acts that can't be simply reasoned or rationalized. They may not be indicative of anything.

The only immediately apparent trend was that all of these seemingly normal children were looking for some kind of revenge over some typical childhood experience—a breakup with a girlfriend, being picked on, dismay at a parents' divorce, etc.—and lived in communities where guns were extremely prevalent. Still, there were no major hints that these seemingly normal children would turn to killing. Though, in retrospect, many saw clues such as the case of Springfield, Oregon's, Kipland Kinkel, who, though apparently no one had taken it seriously, had injured animals, committed vandalism, spoke of building bombs and had just been suspended for bringing a gun to school. His classmates had humorously voted him most likely to start World War III.

This was underscored that same year by a variety of other cases where seemingly nice, middle-class students were accused of committing neonaticide—killing their newborn infants often after keeping it a secret from everyone they were pregnant. In one case, two seemingly well-adjusted college students from suburban Wyckoff, New Jersey, were accused of and later pleaded guilty to killing their just-born baby and depositing it in a motel Dumpster. Eighteen-year-old Amy Grossberg, the daughter of affluent parents who volunteered as an art teacher for children in her spare time, and 19-year-old Brian Peterson, who worked part time for his parents' business, seemed like just a couple of very nice people and were well loved by all who knew them.

One attorney, Jerry Capone, who works with many less advantaged youths conveyed his alarm at the background of Grossberg and Peterson. "These kids from strong family backgrounds should have the proper moral background," he said. "That really frightens me. It means this lack of respect for human life cuts across all economic classes."[21]

More than ever, it seems that there are few reliable indicators to give warning that a young person may have a predilection toward violence. Some psychologists believe there are sometimes signs that can point to the potential for violence in a child who still has not previously exhibited any violent behavior. If a child is an isolated loner, overly fascinated with death, mutilates animals or toys, has few friends or, in the vernacular, just plain acts "weird," maybe therein lies the tipoff. But even these indicators aren't overly reliable, since some kids can exhibit any one of these traits and they don't become violent or unsuccessful later in life.

But it's the growing number of kids who show no outward signs of potential violence that scares many of us the most since we (and especially parents) don't know how to identify them and subsequently watch out for them in our midst.

Never was this felt more deeply than in the Eddie O'Brien case, already noted in the previous chapter, whose trial was, ironically, held in the same Cambridge, Massachusetts, courthouse as the Louise Woodward case just several weeks earlier in 1997.

Eddie O'Brien was a popular 15-year-old growing up in a working-class neighborhood of the Boston suburb of Somerville, Massachusetts, where his grandfather had been police chief for decades. It was a close-knit neighborhood where everyone knew everyone else and the neighborhood kids frequently went into each others' homes without knocking. Eddie was a lovable, sweet-tempered kid with lots of friends. By all accounts, they weren't into alcohol or drugs or fights, and Eddie, although very big physically, didn't even appear to be aggressive enough to play football seriously. He was very good-humored and often almost a clown.

Eddie's best friend lived right across the street with three siblings and his mother, Janet Downing. On July 23, 1995, Eddie passed out ice cream popsicles to some of the younger kids in his neighborhood and then at home put a video of *Sleeping Beauty* into the VCR for one of his younger sisters. It is alleged that, a short while later, Eddie somehow wound up in his friend's house across the street, which was not that unusual. But this time, alone in the house with 42-year-old Janet Downing, he was said to have stabbed and slashed her to death with a knife 98 times. It was an act of overkill so savage in its passionate ritual execution that it was believed only a sexually obsessed psychopath could have done it.

Again, one of the reasons the public seemed so drawn in its fascination to this case is that, in light of the sheer grossness of the monstrous crime, the public was made aware of absolutely no warning signs that such a sweet neighborhood kid as Eddie O'Brien could have committed such an act. He didn't seem to fit any of the conventional profiles. He wasn't a loner, wasn't obsessed with death, didn't practice cruelty to animals or children or exhibit aggressive behavior, didn't appear depressed, came from an intact family and had many friends. So, logically, many who followed the case essentially said to themselves, "If this is true and a regular, seemingly nice kid like this could pull off such a murderous rampage without any warning signs beforehand, how do I know if other seemingly nice people in my life will harm me and my family? How do I protect myself?"

It's this wariness that killers may be in our midst and closer to us than ever that has the public so much more dedicated than ever to meting out harsh punishments. For example, after the alleged Grossberg/Peterson act of neonaticide in New Jersey, there was suddenly a spate of news stories in 1997 about kids killing their just-delivered babies, particularly unwed teens who were able to keep their pregnancies secret.

Surprisingly, in the past, neonaticide was not uncommon. This was particularly so in Victorian times when servant-class girls were sometimes sexually exploited. They were perceived as desperately poor, couldn't afford abortions and, besides, when discovered, scientific methods didn't exist to determine whether the child had just been born dead. Still, in those rare times when they were prosecuted, they were, for better or worse, treated with some leniency.

Not today. Such killers are viewed as overindulged, affluent and callous and are prosecuted without hesitation. In the Grossberg/Peterson case, the prosecution initially sought an unprecedented punishment for this kind of crime—the death penalty—though the defendants ultimately pleaded guilty to get short prison sentences. Forensic psychologist Barbara Kirwin, who has testified at numerous neonaticide trials, sees no excuse for these educated teens who come from apparently nondysfunctional families and have good access to birth control information to commit murder. Kirwin states:

> I don't see it as a mental illness. I see it as symptomatic of a lack of maternal bonding—the baby is seen as a burden, a bother—and of family systems that break down. These families look functional on the surface, but there has to be something wrong that the mother doesn't notice her daughter's pregnancy. I think it's the moral equivalent of benign neglect.[22]

There was another 1997 case of murder which raised the public ire from coast to coast and didn't even have to do with the death of humans. On the evening of March 7, 1997, Chad Lamansky and Daniel Myers, two teenagers without prior criminal records from the rural farm community of Fairfield, Iowa, broke into the Noah's Ark Animal Shelter. Once inside, they bludgeoned to death 16 cats and injured at least another seven. When the owner of the shelter, David Sykes entered the blood-spattered building, there was carnage everywhere. He recounted: "Some had broken limbs, just hanging and flopping. Some had broken jaws, others had bloodied eyes. I remember thinking this was a dream. But it wasn't. A holocaust had hit the shelter."

The vicious crime was pointless, done, as the boys allegedly told their friends, "just for the thrill of it," and they were said to have bragged about it. A debate ensued and many people thought that this shouldn't be regarded as just a "boys will be boys" prank because after all it was only animals, not people. They were demanding decades of incarceration in adult prison—and more. "I would like to see the three drawn and quartered and left in the sun to dry out," said Iowa resident Lou Hill.

Ultimately, they were sentenced to a "taste of jail"—23 days—but were given years of onerous alternative punishments such as community service, payments of the cost of the prosecution, fines and restitution, counseling and an additional four-year suspended prison sentence hanging over their heads.

NO LONGER TAKEN LIGHTLY

Perhaps as the juvenile violent crime rate begins to significantly drop (more than 16 percent in 1995, 1996 and 1997), it's these high-profile horror stories that fuel the rush to abandon all methods of fighting juvenile crime save one—prosecution in adult courts and incarceration in adult prisons.

The above-mentioned case of the 11-year-old facing a life sentence in adult court is no aberration. The previous year, a six-year-old mildly retarded boy in Richmond, California, outside San Francisco, was charged with attempted murder in the near-fatal beating of an infant. As the story was pieced together, he and two eight-year-olds had gone into a neighborhood home looking to find a Hot Wheels tricycle when a one-month-old baby who was alone in a crib there began to make noise. The boy knocked the crib down and later kicked the baby to try to shut it up. It was a shocking crime.

The six-year-old had, to be sure, a young life that was almost designed to eventually create a sociopath. His alleged drug-dealing father had been murdered with six gun shots to the head when he was only four years old and, although he was not around to witness that killing, he always fantasized that he had. The six-year-old had witnessed his mother being frequently beaten up by boyfriends and he, himself, had been tied up and had glasses thrown at him by these men. His grandmother was a profane, loud, violent crack dealer. Often, when drug use was going on in his home, he'd be sent outside at 9 o'clock at night by the adults to "go outside and play." So at these times this kindergartner would stand out in the dark by himself with no one to play with until the adults would let him back in.

Prosecutor Harold Jewett prosecuted the six-year-old for attempted murder. He was detained in a juvenile detention facility where he'd cry every time he was locked into his cell for the night. A judge ruled him incompetent to stand trial because he was too young to understand the proceedings against him. Jewett vowed to still prosecute him once he became competent in the future. In the meantime, the six-year-old was transferred to a group home.

"It doesn't matter whether you're 6 or 106," said Jewett. " If you do something that hurts someone else with knowledge of the wrongfulness of it, you're responsible for it. Period."

Yet it's not just these major crimes. This attitude has trickled down to the lesser offenses. Increasingly, young people who have never been in trouble before are treated harshly by impatient politicians who believe they can please the crowd.

I represented someone I'll call Harris, a teenager from a small New England town with kind and devoted working-class parents. A phenomenal artist winning all kinds of awards in high school, he gained admittance to one of the finest art-and-design schools in the country. Today, a large and extraordinary mural he painted still adorns a wall at the high school. But, as happens, a variety of contributing pressures hit him all at once—depression, anxiety about the future, the breakup of a relationship and an alcohol and drug problem. He was hospitalized for a couple of weeks.

Harris seemed better but, at Christmastime, depression took hold of him again. One night, he found a hypodermic needle which had been left by a diabetic friend and put a variety of cleaning fluids in it including ammonia. He decided to kill himself by injecting the fluid into his arm.

But Harris, blessedly, still must have clung to some small sense of survival because before he did this, he made a final desperate grasp at life. Hanging on to a will to live by a thread, he called a local suicide prevention hotline and let them know he intended to give up God's greatest gift. He spoke to them at length, the phone in one hand, the lethal hypodermic needle in the other. He gave them his phone number, name and address. Following standard procedure, they kept him on the line while contacting the police.

The police were over in a flash. Harris was surprised as he put the phone and needle down on a coffee table and went to the front door. Two police officers asked to come in to speak with him and he let them in. One spotted the needle and secured it. They took Harris with them to a local psychiatric hospital where he acknowledged to them that he had found his friend's hypodermic needle and had planned to kill himself. He was admitted there. Once again, his family rallied to his side, he transferred over to a much better hospital and then eventually was released. The crisis had passed. He continued to improve. Plans were made for him to finally begin college for his art.

It was about a month and a half later that he received a summons left for his arrest. The police had brought a criminal charge against him. What in the world could he have done? Illegal possession of a hypodermic needle was what they came up with.

At that point, I was brought into the case. As Harris and his family sat across the desk from me and I listened to their story, I realized I was hearing one of the "you've-got-to-be-kidding" stories of all time. I empathized deeply with Harris, who was valiantly fighting his inner demons and making real progress in his bid for good solid mental health. This was the last thing he needed. Were they out to undo him? What good would it do to run him through the criminal justice meat grinder and convict him criminally?

In the state where he lived, for such crimes, they don't use a prosecutor who is an attorney. Instead, they use a police prosecutor who is a police officer specializing in going to court and negotiating some of the relatively more minor crimes short of trial. I spoke with the police prosecutor about the purpose of going ahead with the charge. Yes, I agreed that technically Harris did break the law. It is illegal to possess a hypodermic needle without a doctor's prescription. But give me a break. Do you really want to discourage potential suicides from reaching out for help? Do you want to punish them for grasping for life? I made no progress in heading off the police prosecutor from going forward with this charge. Eventually, I accompanied Harris and his parents to the police station where he was booked. At this point, my mind started drifting back to an old black-and-white film . . .

In a scene from the Christmas film classic, *It's a Wonderful Life,* the protagonist George Bailey, played by James Stewart, in the dark night of his soul, stands poised on a snow-covered bridge about to jump in and end his life. But before he is able to do so, he is surprised by someone else jumping in. Unbeknownst to him, it is his guardian angel, Clarence, who knows that the good-hearted George will abandon his own plans to kill himself in order to try to rescue another. In the next scene, wet and freezing, they are in the bridge tollhouse in the company of the tollkeeper as they attempt to get dry and warm.

In an amusing dialogue, Clarence tries hard to explain to George Bailey and the tollkeeper that the reason he jumped in was, ironically, to save George from going ahead with his suicide attempt. With deadpan earnestness, the tollkeeper immediately remarks that it's against the law to commit suicide.

The line, as delivered in the film, about being subject to arrest after killing yourself, is a light comedic line which reaches for a laugh. Actually, it is true that many states do have such laws, but how ever would you enforce them? It would also take a rather grim prosecutor to charge someone with attempted suicide since a jury would have little stomach to convict a self-abusive depressed person. Or so you'd think.

Sometimes, as in the case of Harris, they don't exactly charge you with the crime of attempted suicide. They just find something else related to the event to charge you with. It's much more subtle. The key was to get this teen with something—anything. Ultimately, I was able to help protect Harris' future by keeping him from getting a criminal record, though not before he was dragged through hell.

The attitude is pervasive. A school suspension was also given out in 1997 to a five-year-old in Worcester, Massachusetts, for bringing a plastic toy gun to school. This was in violation of a school rule forbidding toy guns.

Later that same year, a junior high school student was suspended from DuPont Junior High School in Belle, West Virginia, for giving another student a nonprescription cough drop because school officials there said there's no such thing as harmless medication.

The question is, if these students did, in fact, break the rules or were troubled in some way, would a suspension be the most effective way an educator could help them or others with their problem? Of course not. How would having them no longer participate in being educated turn them around? If anything, insisting a child get educated would make more sense than forcing that child away from education.

At the time the five-year-old Massachusetts boy with the toy gun was suspended, violence prevention expert Deborah Prothrow-Stith, appearing on the March 25, 1997, newscast of Boston station WHDH, commented, "At some point we've got to use professional judgment; we've got to use common sense. Suspending children from school is probably one of the least effective ways to deal with their behavior."

Another person said, "It's overkill. I think that people are pushing it way too far." This was followed by one more person commenting, "Part of the time, we need to just lighten up a little bit and let kids be kids."

This was particularly true in the case of the 15-year-old Lakeside, Michigan, honor student who regularly attended a Baptist church study group and never had been a discipline problem. She had long had a collection of "weird" pens. Then, in 1996, when she was on a visit to Chicago, she bought a pen that had the words "real pot seeds" and then had the word "sterile" written on the side. This meant that the seeds encased inside were unusable and therefore legal under Michigan law. Despite a huge protest, the school suspended her for 45 days giving her a zero for everything she missed and not letting her make up the work so that her college future would be jeopardized. But that wasn't sufficient for her principal, who turned matters over to the police. She was charged with possession and distribution of a controlled substance. But since it was sterile and therefore powerless, the charges, of course, had to be dropped. Even though it was proved not to be a drug under the law, the principal didn't stop the suspension because of a peculiar and vague school rule forbidding not only drugs, but an undefined "lookalike drug."

In late 1997, two ten-year-old girls were hauled into court in Mount Clemens, Michigan, a suburb of Detroit, and ordered by the judge to play nice or they could go to jail. Circuit Court Judge Michael Schwartz told them, "No more harassment, no more threats, no more obscenities or vulgar names, no more pulling hair. If one of you causes problems to the other, I'm going to put you in the juvenile hold."

This court case caused great turmoil in Mount Clemens, where educators said such actions usurp their role in teaching kids how to get along, and prosecutors referred to it as an abuse of the court system. "Where did we get this idea that every dispute between children has to wind up before a . . . judge?" asked Carl Malinga, a Michigan prosecutor who was not involved with the case.[23]

It is not disputes alone. More and more aspects of childhood are being legislated, codified and dealt with in court, for better or worse.

An example of the abdication of teachers in favor of the courts happened in Largo, Florida, in 1997. There, a six-year-old threw a tantrum and wouldn't listen to her first grade teacher when she and others were told not to sit too closely to a TV set where a visiting police officer was showing a crime prevention video. She was arrested, charged with a felony and whisked off to a detention center where she was held for hours.

This was similar to the ten-year-old Las Vegas boy who in 1997 wrote in some freshly poured cement. He claimed he had done so at the invitation of one of the cement laborers. He was yanked out of his third grade class, charged with a delinquent act of vandalism, strip-searched and left for five hours in a holding cell before his mother was notified. Again, his behavior was poor and should be addressed. But aren't schools capable of or interested in handling and disciplining students any more? Must so many things be referred to the police where the children are incarcerated and face gaining criminal records which can follow them forever and damage their careers before they even begin in life?

A WAR ON CHILDREN

Rather than go after the root sources of what causes children to finally engage in crime—things that they may not have created such as the disintegration of the family, poverty, our disinvestment in children, the media—we just wait for them to get in trouble and then go after the kids.

"Today, running short on villains, we're back to blaming the kids themselves—or at least teenagers," wrote Richard Louv, senior editor at Kids Campaigns and a columnist for the *San Diego Union-Tribune*. "With the exception of a few noteworthy programs, we're turning our backs on young people. Instead of acting like adults—instead of doing what it takes to build strong families and offering children and teens a sense of meaning by investing more in education, recreation and mentoring programs—we're demonizing children and building teen centers called prisons."[24]

That's why politicians now score points going after young people. They don't work to help them or intervene in their lives to prevent crimes and spare victims. They just go after them in their endless dance for votes.

In April 1998, a 10-year-old boy in Miami was arrested, handcuffed and jailed overnight after a waitress allegedly saw him kick his mother at a restaurant. Miami-Dade police Detective Ed Munn said that they had no choice to make the arrest because the domestic violence law required the fourth-grader to be arrested. Both the judge and juvenile officials criticized the rules following the child's arraignment on charges of domestic battery. But none were as angry as the boy's mother, Arlene Martin: "To be arrested for something like that? It was ridiculous. I couldn't believe it was happening. When they put the handcuffs on him, I was completely shocked. He just sort of brushed my leg. It was nothing."

In 1997, one elected politician, Sheriff Joe Arpaio of Maricopa County, Arizona, predictably announced he planned to extend the use of chain gangs and tent jails to juveniles. In order to humiliate them, Arpaio announced, "My philosophy is, they will eat the same bologna, wear the same pink underwear (as adult inmates). They'll be treated the same."[25]

It's such acts that caused Bruce Shapiro to write in a July 7, 1997, editorial in *The Nation*:

> Not so long ago, politicians campaigned by kissing babies. Today, they lock children in jail. Never mind that juvenile crime rates are falling. Washington is in a bipartisan fever to incarcerate middle-schoolers in Attica, Huntsville and other penitentiaries alongside adult robbers, rapists and killers.

Politicians feel they have nothing to lose by putting children in adult institutions where, in contrast to juvenile facilities, they are:

- Five times as likely to be sexually assaulted
- Twice as likely to be beaten by staff
- Fifty percent more likely to be attacked with a weapon
- Eight times as likely to commit suicide.[26]

Louv quotes Nancy Ajemian Sherman, director of Harmonium, a social service and counseling program for teens and families, asking, "Have we declared war on teens? We've done worse than declare war on them. We have made them invisible. They are treated worse than any minority."[27]

Attorney Phillip Kassel, who works with young people, argues that people can like their own kids or kids they know on an individual basis, but still have no sympathy for youth in general terms. He says:

> I think people see kids in groups and are intimidated. They don't compare them to their own children and identify any sense of their hopes and fears and anxieties and aspirations, and they see them as threats. It's a dehumanizing way of looking at it, so they're scapegoats. And again, I think, in the popular culture, there are always images of sociopathic, cold-blooded killer children that get internalized. I don't think

they're particularly accurate. I mean, there are some children like that, who get so demonized themselves, that perhaps they meet that description, but they're few and far between. Cops tell you that.

Rebecca Young, director of Citizens for Juvenile Justice, believes this very attitude held by many concerning the lack of importance of children may be directly attributable to the fact that they can't reach the ballot box. She said:

> I really believe that they can't vote is not irrelevant. I really think that the fact that they have no voice of their own is a problem. I mean, they're a powerless group, and if the rest of us, if the adults, fail to say, "Look, it is our job in life to protect them and to help them grow so that someday they'll be like the rest of us who aren't committing crimes," then we've sort of failed in part of our basic goal in society.

But despite the difference of opinions on the appropriate approach to dealing with troubled young people, the question still begs to be asked—are young people today radically and fundamentally different from previous generations? Though it may be a generalization, are young people today less moral, more lost and more dangerous than ever before?

No. But things are being done to some young people differently from before—they're being abandoned, given an absence of older people in their lives, being flooded with guns and flooded with violent media images. So, a very small segment of the juvenile population, originally victims themselves, without adults or any guidance in their lives, does pose a risk and they are a segment to be reckoned with. This is particularly so when guns are so pervasive in their lives. Juveniles are somewhat, but not significantly violent in greater numbers than they were in the past. But when they actually are violent, the violence today is so much more deadly. Today, a kid settles a schoolyard affront less often with a punch or a shove and more often with a gun. Juveniles aren't a great deal more violent today; they're just more lethal.

One prison inmate in his mid-40s whom I spoke with, gave his perspective to me on the youths he sees coming through the prison gates:

> People try to make distinctions between generations—whether or not this generation of youth is any more violent than its predecessor. Some law enforcement agencies or zealous politicians even refer to them as superpredators. But I don't think there is much of a difference. I think the difference lies in the availability of weapons and drugs and the fact that every generation of youth feels more and more locked out of the economic mainstream.

Children are often impulsive and therefore aren't always the best and most reasonable problem-solvers. Hence, the all-too-common punching and shoving. But with some kids so much better armed today, they'll simply use the weapon where a punch might have sufficed for them if they didn't happen to have the gun with them.

According to noted criminologist James Alan Fox, dean of Northeastern University's College of Criminal Justice, using a phrase made popular by his colleague Jack Levin, "It's always been that teenagers are impulsive. One might call them 'temporary sociopaths.' But now they're armed."[28]

Youth crime rates for nonviolent crimes didn't go up either. It's guns, guns, guns. Guns are the sole area of youth crime that has shown a marked and significant increase.

"This is really a gun story," says criminologist Alfred Blumstein. Blumstein believes that the rate of gun homicides began to move upward in 1985 at the same time that massive amounts of crack cocaine were introduced into inner-city neighborhoods. The drug industry began to recruit young people into the drug business and to arm them. Soon, kids not even involved with drugs began to arm themselves for protection and status.

Guns are more deadly than anything else. First of all, I'd much less rather face someone in his early teens with a gun than a person in their 30s or 40s. A youngster is not only less well trained with firearms, but also tends to be more impulsive. Not only that, but it's just easier to kill with a gun than if you had to perform the murder up close with your bare hands or a knife. The killing is more remote and less real and personal psychologically if you can do it from farther away. So you can kill more readily over less important things.

Fifteen-year-old Tyrell explained to me the incredible triviality and frightening values which can lead to shootings in his rough urban neighborhood:

> Like you could be playing ball with someone and you could foul them. A person could just get mad, go off and shoot you. Over something little like that . . . maybe just over words. Because that person don't like that. Some persons can't take that. Some people are very sensitive. A person could just get mad over someone saying a certain word they don't like. 'Cause a person feels if you disrespect them, you take away their manhood or girlhood. . . . People dying left and right. It shouldn't be like that . . . over a little disrespect or whatever.

For some, it's almost as if they don't understand that, unlike all the TV they watch, this is not a game, death is for real and permanent and the victim won't, later on, get up and walk off. This is the very small segment of the youth population without anyone to give them direction and there is a marked risk here.

DISINTEGRATING FAMILIES, GROWING POVERTY AND THE MEDIA

What made this particular group that way? No one is born bad, although some tiny fraction emerge at birth with some kind of organic brain damage, mental illness or the ill effects of a parent's substance abuse. The once popular theory that there is a "crime gene," perhaps an extra Y or X chromosome, has long been discounted. Though currently, serious research is being done on whether serotonin levels in the body affect behavior and impulse control.

Aside from that infinitesimally small group, what happens to pure healthy babies somewhere between birth and their criminal act which takes places perhaps in their early teens? Something must have gone on; there must have been a reason. Something happened, and, if we can understand it, we can do something about it in the future. The situation is gravely serious, but there is absolutely nothing hopeless about it.

A variety of experts cite such things as today's disintegration of the American family, poverty and the relentlessly violent media upon which so many are weaned. Certainly, all these factors exist and contribute.

The era of two parent families with one at home is rapidly fading:

- In 1970, 85 percent of the children in the United States lived with two parents. By 1996, this number had dropped to 68 percent (75 percent for white non-Hispanics, 64 percent for Hispanic children and a sadly disheartening 33 percent for African-American children).
- A survey of college freshmen released in 1998 showed that 28.5 percent of them had parents who were divorced or separated, three times the level recorded when the question was first included in the survey in 1972.
- The percentage of births to unmarried mothers rose from 5 percent in 1960 to 32 percent in 1995.
- By 1994, 76 percent of all births to teens took place outside of marriage, compared to 15 percent in 1960. (In 1994, 67 percent of

births to white teens, 70 percent to Hispanic teens and 96 percent of births to African-American teens were nonmarital births.)

- "Out-of-wedlock" teen births have continued to increase, despite the encouraging news that the overall teen birth rate moved downward during the 1990s. Both government and private studies released in 1998 attributed this to both less sex and more birth control. Additionally, this study noted that dramatic drops in this rate have been made among the African-American community through that community's own strategy of community leaders, schools and religious leaders letting young people know how limiting it will be to their future. "If you think you have a future, you put off having babies," said Donna Shalala, secretary of Health and Human Services.[29]

While passing absolutely no judgment on the morality of premarital sex for teens, it is irrefutable that there can be a number of negative consequences. Although this is only a generality and there are certainly exceptions, a child born to an unmarried teen is generally less likely to garner the sort of emotional and financial resources that would be most helpful in making him or her into a happy, stable, productive, well-adjusted adult:

- 62 percent of young women who had a child while in high school dropped out of high school.
- Studies show that children with mothers who are age 17 or younger:

  —have lower cognitive test scores and more difficulty in school
  —have poorer health and receive less health care
  —have less stimulating and supportive home environments

  —have higher levels of incarceration
  —have higher rates of adolescent childbearing themselves

- Almost 60 percent of families who receive Aid to Families with Dependent Children funds are headed by women who were teenagers when they had their first child.
- A child born to an unmarried, teenage, high school dropout is 10 times as likely to be living in poverty as a child born to a mother with none of these characteristics.[30]

The typical profile of an unmarried woman giving birth is not the successful, affluent career woman who makes the choice and then has the financial wherewithal, support and education to raise a flourishing child. In 1998, the Census Bureau reported that single mothers were eight times as likely as married couples to live in poverty.[31] Essentially, on average, a single mother raising a child tends to have a much lower income, less education and frequently the severe emotional stresses that go along with those features. The sad result is that rising out-of-wedlock births clearly has had an effect on crime:

- 43 percent of all inmates grew up in a single-parent household.
- Men from single-parent families are twice as likely to commit crimes as men from two-parent families.
- The sons of adolescent mothers are 2.7 times more likely to be incarcerated than the sons of mothers who delay childbearing until their early 20s.
- A state-by-state analysis by the conservative Heritage Foundation found that a 10 percent increase in single-parent homes typically led to a 17 percent increase in juvenile crime.
- A 1 percent increase in births to single mothers appears to have increased the violent crime rate about 1.7 percent, according to one study by the Cato Institute.[32] The babies of young, unmarried, poorly educated women are far more likely than other infants to be victims of homicide. The babies of girls under 17 are more than three times as likely to be killed. Having more than one child before the age of 19 increases the risk of infant homicides a whopping ninefold over children born to parents over the age of 25.

Some of this may be attributed to the combination of desperation, lack of real interest, immaturity and inexperience of adolescent mothers. One study of children in Illinois found that children born to adolescent mothers were twice as likely to be victims of abuse and neglect than even children born to 20- to 21-year-old mothers.[33]

But even two-parent homes can produce children with a higher crime rate when both parents are absent, usually due to their jobs. Additionally, there are dozens of studies over the decades which show that, even when an intact family with two parents exists, if the parents' relationship is characterized by discord, strife and/or spousal abuse, their children are much more likely to commit crimes.[34]

Robert Sampson, professor of sociology at the University of Chicago, states, "There are higher crime rates in places where communities are not characterized by strong families. The research has been fairly consistent, showing a small to moderate positive relationship between individual delinquency and family breakdown."[35]

Even in very high-crime neighborhoods, if the intact family is close knit, there is little chance that the child will commit crimes. And families do come in different forms. Seventeen-year-old Linda's impoverished, immigrant single mother worked all the time to support her children and was rarely around. Yet Linda told me they put together a system that worked:

> My older sister had to be a role model to us because my mom had to go to work all the time and she was like really strict on what we had to do. My sister had to answer to my mom if the rest of us did anything wrong, so my sister was like a mother to us. My mom couldn't take the pressure, maybe because my dad had left, I don't know why. So my sister told us how to act.

Despite her rough urban surroundings and the fact that most of her friends were in gangs, Linda always managed to stay out of trouble, is an excellent student and has a paid job as a youth outreach worker in the community.

The importance of family is particularly clear when we note the now well-known, but still surprising, fact that most crimes by young people are not committed late at night, but rather between 2 in the afternoon and 8 in the evening—those hours when school is out, but the parents have not yet come home from work. In fact, at the witching hour of 3 p.m., juvenile crimes begin to triple.

In fact, it's not just violent crime, but all kinds of regrettable behavior that occurs among unguided juveniles in the afternoon. A University of Southern California study showed that eighth-graders left unsupervised after school were more likely to smoke, drink and use drugs than those with some sort of afterschool oversight. They were also more likely to get poor grades and behave badly, according to another study. In fact, 75 percent of all first-time sexual liaisons occur inside the juveniles' homes. It's easier today now that the parents aren't home. Note that 60 percent of all sexually transmitted diseases are contracted by teenagers. "We had to use Chevys," mused criminologist James Alan Fox. "Now kids don't need cars. When the cat's away, the mice will have sex."[36]

The solution is simple. More schools should be open and have afterschool activities. Today, only about 30 percent of the schools in America are open in the late afternoon. Many more used to be open, but with cost cutting, this is the first place many municipalities have been slashing. Prior to 1978's Proposition 13, all Los Angeles schools used to be open for afternoon programs. Now, with the exception of school sports, they're all shut tight. It is part of this country's trend toward an all-around disinvestment in children. Of the American schools that are open in the afternoon, most charge fees. Only the moneyed classes can take advantage of it. This is wrong. Considering that juveniles who become career criminals will cost us over $1 million each in their lifetime, not spending a pittance of money on afterschool programs will cost us too much.

Northeastern University professor Jack Levin, one of the nation's premier violence experts, is also one of the prime backers of the movement to keep schoolhouse doors open after school. He says:

> Of course, it would be wonderful to increase parental responsibility and it is happening to some extent. But, the schools can play a critical role if, and only if, local community members allow it to happen. I would be in favor of expanding the school day so what we call afterschool programs now are incorporated throughout the day.[37]

Police Commissioner Thomas Frazier assigned over 50 officers along with other staff to operate 27 afterschool programs all around Baltimore. "In the high-crime area where we opened the first center, neighborhood crime dropped 42 percent in the program's first year," Frazier said. "But we still reach barely 1 in 10 kids. Like most cities, Baltimore needs the resources to do more."[38]

The daylong absence of the mother and father in two-parent homes is felt hardest among the very youngest children. Fresh research on the brain hammers home the point that it's the beginning experiences which have the deepest effect on the child's mental, social and emotional development. Yet today, more than half of the mothers of children under four are working. And nearly half of the 15 million infants and toddlers whose parents are working are in nurseries and day care centers.[39]

But much of day care was originally designed as a sort of lengthy babysitting service or friendly warehousing, and today it's still not that good. Now that it's being used for such a massive percentage of the populace, we have the youngest children growing up often without any real parenting during most of their day.

Roberta Bergman, of the Child Care Group in Dallas, Texas, wrote, in a letter appearing in the November 24, 1997, edition of *Newsweek*:

> [T]he need for fundamental change goes beyond money. Child care
> has largely been created as a consumer service for working parents,
> designed for efficiency in managing children in groups. But for chil-
> dren who are spending more of their waking hours in child care than
> with their families, it is a powerful influence on how they develop.
> Child care must replicate what the family offers: learning through
> close, continuous nurturing relationships.[40]

Since children's minds are so pliant and flexible at the very youngest
ages, day care can even make inroads against bad parenting by, at the very
least, providing a safe and stirring environment.

But most of the hodgepodge of child care situations springing up all
over the country, both informal and formal, are unregulated and unli-
censed with extremely low-paid, untrained staff at inadequate facilities.

"We require licenses for beauticians and caterers," according to
Sharon Lynn Kagan, the author of *Reinventing Early Care and Education*.
"It's ludicrous that we don't require licenses for child care workers."[41]

They can get away with providing such poor day care in this country
because there is such a desperate lack of it that parents are grateful to get
their children in anywhere they can. In Massachusetts alone, there are
more than 12,000 kids on waiting lists for day care.[42] Unfortunately, what
they are waiting for is not so good. A 1997 national study by Yale University investigators found that 86 percent of the child care centers in the survey offered poor to mediocre care.

Syndicated columnist Ellen Goodman on January 15, 1998, also expressed concern about the failure to truly recognize the worth of those
who work with children:

> Every once in a while when you dig through the dusty archeology of
> statistics, you come across something of value. Or at least something
> about values.
>
> Consider the numbers from the Bureau of Labor Statistics show-
> ing that a worker who helps bury people is worth about a dollar more
> than one who helps raise them. The median wage for a funeral atten-
> dant is $7.16 an hour; the median wage for a child care worker is $6.17
> an hour.
>
> If that doesn't strike home, consider that we pay someone in pest
> control $10.25 an hour. That's about $4 an hour more to get rid of bugs
> than to take care of kids.[43]

When President Clinton, in 1998, proposed a $21.7 billion package of
grants and tax breaks to help working families pay for child care, his
thinking was that it would strengthen the American family. He said, "We

know that the government cannot raise or love a child. What the government is supposed to do is to help to create the conditions and give people the tools that will enable them to raise and love their children while successfully participating in the American workplace."[44] But predictably, the package was met with resistance.

George Will wrote in his January 19, 1998, *Newsweek* column that the package would

> encourage illegitimacy—the principal cause of chronic poverty and attendant social pathologies—by making its consequences less burdensome for the irresponsible. The package would encourage parents to spend less time with their children. . . . His plan also is balm for the consciences of millions of married couples. They are, and ought to be, uneasy about their decisions to consign their young children to day care so that they can both work. . . .[45]

It's a difficult dilemma. In a perfect world, it would usually be best for the child to have at least one parent at home with the children throughout the day. But, in order to keep the family together, nowadays usually both must work. Even if, hypothetically, Americans could be restored to an economic era similar to that of the 1950s when one income per family was sufficient, who's to choose which parent would stay home? Today we're stuck with the reality that it's frequently vital that both parents work. So, although two-parent families are still so very favored against the otherwise deteriorating American families, the end result is that children may nevertheless be left without real guidance most of the time.

Still, regardless of whether they're living with two parents or one, more American children than ever exist below the poverty line. It's interesting to note that between 1950 and 1978, Americans in general got richer and that rise was felt both by rich and poor. There was real growth in income and the standard of living in all segments of the population.

But that trend stopped. Beginning shortly before the 1980s, there developed an increasing gap between the rich, who got richer, and the poor, who slid backward:

- In 1972, 14 percent of American children lived below the designated poverty level. By 1992, that number rose to 23 percent of American children. Since then, it's reached the 25 percent mark. (Keep in mind that many believe the official U.S. poverty line is too low. Many people have an income above the official poverty level, yet still live in desperate circumstances.)

- By the mid-1990's, America had the highest child poverty rate among 17 developed nations.
- The percentage of children living under the poverty level in the following countries from 1984 to 1987 was:

—United States	20.4	—Australia	9.0
—Sweden	1.6	—Netherlands	3.8
—Canada	9.3	—Germany	2.8[46]
—France	4.6		

The poverty of children—the most powerless people in society—was particularly accelerated by (1) an increase in single parent homes; (2) a failure of many fathers to support their children, with child support enforcement so lax that, even of those few ordered by the court to pay, only 40 percent do so; (3) the falling value of wages; (4) the move by states to shift funding away from child care thus hurting the working poor more than those on welfare; and (5) the inaction by the states to prevent inflation from eroding the budgets of many programs supporting children. Also, according to a 1998 report by the National Center for Children in Poverty, the states that had the greatest rise in child poverty—California, New York and Texas—also had the greatest recent rise in immigrants, many illegal.

It is startling to many that most of the poverty stricken children in the United States aren't the children of the jobless. When the new poverty rates were announced on May 4, 1998, it was revealed that between six and seven of 10 of our poor children live in families where someone works. Even though unemployment is down, there are a lot of people who are working at below poverty wages and just not getting by.

This is the increasing phenomenon of the working poor. Up until around the mid-1960s, a young white male with a high school diploma who wanted to work hard could get an excellent-paying blue-collar job with good benefits and full insurance and own his own home, all on a single income. Today, it is more likely that a blue-collar worker without an effective union can only get a low-paying job with few if any benefits. He is dependent on a spouse's second income to have any hope of owning his own home and even then that second income may barely help make ends meet. However, in 1998 the Census Bureau announced, for the first time in decades, the percentage of Americans in poverty had gone down, just as the crime rate had.[47]

We need to do something about reversing the poverty of so many of our children, not merely out of sympathy for them, but because of the enormous burden they could eventually become as they grow older. They won't have education or be employable and they'll sap all our resources in unemployment, welfare, medical bills, the costs of their thefts and victim's restitution and the need to imprison many of them.

Disintegration of the American family and poverty—growing up poor in a poor area without adults around—can be, at least, a partial prescription for children to both be in danger and create that danger. Many young people lack a sense of hope, seek immediate gratification and are heedless of risks. They aimlessly drop out of school, have a baby, sell or use drugs or commit crimes. There appears to be no expectation or optimism that their own actions can control their destiny and get them to a better life. Criminologist James Wilson, a former UCLA professor, stated in a December 4, 1997, speech before the conservative American Enterprise Institute:

> In these families where either neglect or abuse or both combine, children do not learn that what happens to them will be a consequence of their own behavior. . . . If you live in a neglectful or abusive family, you do not learn the lesson that your behavior affects what happens to you. You learn that what happens to you is the result of a random process. Your mother was mad this day so she slapped you. Your father was drunk this day, so he beat you. Or neither mother nor father was there and you were left to your own devices.[48]

It is in this atmosphere of poverty with no functioning family structure around that our children are most vulnerable to the media's effect. This is because the media, with all its other wonderful positive aspects, bombards us with violence. But violent media by itself might not be so much of a problem. Take Japan, for example, whose media is as violent, if not more so, than America's, yet of 9 million teenagers, they had just 35 murders in 1992.[49] Media violence in and of itself is not the problem. So censorship is not the answer. But here in the United States when you combine this media violence with children growing up in great poverty with the lack of family and community, the combination becomes deadly. So, as will be explained in more detail below, the violent media, which is ubiquitous in our lives, can make a negative contribution when it acts in concert with these other, more significant and more dangerous factors. But the greater wrong is that with so much insipid nonsense and violence taking up the precious air time, television fails to meet its enormous potential as a towering educator and inspiration to children. It is a legacy unfulfilled. The following is what is swallowing up so much television air time, filling our motion picture and computer screens and having a lopsided presence in the music to which we listen:

- By the time the average American child finishes high school, he will witness on television 40,000 murders and 200,000 other acts of violence.
- Although prime-time television features on average five violent scenes an hour, there are 25 violent acts an hour on Saturday morning cartoons which are most watched by children. That's only network television.
- A survey by the Center for Media and Public Affairs determined that on one particular day in 1994, a look at all programming including cable in one city tallied 2,605 acts of violence.
- The body count of motion pictures continually rises to impress a youthful audience that has become almost inured to violence. The first *Die Hard* movie had 18 deaths, while *Die Hard 2* had 264. The first *Robocop* film had 32 deaths; the second 81.[50]

In concert with no adult supervision in one's life, this exposure can create a mindset where some kids often can't tell the difference between reality and fantasy. It's what George Gerbner, former dean of the University of Pennsylvania's Annenberg School of Communication and the long-time head of the Cultural Indicators project, refers to as "happy violence," where death is quick, often funny and the film comes to a happy ending. Besides, they learn that for the most part their heroes come through all right.

They assume that in real life if you shoot somebody, it may not be forever. The dead victim may just get up and walk away after 20 minutes. They don't perceive the finality of the killing and the hellish, brutal pain that rips into the victim's family.

"How many deaths will teenagers witness of the stars of their favorite movies?" writes Theodore Fenn. "I dare say, not too many. Role models are so important to kids, and a role model that never dies and wreaks havoc among the 'bad guys' is enticing yet possibly dangerous."[51]

But even the death of the bad guys may not be all that convincing. Lynda Rowan was a warden in numerous adult prisons before taking charge of the Adapt Program in Hartford, Connecticut, which provides al-

ternatives to incarceration for youths in trouble with the law. Her experience with juveniles has given her the impression that, "You see so much
violence on TV and the movies, but then you see the guy who got killed
show up in another movie a month or two later. So you think nothing
happened."

This occurrence is dramatically underscored in the children's cartoon
show *South Park* which debuted on the Comedy Central network in the
late 1990s. A running "joke" on the show is that one of its characters, a
child named Kenny, is killed on almost every single program, only to appear on the following week's show to be killed again. Kenny became such
a cult figure that kids started wearing T-shirts with slogans on them such
as "Oh my God, they killed Kenny."

Perhaps this is why all the big-headline mass shootings in schools which
took place from 1997 to 1998 represented a trend away from traditional one-
on-one incidents of school violence to dramatic movie-style scenarios of massive body counts. Despite a general drop in school shootings across the
country, were the children in the high-profile school shooting incidents such
as Jonesboro, Arkansas, and Springfield, Oregon, acting out scenes of cine-
matic violence in imitation of the mayhem they had seen on the screen?

A comprehensive national study released in 1998, which determined
that a massive 67 percent of all prime time shows depict some violent behavior, backs up this viewpoint. It found that most violence on television
goes unpunished, is unjustified, has no lasting effect on the victim and is
committed by an attractive hero. In fact, nearly 40 percent of television violence is committed by the good guys. The danger here is that children are
likely to imitate characters whom they see as captivating.[52]

Fifteen-year-old Tyrell told me how he and his friends use the violent
characters on screen as their role models: "When, like, *Scarface* came out,
people was like 'Oh, he big time. I think I can make money like him. He
livin' large.' "

Additionally, the 1998 study found that violence in cartoons is glam-
orized and sanitized, making it dangerously seductive to young children.
The very youngest children, who aren't always exactly sure what is real
and what is fanciful, may try to emulate the fantasy violence.

It's not so long ago, in 1977, that 15-year-old Ronny Zamora shot and
killed his 82-year-old Florida neighbor and, in a then novel defense, tried
to plead not guilty by reason of having watched too much television. His
lawyer, Ellis Rubin, said Ronny had been inured to violence after suffering
from "television intoxication." At that time, it seemed like the entire na-

tion, upon hearing of this sensational case, either reacted with laughter or total disgust. The jury didn't buy this then outrageous-sounding defense one bit, and Ronny was found guilty. Today, more than 20 years later, one could speculate that jurors would still find Zamora guilty as they would not buy Zamora's refusal to take personal responsibility. But one wonders if now either jurors or the public in general would find Ronny Zamora's defense either laughable or so outrageous.

It's not just the entertainment industry which evidences our lopsided encounter with viewing violence. From 1993 through 1996, the country's homicide rate dropped by 20 percent. Remarkably, during that same time, there was quite a different picture on the network news where coverage of murders soared by 721 percent, according to one study, by the Center for Media and Public Affairs.[53]

Perhaps it was the number of high-profile killings the media covered which the public seemed to devour, such as the O.J. Simpson murder case, which served to encourage the media to greater proportions.

In fact, in a January 1997 survey of adults conducted by the Roper Center for Public Opinion Research, the Newseum and the Media Studies Center, 68 percent of those polled declared that they were either extremely or very interested in crime news.

Crime and criminal justice stories took up 29 percent of the early-evening newscasts in eight cities in 1997, according to a survey directed by University of Miami communications professor Joseph Angotti, a former network news executive. "If it bleeds, it leads," is still the operative cliché of local news.

My own experience as a local television news reporter also taught me that fresh crime scene stories are usually the easiest and cheapest thing to cover. Rather than spend the time and energy setting up thoughtful and important stories where you travel from place to place getting interviews in various locations and taped footage in a number of other places, it takes very little to just show up at a shooting scene. Everything is generally right there with no advance setup—the dramatic video, the sound bites, the crying relatives. It's the path of least resistance. It's true that many crime stories are important and can't be ignored, but currently the coverage far exceeds their place among other areas of news coverage. The headline cases prevail despite the fact of dropping crime rate.

During the first week of October 1997, the government came out with the statistic that for the second year in a row, violent crimes by juveniles had gone down—way down. Yet during that very same week, there were several truly horrifying and reprehensible murders committed by youth. This was the week that a 16-year-old in Pearl, Mississippi, stabbed his mother to death, then went to his school where he killed two students and wounded six others with his rifle. At almost the same time, an 11-year-old New Jersey boy selling candy for charity door to door was sexually assaulted and strangled by a 15-year-old boy who himself was being abused by a middle-aged male he had met over the Internet.

The airwaves were, of course, filled with discussions about charging children as adults. Typical was the October 1, 1997, broadcast of the CNBC program "Rivera Live" with the obvious segment title "Adult Crime—Adult Time." The substitute host John Gibson summed up a prevailing viewpoint when, in spite of the contrary statistical data, he asked the panelists:

> Have you seen the spate of these teen killings that are crossing the wires today? We picked out two examples. They're the most heinous. But I must have rejected five others that were on the wires today. Do we have a wave of teen violence that we have just been too soft on and we've got to toughen up?

It's these cases that are encouraging frustrated politicians to want to send all children who break the law to adult prisons. It's an overreaction. Aside from the major cases that have captured the attention of the media, the juvenile court system can handle these cases more to society's benefit.

With young people watching, on average, 27 hours of television a week, according to the *Journal of the American Medical Association*, Gerbner views television as equaled only by religion in acting as a cultural force. "Whoever tells most of the stories to most of the people most of the time has effectively assumed the cultural role of parent and school," says Gerbner, ". . . teaching us most of what we know in common about life and society."[54] Gerbner frequently quotes the Scottish patriot Andrew Fletcher, who in 1704 wrote, "If I were permitted to write all the ballads, I need not care who makes the laws of the nation."

This reminds me of an old tale I once heard about an ancient army in some year B.C. being captured by their enemy. The bugler of the captured forces argued that he should be treated more leniently since he never actually carried a weapon and never fought against the victor's forces. He only trumpeted them as they rushed into battle. The unfortunate musician was told that, in light of that, he would be treated harshest of all. He was told that he, in sounding their call to battle and heralding them on with his encouraging blows on his horn, was even more responsible than the actual warriors. There's actually a certain logic to this fable.

If, as a 1994 *Los Angeles Times* poll cited, 65 percent of us say our feelings about crime are based mostly upon what we see in the media rather than our own personal experience, then the media (our modern-day version of the ancient trumpeter), decides how our entire culture will look at and then act against crime. When you combine this knowledge with a 1997 study in the *American Journal of Public Health*, which found that 55 percent of the television stories on youth involved violence and 68 percent of the stories on violence involved youth, it's easy to see why everyone's going after youth.[55] But this is misleading, writes columnist Derrick Z. Jackson:

> Of course 55 percent of teens are not committing violent crimes. Less than one half of one percent of youths aged 10 to 17 were arrested for a violent crime in 1994, according to FBI statistics. And youths are not committing 68 percent of violent crimes. The juvenile proportion of violent crime is 14 percent.[56]

The headline of Jackson's column says all—"No Wonder We're Afraid of Youth."

But nowhere is the ancient trumpeter analogy updated more persuasively than in the music industry. Dr. Joseph Stuessey, professor of music history at the University of Texas, testified before the U.S. Senate in 1995:

> Music affects behavior. This simple fact has been known intuitively for centuries. . . . In the 20th century, especially in the last four decades, tons of research has been done on the interrelationship of music and human behavior. . . . It affects our moods, our attitudes, our emotions, and our behavior. It affects us psychologically and physiologically.[57]

Can it be true that a relentless number of popular rock songs cheerfully extolling the coolness of violence might have an encouraging effect on impressionable youth? Will the 1997 song by Time-Warner's techno group Prodigy, entitled "Smack My Bitch Up," give spirit to a violence-prone teenager? In fairness, Prodigy claims their song has nothing to do with violence against women, but rather was slang for raising the level of whatever one is doing. Still, the general public did not perceive it this way. How about the group Rigor Mortis' hit entitled "Body Dismemberment," with the lyrics describing how the passion increases with each slice of a body. Or the group named the Dead Kennedys whose song, "I Kill Children," heralds the joys of watching children die with the object of making their mothers distraught? Again, it is unlikely that any one individual song will incite a person to violence. There have been violent ballads throughout history. It is only the sheer volume of all violent media coupled with the absence of positive influences such as family that has strengthened this link. Surround a child with a loving family and caring adults and he is likely to remain impervious to any negative influences of popular culture.

It's also in the games children play. All too typical is the computer game called *Postal*,[58] where a deranged postal employee goes into a homicidal rage on the street. The player gets credit for napalming a marching band and killing police officers, churchgoers, a bomb-throwing Santa Claus and pedestrian targets who beg for their lives while they lie on the ground. You can work a button to execute someone or another button to commit suicide.

In *Quake II*, you get extra points if you shoot a final blast of gunfire into your falling enemy and he blows up into bloody clumps of flesh. If you play *Carmageddon*, speeding cars drive onto sidewalks and plow down innocent pedestrians in their path. The higher the body count, the better the score.

There have been so many thousands of studies over time that it's no longer even much of a point of contention whether popular culture has an effect on violence. In fact, prior to 1971 alone, there were 3,000 studies indicating a powerful correlation between television watching and aggression.

Aside from all the humorless, dry statistical analyses, the best example of this point is something I saw with my own eyes. It was in the mid 1970s when, for a few months, I was in, of all places, the Fiji Islands in the South Seas. I was in some very remote places there. In fact, I entered and stayed in some villages where at least the youngest children had never seen a white man before.

One day I was in a small village where they had a wooden building where, once a week, they used it to show a movie. As is true in many countries where the native language is rather obscure and they don't make films in their own language, the foreign movies they'd show would be heavy on action or old-fashioned physical slapstick comedy since the audience might not understand, for example, the English-language dialogue. On this particular night, there was a martial arts movie. You really didn't have to understand much of the dialogue. It was enough just to watch the good guys and bad guys lunging at each other with the usual kicks and holds and locks and jabs. The audience was thrilled and they cheered and booed and even made mocking clucking sounds during the obligatory kissing scenes.

When the film ended and everyone left the structure, I looked around and there I had my revelation. There were dozens and dozens of kids all gleefully and merrily imitating what they had just seen. None of the children really knew what they were doing, but they were awkwardly and happily giving each other fake karate kicks and chops. I said to myself, "Gee, this is exactly what my friends and I back in the States would have been doing when we were 8 or 10 or 12 and had just seen something like this." It dawned on me that even across cultures, kids are the same. Kids are kids.

At the time, I thought it was a rather positive revelation saying something about the universality of mankind and the common high spirits that we in the family of man share. I still believe that. But there's another, just as obvious lesson here. Children are strongly influenced by and will imitate what they see in popular culture.

We've always had violence in popular culture for children. In *Hansel and Gretel*, the witch gets pushed into the oven. In *Little Red Riding Hood*, there's a murderous wolf who eats people. Grimm's fairy tales were just that. Grim. Road Runner cartoons were one attempted murder and maiming after another with the coyote "humorously" being blown up, crushed by rocks, set on fire, run over by trucks, run through with arrows, etc. And is it even worth mentioning the Three Stooges?

The difference is that with a strong family structure and supervision around, violent books and films and music and games don't have too much of a bad effect. Part of the reason for that is that, in the past, when a child would see a play or read a book, he or she might do it under the supervision of a teacher or parent. Even watching television or listening to the radio used to be a family affair, with everyone gathered around the set. Now, kids are alone and unsupervised without parents around and no one selects what they see. It is ironic that years ago, a common complaint was that families were talking among themselves less and watching TV together more. But at least, the families would watch the one family television set together. Ed Sullivan and Disney were a shared experience. Now children sit alone fixated on the hypnotic bluish glow of the screen. They just look at the television, and the endless scenes of violence just keep coming and coming at them more graphic than ever without any filter or barrier or perspective to help interpret what they see. The family could counterbalance the endless drumbeat of the violent media—they were around.

This isolated activity is inherent with other problems for youngsters, according to criminologist James Wilson. He said in a November 27, 1997, lecture at Claremont McKenna College in California:

> First, by inducing people to engage in solitary behavior, watching television to the exclusion of other ways of spending your time . . . solitary behavior is the enemy of the natural sociability of mankind. We are social animals. Our moral code grows out of an attempt to moderate and deal with societal reality. If you grow up in isolation, if you grow up not playing with young people, not doing what the teacher wants, not struggling to get ahead in the corporation, but simply indulging yourself in the fantasy world—the fantasy world can be supplied by motion pictures or supplied by television or supplied by drugs—you are indulging in an activity that encourages your personal social isolation.

Surprisingly, only "live" language, not television, helps infants and toddlers build vocabulary. You might think that the endless amount of talk on television would incite and invigorate language development. But Janellen Huttenlocher of the University of Chicago says she suspects that "language has to be used in relation to ongoing events, or it's just noise."[59]

NO COMMUNITIES OR ROLE MODELS

It's true that the crumbling of the American family, the increasing poverty among children and the relentless drumbeat of a graphically violent media are strong factors of childhood crimes. But it's the older generation that offers a reality check to overreliance on the belief that these are the main causes of increasing juvenile crime. They say something like, "We grew up poor during the Depression and my father died when I was very young, but we didn't turn to crime. You still haven't answered the question why this younger generation turns to crime. If I was poor and from a family that wasn't intact and I didn't hurt anyone, what's the difference with these guys?"

As best as I can determine, the difference is that, in the past, even if you grew up poor in a broken home, you at least had a better chance of growing up in a cohesive community. There were plenty of role models, mentors and surrogate parents around. Perhaps your father was dead, but a neighborhood priest stepped in or perhaps your friend's dad. In many old neighborhoods, everyone knew everyone from the neighborhood grocer to the corner shoe repairman and kept an eye on each—other even in a peripheral or nosy, intrusive way.

Fran Lebowitz, the gifted and curmudgeonly novelist and humorist, wrote in the January 1998 issue of *Vanity Fair*, in a comedic and complaining way, about growing up in such a close-knit community. But still, her funny grumbling is evocative of a more caring era:

> . . . and all the parents watched you. There were approximately one million mothers. You couldn't do anything. I grew up in a small town. You did something in the street ten blocks away, the mother standing in that street called your mother. It was like living in East Berlin. If there was one thing I knew, it was that the phones were tapped. I knew that no matter where I was, I was being spied on. Someone was going to tell on me.[60]

General Colin Powell said much the same thing in an essay aptly titled, "I Wasn't Left to Myself." He wrote about growing up in the Banana Kelly community of the South Bronx:

> The tough neighborhood of Banana Kelly where I grew up had a heart: people cared about kids. I was surrounded by family, church and a wonderful public school system. And when I set off to school each morning, I had an aunt in every other house, stationed at the window with eyes peeled, ready to spot the slightest misbehavior on my part and report it back to my parents. The instant communication of today's Internet pales in comparison to the "Aunt-Net" I remember from my childhood.[61]

The authentic family can never be replaced. Anything else is second-best. But sometimes, just having nonfamily role models and mentors and older people—whether teachers or coaches or kindly neighbors—to give you direction and guidance and a set of values can be enough to set you on the correct path. This, in spite of the fact that it's second-best.

But today, all too often, not only are your parents not home, but there is no extended family around such as grandparents. Yet, neither are the neighbors. Besides, you don't know your neighbors. Instead of hanging out with the nearby residents on the stoop or in the park, you sit in darkened rooms and watch a videotape. Instead of strolling down the street to your destination and greeting your acquaintances, you drive silently in your car. Instead of talking with the local shopkeepers, you do your commerce in anonymous malls with an ever-changing sales force. Not only are there latchkey kids; there are latchkey neighborhoods. A kid can be all alone in his surrounding world.

This definitely has an impact on whether young people turn to crime. In a landmark five-year study released in 1997, it was determined that the level of violence in a neighborhood is influenced more by cohesion among its residents—a strong sense of community and shared values—than by poverty, racial makeup, immigration factors and the transience of the population. Things like neighbors looking out for each other's children, stopping graffiti painting, truancy, hanging out on street corners and generally minding other people's business are the key. In other words, a "willingness by residents to intervene in the lives of children" was what the researchers called a "shared efficacy."

One of the authors of the report, Robert J. Sampson, a sociology professor at the University of Chicago, said the report indicated hope and optimism that something can be done. He remarked, "It suggests people can reclaim their neighborhoods."[62]

Not surprisingly, many youngsters yearn for a connection with roots and with the past. Linda is a 17-year-old Cambodian immigrant who has lived on her own for the past five years. Somehow, she has escaped the gangs and violence of her rough neighborhoods and is a successful student who has a paid job with a community action group. Still, whenever she does get together with relatives she mourns the fact that she never really has gotten to learn much about her heritage. She told me:

> One thing I regret is that I don't know a lot about my culture. When I go out with my family and am with a lot of family, I'm always wondering if I'm doing the respectful thing in my culture because I don't really know. I wonder if I would have stuck around my mom for a longer time I would know. I wonder if elders would expect more.

This need for a community of responsible older people in their lives is exactly what Richard Rodriguez wrote about in the January 21, 1996, edition of the *Los Angeles Times* when he noted the wrongheadedness of calling children in trouble "superpredators." He stated:

> We adults now name the young criminals superpredators. Perhaps we should think of them as super-alones. There are children in America who have never been touched or told they matter. Inner city mama is on crack. Or suburban mama gives the nanny responsibility for raising the kids. Papa is in a rage this morning. Where are the aunts to protect the child? Where is there a neighbor who cares?[63]

Navy Lt. Commander Robert Sanders helped start an afterschool youth center in a converted armory in Jacksonville, Florida. Following this, youth crime in the area nose-dived. Sanders says:

> I think back to the kids I grew up with who are not dead or in jail.
> What did we have in common? Those who succeeded had some kind
> of structure that let us go on to the next level. A few years ago the big
> thing was to say that kids had to have food in their stomachs to think.
> But that's not enough. We have eight year olds raising three-year-olds
> and they're supposed to grow up to compete in the world economy?
> Our whole future, our national security, depends on what kids can do
> tomorrow.[64]

It all seems to point to the wisdom of the old African proverb that it
takes a village to raise a child. Yet when the First Lady used that expression
for the title of her book, she was met with a thunderstorm of criticism. This
is worth looking at because ultimately both she and her critics are right.

Mrs. Clinton said she choose to title her book *It Takes A Village* because
"it offers a timeless reminder that children will thrive only if their families
thrive and if the whole of society cares enough to provide for them."[65] Her
book was a clarion call for the strengthening of and support of the American family. It suggested that in those cases when a family wasn't thriving,
Americans, whether through churches, individual volunteers, the government or community groups, should give each other a hand.

It sounds innocuous enough. Few can argue that we shouldn't grow
up in a kind nation where we all shore up children and each other. That's
why it was initially surprising when Bob Dole, in his convention speech
accepting the 1996 Republican nomination for President, appeared to take
shots at Mrs. Clinton for this very concept. He said:

> And after the virtual devastation of the American family, the rock
> upon which this country was founded, we are told that it takes a vil-
> lage—that is, the collective, and thus, the state—to raise a child. The
> state is now more involved than it has ever been in the raising of chil-
> dren, and children are now more neglected, abused, and mistreated
> than they have been in some time. This is not a coincidence, and, with
> all due respect, I am here to tell you: it does not take a village to raise
> a child. It takes a family.

At first, it seemed curious that Dole, of all people, would knock the "it
takes a village" theme. During his campaign and, in fact, all throughout
his public life, Dole related strongly evocative and deeply moving stories
about his boyhood in Russell, Kansas—the epitome of nurturing small-
town America. This was the heartland town where, when Dole returned a
gravely wounded and devastated young veteran of World War II, the people of Russell rallied around their beloved son with financial and spiritual
support. In a story that's become part of political legend, the people of

Russell chipped in what money they could into a cigar box at Dawson's Drug Store to pay his hospital bills. They kept track of the donations on a piece of paper. Throughout his life, Dole kept that piece of paper and cigar box in his desk to remind him of the support his village gave him when he was most down on his luck. Dole once said:

> Anyone who wants to understand me must first understand Russell, Kansas. . . . The Russell of my youth was not a place of wealth. Yet, it was generous with the values that would shape my outlook and the compassion that would restore life's richness after I had begun to doubt my future following the war. Ever since, I have tried in my own way to give back some of what the town has given me. I have tried to defend and serve the America I learned to love in Russell.[66]

Again, it initially seemed strange that a man so grateful for the way his village and community helped raise, encourage and support him along with his wonderful parents, would knock the idea of "It takes a village to raise a child." But what Dole was apparently saying was that he was wary of government programs substituting for the family. This is a healthy reminder of a valid concern and should be heeded.

Many conservative commentators echoed the same reaction. Kerby Anderson of Probe Ministries International and Penna Dexter of Concerned Women for America wrote of Hillary Rodham Clinton's book:

> It represents the new paradigm of feminist and socialist thinking. At its face, there is nothing controversial about the idea that it takes more than parents to raise a child. Grandparents, friends, pastors, teachers, Boy Scout leaders and many others in the community all have a role in the lives of our children. Mrs. Clinton does acknowledge that "parents bear the first and primary responsibility for their sons and daughters." But she also extends the village far beyond the family to various organizations including the federal government. . . . Families don't need more government—they need less. It may take a village to raise a child, but that doesn't mean it takes the government to raise a child.[67]

Again, the point is well taken that parents and families mustn't be replaced by government bureaucracies in some sort of social engineering scheme. Seventeenth century poet George Herbert was right when he said that one father is more than a hundred schoolmasters. There's also similar wisdom in the old Spanish proverb that an ounce of mother is worth a ton of priest.

Actually, any combination will work. A 15-year-old I'll call Victor gave me a number of reasons why he was one of the very few in his urban neighborhood to escape the gang life. He said:

> I almost joined because my brother was in a gang. But my mom was crying when he went to jail and everything. I thought about it and that got to me. I couldn't do it to her. Lucky enough, I had people to help me, like teachers. Now I have a positive attitude about myself.

But anything to shore up the family and support its own sacrosanct role should be done—and done on the smallest level whenever possible. Neighbors helping neighbors; ministers and teachers and coaches supporting the people around them in their lives. As the very last resort, when a child is completely abandoned and the particular family is completely broken down (if it in fact was ever intact), children must not be abandoned and left to their own resources. A government program to bring real role models, health care, education or support into the lives of children is an admittedly poor second-best to the family or private individuals, but will still save children and lives. It need not even be done out of kindness, but out of social necessity. Turning out an uneducated, unhealthy, immoral generation who won't work or abide by the law will drain and endanger us all. Conservative criminologist James Wilson argues:

> Children are not raised by programs or governments or villages. They are raised by two parents . . . two parents who are fervently, even irrationally, devoted to their children's well-being. Though the benefits of two parents are beyond dispute, some children—in some big cities, most children—are raised by one parent. There is, however, evidence that early intensive intervention can help even the children of single mothers.[68]

It is sad that families and neighbors today aren't always there. I agree with the spirit of the letter to the editor submitted to the November 24, 1997, issue of *Newsweek* by Margaret Baird of Metairie, Louisiana, which said, "Liberals must understand that parents, not taxpayers, are responsible for their children."[69]

Baird is right, but so, on the other hand, is columnist and author James Carroll, who wrote that, be that as it may, it's still unfortunately crucial that someone step in to help and save the children if parents and families aren't fulfilling their ideal roles. Thus, they and their families must serve as miner's canaries, warning us of a larger danger:

> The broader society has a crucial role to play in each family's life. If the mechanisms for that interplay disappear, we are in trouble. Neighbors and friends, teachers and doctors, religious leaders and social workers—what we used to call the family of man—is the necessary network. If society's role occurs only after murders have been committed or abuse has been exposed, then more and more canaries will die. . . .

> We regret the loss of social cohesion that once enabled neighbors and friends to play this role discreetly, but when police or reporters are the first to know a family's darkest secrets, perhaps, instead of clucking, we should ask two questions, one personal and one political: Whose neighbors and friends are we? Must the reinvention of government isolate families even more?[70]

A 15-year-old, whom I'll call Alvarez, had a nightmarish early childhood in a very tough urban ghetto where he still lives—that is, until he was taken away from his parents and placed in foster care. Alvarez wasn't very talkative or articulate when I spoke to him, but he managed to say a few words about the impact of his foster father. He said, "He changed my life around. He makes me do my schoolwork. He has me play sports."

BLAMING THE CHILDREN

It's clear that some of the chief components in the creation of youth crime are the breakup of the traditional American family, increasing child poverty, the media and, most important of all, the lack of any cohesive community. Why then, do so many politicians, as their only weapon in the arsenal against youth crime, just angrily go after the children in a rage? Their one and only solution is to increase punishment.

Sure, children must take responsibility for and accept the consequences of their own actions. But why do many of the politicians blame only the kids as if they were the sole cause? Youth worker Molly Baldwin is certain this is just wrong:

> I mean, we're the grown-ups. These are our children. These are our kids, not someone else's kids. It's not like Mars came and planted them. If you don't raise them and you don't love them and you don't nurture them and you don't pay attention to them, then we get all upset 'cause they're acting up. And I think we're just really good at trying to find a scapegoat with the kids.

Jennifer Wynn, editor of *Prison Life* magazine, said much the same thing against the "only blame the kids" point of view, when, in a letter to the editor in the June 16, 1997, issue of *New York* magazine, she wrote, "Inner-city kids join gangs because their communities are devoid of role models, their playgrounds are bereft of equipment, and their parents are either on dope or in the joint."[71]

A perfect case study in the evolution of a law-abiding, straight-A student to violent gang member can be found in a young man named Saroeum Phoung whose family stuck together through the extreme violence of Cambodia's killing fields and, through a circuitous route, found themselves in a tough area of working-class East Boston, Massachusetts. When I spoke with Saroeum, he had already turned his life around and was working full time with troubled young people. By listening to his story, I was able to follow why he had taken the path that he had once he had settled in the United States:

> The school system wasn't ready for us. They weren't ready to teach us anything. They weren't prepared for us to go there . . . the teachers. Everybody speaking and I couldn't speak English. I couldn't understand what the teachers were saying, all this racial problem that wasn't first told to us. . . .
>
> When I came here, I never see or play video games. In East Boston, they have this place where they have all these video games and I don't have any money so I would collect cans, friends, we'd just turn them in for money and then we made like five, ten dollars . . . we'd go down there and play games. And East Boston, the majority of people that live there is white, so what happened is that they called us names. I really didn't speak English much during that time, so they would call me motherfucker. I would say hi to them.
>
> So we'd go out there and we'd play and then they'd smack us around. They'd dis us around and I remember they burned my jacket and everything. It was just a bad feeling. It was my favorite jacket. It was a New York Giants. It was my first jacket I got and I was pretty much upset about it
>
> Well, I guess when I was a kid, I'd take so much of it and then I couldn't help it no more. Then I say, the hell with it. They want to fight. They want to swear at us, they want to do this. You just can't take it no more. And what happened, the worst part of it is that when you come to this country, not knowing the racial problem and your parents don't know how to deal in the new society and the system, that makes it even more difficult, and sometimes when your parents are working long hours, you don't really have nobody to talk to and nobody really to listen to.
>
> My mother was working long, long hours from morning to night. Every day. My father . . . he don't work. I think my mom let him not go to work and she just wanted him to go to school and learn English. He didn't. He made friends and he drinks a lot. My father during that time he gambled a lot. He'd lose a lot of money and he started to abuse my mom and everything and everybody in the family. So they both filed for a divorce and that's when things really

screwed up for me. Until that time, I was a straight-A student in class. I just couldn't understand why. Because we came from a long way from Cambodia to here, we struggled, we fought, and the reason why we're here is because we work as a team. And now that we get here, there's our goal and they divorce. So, I was a kid. I didn't understand that.

And so mom used to pick on me all the time. She don't have nobody to talk to, to complain to, to yell at, so she always used to yell at me. She said, "You don't like it, just leave me alone, get out of this house." It triggered me. It was like maybe she doesn't love me no more. So that's why I took off. I ran away from home.

It was then that Saroeum found acceptance, comfort and society with other youngsters in crisis. He started getting into serious trouble with the law. But nothing like what began to happen when he headed to another city in Massachusetts, Attleboro, to be near another young relative:

Your friends would share the same type of pain, same boat, same feeling. And then you get together and something just triggers enough is enough. We need to stand up and fight back. . . .

The school didn't want me cause I was a little bit crazy already so they kicked me out. By this time, I started stealing cars, stealing radios, breaking into some stores and stealing some stuff. Some of my friends moved with me because we were really close. It was like "the hell with school." So these are the kids who supported each other for a long time. It was pretty crazy. And then we started to go out to parties, stealing parties, and then we'd get into fights with different gangs . . . mostly Cambodian gangs and other gangs like Latino, African-American and the skinheads. When we got into too much trouble that's when we stood up and said, "If all these people think we're a gang, why don't we make up a gang?"

We had knives, ax, butcher knives, machetes. We're getting into a lot of trouble now in Attleboro, the police didn't want us there, so we moved to Providence, Rhode Island. When we got there, there's heavy artillery involved. Like, we had guns, we had manpower. There's like 15, 16 of us . . . I wouldn't say heavy, heavy, but we had like Tech 9's and stuff, like machine guns, hand guns and almost like every week, we'd have a shoot-out with a different gang. When I was in a gang during that time, to be honest with you, I never thought about dying. All I ever thought about was colors, was gang, retaliation, my enemies, my friends. You know, I was a very, very violent person when I was in a gang. They called me butcher man because I used a butcher knife.

The ultimate transformation of Saroeum into a very law-abiding and contributing citizen is remarkable, but this early part of his story is a text-

book lesson in how to turn a young and naive child into a violent offender. Throw him into poverty without an intact family or any outside
adult community support—no adults in his life—and he may turn to the
only community offered to him: other disenfranchised, embittered youth
who band together misguidedly to protect each other from the violence
against them.

The answer is to prevent youngsters from becoming criminals rather
than punish them after their abominable tragic crimes have occurred.

THE DIRTY LITTLE SECRET OF YOUTH CRIME

There's a dirty little secret about youth crime that's often overlooked,
and it is perhaps the main point of this chapter. As the number of violent
acts and murders by youths rose from the mid-1980s to the mid-1990s, the
number of child suicides soared in tandem. They were killing each other,
but they were also killing themselves. What was going on to make them
plunge into such despair that life, especially their own, seemed to have
such little value?

After 15-year-old Kipland Kinkel shot to death his two parents, then
entered his Springfield, Oregon, school cafeteria, killed two more people
and wounded 22 others, he was finally tackled and held down by other
students. His words then were, "Just shoot me. Shoot me now." Fourteen-
year-old Joshua Ryker, one of the heroes who helped subdue Kinkel, says,
"It was like he didn't care, like he had nothing to lose."

On that bloody day, Oregon Governor John Kitzhaber rhetorically
asked the question, "We need to ask ourselves what kind of despair drives
children to this kind of violence. We need to answer and resolve what it
implies about our own responsibility."

Clearly, Kipland Kinkel had no regard for others. But he had no regard for himself either. He is part of a growing number of anguished
youngsters who would kill others, but would just as soon kill themselves.
One African-American youth said, "I been dead since I was 12 so I'm not
afraid of dying. I'm just waiting to get kicked into the grave."[72]

Fourteen-year-old Rosa told me that in her inner-city neighborhood:

> My friends, they be like, "Oh, I feel like killin' myself" or somethin'
> like that. 'Cause she upset or she mad at somebody or somethin' like
> that. She be like, "I'm gonna kill myself 'cause I don't have to deal

with nothing, no more problems, no more nothing." So sometime she
feel like killing herself.

As might be expected, popular culture glorifies suicide. A Marilyn
Manson concert T-shirt reads, "Just kill yourself. Hang yourself."

It's important to note, as the following statistics show, that during
this time, child abuse and neglect also skyrocketed and children became
the greatest victims of virtually every kind of violent crime. As their families fell apart, as the rates of children in poverty rose, as drugs and guns
were handed to them and the media showed them unprecedented death
and violence, they began to place less and less value on human life—especially their own. Why, then, is the politicians' only answer to youth
crime to blame the kids who are initially the first victims and then go after
them with a vengeance, speaking only of retribution and harsh punishments?

- Between 1980 and 1994, the suicide rate for 15- to 19-year-olds
  rose 29 percent, according to the Centers for Disease Control and
  Prevention. (The risk of suicide is five times greater for those living in a home with guns.) Among 10- to 14-year-olds, there was
  an increase of a whopping 120 percent. In fact, in a survey released in November 1998, one-quarter of all high-achieving high
  school students claimed they had considered committing suicide.
  Incidentally, incidents of suicide by African-American youngsters
  soared from 1980 to 1995, more than doubling.
- Complaints of child endangerment in the United States over the
  last decade soared from 2.2 million in 1987 to 3.1 million in 1996.
- Fatalities from child abuse or neglect increased 20 percent from
  1985 to 1996, according to the National Committee to Prevent
  Child Abuse.
- Child abuse and neglect nearly doubled between 1986 and 1993,
  according to the U.S. Department of Health and Human Services.
- During the 10 years between 1984 and 1995, the number of children in foster care shot up from 280,000 to 494,000—removed
  from their families as a result of abuse, drug addiction, neglect
  and the erosion of their families. Many turn 18 and are set free out
  on their own without ever having had a permanent family.
- Children who are victims of violence are 24 percent more likely to
  engage in violence themselves during adolescence.

- From 1984 to 1994, there was a 44 percent rise in the number of times juveniles age 12–17 were themselves the victims of violent crime.
- Persons aged 12–24 comprised:

  - 22 percent of the population
  - 35 percent of murder victims, and
  - 49 percent of serious violent crime victims.

- Serious violent crime victimization rates for persons age 18–21 were 17 times higher than for persons age 65 or older.
- The number of juveniles murdered in 1994 was 47 percent higher than in 1980, while overall murders rose only 1 percent during that period.[73]

One of the most appalling examples was a widely publicized case which began on a February evening in 1994 on Keystone Avenue in Chicago. Police officers entered a filthy and freezing rat- and roach-infested apartment with 19 children crammed inside. There were even more children who just weren't in the apartment at that time. There was rotting food and garbage strewn about and some of the children had been brutally beaten and tortured. The scene was beyond something out of Dickens.

In the most heartrending moment, one of the little girls looked up at one of the female police officers and simply pleaded, "Will you be my mommy?" The little girl did, in fact, already have a mother. But she and five other, mostly drug-addicted mothers who lived there, all collecting more than $4,500 a month in welfare and food stamps, weren't around much. The children were immediately removed from the squalid apartment.

All six mothers were ultimately found by the court to be unfit, unable or unwilling to parent. This was so despite Herculean efforts by the courts over the next several years to reunite the children with these natural parents, even offering the mothers parenting classes, job training, drug treatment and peer support meetings. A battery of therapists, social workers, lawyers and counselors got involved, but one by one each of the mothers failed to follow through. One of the mothers of four of the children was actually honest enough to concede, "I'm not ready to grow up at this time."

The judge, who eventually ruled against their custody, wrote in her decision that the argument of their lawyers giving poverty as an excuse for bad parenting, "is an insult to the poor people who run their homes and raise their children with love and devotion."[74]

Within a handful of years, most of the "Keystone Kids," as they were called, were doing rather well in foster care, with some on their way toward adoption.

The Keystone Kids weren't alone. The number of American children entering foster care has surged. In the five-year period between 1990 and 1995, their numbers rose 19 percent. This has often had tragic results in that the overwhelmed foster care system has become a disorganized bureaucratic mess where children often fall through the cracks. It has been characterized by poorly trained judges, inexperienced lawyers, overworked social workers and uncaring agencies without even a view as to their mission. Children frequently suffer irreparable harm over the years as they bounce from home to home neglected or abused by foster parents ill equipped to raise children.

Journalist John Gibeaut examined one such incident in a story he wrote for the December 1997 issue of the *ABA Journal* entitled, "Lucas Deserved Better." It was the story of seven-year-old Lucas Ciambrone who, brought in unconscious to a hospital in Bradenton, Florida, was found to weigh just 26 pounds (half the normal weight) and to have had more than 200 injuries. He died. His foster parents, Joseph and Heather Ciambrone, who by then had adopted him, were charged with having beaten and starved him to death. Joseph was found guilty and given a sentence of life without possibility of parole. Heather was, at least temporarily, found incompetent and her trial was delayed.[75]

But almost as disturbing as his foster parents' alleged behavior was the assertion that the agency licensing the foster parents had used their home as "basically a dumping ground"; had failed to investigate and document numerous abuse reports from neighbors, physicians, schools and psychologists; had permitted the adoption without the required detailed study of the home environment; and had such a high turnover in its office that no single person had an overview of the case. "Lucas Deserved Better" was, indeed, an apt title for the article.

"The legal system's inability to deal with these kids, even though we know who they are, contributes to their repeated injury," says Michael Petit of the Child Welfare League of America. Unfortunately, once these damaged children start causing trouble themselves, the legal system may deal with them, angrily punishing them. This, rather than save the children before they enter the world of crime.

Clearly, our children are being victimized in astronomical numbers without precedent and this continues to be glossed over with little attention paid to it. Politicians don't want to hear it. Yet, they are quick to squash a child who lashes out in anger and despair.

According to Dr. Bruce Perry of Baylor College of Medicine, although trauma can change an adult's behavior, it "literally provides the organizing framework" for the infant's brain. In other words, if a child has experiences again and again such as fear and stress, then the neurochemical response to fear and stress actually changes the structure of the brain. This causes hyperactivity, anxiety and impulsive behavior. Trauma also scrambles neurotransmitter signals which, when children are subjected to chronic and unpredictable stress, makes it so the child will have problems in his or her ability to learn. "Some percentage of capacity is lost," according to Perry. "A piece of the child is lost forever." Additionally, children who go without love and tender care may not biologically have the ability to feel compassion or deep empathy. The brain region for emotional attachments may never be developed properly. What this all means is that babies and young children who are subjected to abuse actually develop actual physical or chemical reasons why they ultimately turn to crime.[76]

It's true that once a previously victimized teen becomes extremely violent and even murderous, we can't make excuses for him and he may have to be locked up at length to protect the public. But if we could only protect these youthful victims in the first place, then we wouldn't need to come up with the inevitable, expensive, severe punishments.

Dr. James Gilligan, a renowned expert on violence, forcefully argues this point:

> When you look at the amount of outrage that is expressed at young children today by many of our politicians, you would think these kids are young punks and they're evil and all they're doing is going out and killing people and we need to get tough on them and punish them more because that's the only thing that will stop them. But if you look at this, it will make you stop. They're not just killing other kids. They're killing themselves. One thing I think that tells us is something is going on in our society today that is leading to a level of despair and hopelessness among our youth that is leading them not only to kill each other and to get killed by each other, it's leading them just as rapidly to kill themselves.
>
> It becomes much harder to see these kids as simply victimizers and tough punks who we need to punish more, when you realize

something is going on which is leading them to kill themselves. We need to ask ourselves what is going on in our country today.[77]

Why is it that we vilify violent youth when their incidents of violence are so fewer than those committed by adults? For example, parents are six times more likely to kill kids than the other way around.[78]

I would argue that we need to eradicate abuse of children not simply as an act of kindness and humanity to children, but also in the pure selfish self-interest of us adults. This is because, inevitably, almost every time we hear of a horrendous killing by a juvenile, we ultimately learn that that killer had been abused. It is almost without exception. This is, of course, an explanation—not an excuse. But we know that 75 percent of very violent youthful offenders were seriously abused by a family member and nearly 80 percent witnessed extreme brutality in their young lives such as beatings and killings. A 1995 study by Mark S. Fleisher of almost 200 inner-city street criminals was essentially a litany of parents who "beat their sons and daughters—whipped them with belts, punched them with fists, slapped them, and kicked them."[79]

Part of it has to do with our increasing sweeping disinvestment in youth. One experienced public school teacher who's a friend of mine complained to me that, in the past, when children from chaotic and abusive homes came into her classroom, she could identify them and get them special help. Those sorts of programs are now eliminated or cut way back. This is part of this "disinvestment." She says:

> I've seen kids shut down where they seem to have no affect at all and that's a sign of depression or possible abuse. You can encourage them, hold them accountable and give them consequences and they'll look at you with no response, not even caring. These are kids who have few skills to handle a problem. These are skills which have to be learned and if not learned at home then they need them taught even more at school. Years ago, these children who had difficulty functioning in the regular mainstream classes and getting along with other children were often put into special smaller classrooms with more personnel, lots of extra help and less distractions. Today we can't do that. So, we're not servicing the kid. He is absolutely disrupting the learning environment for everyone else and I don't see that we're helping them, especially the very angry children. . . . And when a child will, at six, seven or eight years old threaten to physically harm a teacher or otherwise show that they're an angry child, that kind of anger will translate into crime later on.

Phillip Kassel also bears witness to this disinvestment in children after having represented so many juvenile offenders in the role of their attorney:

I talk with them in their jail cell, in their isolation chambers, and the overwhelming reaction that I have is that they are vulnerable, as kids are . . . I think they're as vulnerable, perhaps more vulnerable than they have been in prior generations, particularly in the last 10 years when the governmental support system has been pulled out from under poor people, and particularly poor kids. So they suffer more now. Their families are more disrupted.

NO YOUTH CRIME WAVE OF SOCIOPATHS

So, the initial question of this chapter remains. Are young people today more dangerous with less conscience than young people of prior generations? Is there a coming youth crime wave by a nation of sociopaths?

The answer is, generally, no. But that's only speaking in generalities.

There is a segment of young people raised usually in poverty, without responsible adults in their lives, without a cohesive supportive community around them, without religion or any spirituality, influenced by an increasingly violent media and with guns plentiful and available. In most of the cases, they are abused. It's a small segment. Even in the peak youth crime year of 1994, less than 0.5 percent of young people were arrested for violent crime.[80] It only seems so much worse, even today now that the youth violent crime rate is dropping, because it is fueled by the few horrendous high profile media cases.

"I certainly think there are a larger number of kids who are growing into teenage years who have raised themselves, not even having a single parent, certainly not two parents helping them get through the pitfalls of life," says Steven Weymouth of the Youth Advocacy Project. "So again, there are kids out there who are violent and full of anger and have very little remorse, but I think it's a small minority. I really do think it's a small minority."

As stated, the rate of violent youth crimes hasn't risen much in the last few decades with the sole exception of gun crimes. While every other kind of youth homicide stayed flat, gun deaths quadrupled.

In 1974, 12.5 percent of all violent crime in America was committed by juveniles. In 1994, the high watermark year of juvenile violent crime just before its decline, it still had only risen slightly to 14.2 percent.[81] In other words, actual incidents of violent crime had barely risen. Regrettably though, the difference was that more of those violent incidents were lethal.

Also, as previously noted in this book, although the nation was shocked by a horrific series of highly publicized school shootings by children between 1997 and 1998, violence in schools was actually on the decline. Violent youth crime was also very limited geographically. Crimes by juveniles in the United States were highly concentrated in just a few locations. In 1995, a third of all killings by juveniles took place in just 10 counties. Eighty-four percent of all counties in the United States didn't have a single homicide caused by a youth. Any killing by a youth is one too many, but it's just not widespread. In fact, half the killings by children take place in six states—California, Florida, Illinois, Michigan, New York and Texas. One-third of all murders by juveniles took place in just four cities—Chicago, Detroit, Los Angeles and New York.[82]

Not only are there areas where the crimes are concentrated, but there are individual victims upon whom crime is concentrated, according to Wendy G. Skogan, professor of political science at Northwestern University:

> It turns out that what appears to cause crime to pile up very heavily in high crime areas is to a certain extent because more people are victimized but, more so, because some people are victimized repeatedly. They may be commercial establishments, they may be organizations, they may be individuals, but that piling up of repeat multiple victimization is mostly what makes a high-crime neighborhood a high-crime neighborhood.[83]

The fact that we've identified the reasons for youth crime and its geographical locations give us much room for hope. This is because if you attack these reasons at these locations, you can make the rate of youth crime go down. Don't accept this on speculation; this is exactly what's already happening. Many criminal justice experts were shocked when the rate of violent youth crime turned around and began to plunge in 1995 and 1996. It was particularly encouraging that this rate made its most significant decline among the very youngest juveniles. Much of the reason for the declining youth crime rate is that a mere handful of cities such as Boston, Detroit, and New York really made extraordinary and conscientious declines in violent juvenile crime. They did this not by jailing more adults and children, but by a variety of initiatives including community policing and partnerships among the churches, community groups, the police and the schools.

It's not rocket science and it's not expensive. It's long been known, not just by the experts but by any parent, that kids need lots of time and attention from the critical adults in their lives. Kids are natural learning machines. That's the bottom line.

So we can and are pushing back against what seemed like an inevitable rising tide of violent crime by children even as we expect to hit a huge bump-up in the number of youths who will be hitting the peak crime-committing years soon after the turn of the century. But, it's not a done deal. We must continue to do what we're doing. So don't breathe easy yet.

When Benjamin Guggenheim, "the millionaire playboy," stood on the deck of the sinking Titanic in 1912 and realized that there were not even enough lifeboats for women and children, he declined the offer of a seat on a lifeboat. It had been bestowed on him because of his exalted social rank. Yet, instead, he went back to his stateroom, took off his sweater and life jacket and put on formal evening wear. He remarked that he and his valet would "meet death like gentlemen."

Guggenheim's remarkable decision to give his life because unfairly cutting ahead in line and, therefore, causing the death of a less wealthy female would not be gentlemanly, was an extraordinarily admirable adherence to a rigid moral code. It represented the extreme test of one's compassion and ethics. But, generally speaking, one's morality can still be lived day by day in less dramatic ways. Yet, there usually must be older people there to have presented the role model.

According to Dr. Robert Coles, the Harvard child psychiatrist and author of The Moral Intelligence of Children, *it's up to the parents to teach children a sense of morality and ethics, not necessarily by long lectures, but just by showing them through hundreds of the little things they do and say every day. It's stunning how even infants can pick up on the ethical rules just by watching the many, seemingly insignificant decisions of their moms and dads. "It's those everyday, minute-by-minute cues that the little ones pick up on," says Coles.*[84]

A better illustration of this can't be found than in the childhood memory of my friend Martha whose father Sam Mattox was the mayor of the small southern town of Radford, Virginia, at the same time that he was the manager of a local department store. She recalls:

> From time to time, he had to run down to the store on a Sunday when it was closed to do something. It was always great fun for me or my sister to accompany him because nobody was in the store.
> I remember one time we went there. I was probably 10 years old. My father was in the office and he wanted to mail a personal letter. He ran the letter through the store's automatic stamp machine and when he finished, he reached into his pocket, pulled out 3 cents and he put it in the drawer. I just noticed it. Even back then when stamps were 3 cents, 3 cents did not seem like a whole lot of money. I mean nobody was looking. He didn't have to put 3

cents in the drawer. But he did and it just made a huge impression on me about honesty when nobody's looking.

Martha's mind then raced forward years later to her final visit to her father who was dying. She had flown in from a distant state to spend time with him. Then she was about to leave.

> *He knew and I knew that it was the last time that we'd see each other and we'd been sitting in the den kind of talking. Then he stood up and I stood up and he sort of shuffled across the room and we hugged. It was pretty poignant because I knew it was the last time I'd ever hug him. I knew it was the last moment we'd ever be together alone and I didn't know quite what to say. I guess he didn't either. He gave me a good hug and he said, "Well honey, just be honest." It was tough, but it was wonderful to hear.*

Martha's memories draw in broad strokes exactly what Coles noted: that it's the day-to-day little things that the adults in our lives do and say that make major impressions on the content of the character of our young minds. The adults should ideally be parents, but as a lesser alternative, neighbors, coaches, teachers, clergy and friends can also give direction through their day-to-day examples. Whoever it may be, children will always model themselves after someone. What Aristotle said in ancient Greece still applies: "The soul never thinks without a picture." Without the adults, a kid can only make it up as he goes along. Occasionally it works. More often it doesn't. Kids are kids. They start out no different today from how kids ever did. But the growing segment who spend their childhood without any older role models in their lives could ultimately endanger us. Punishment, after the fact, or the threat of punishment is irrelevant. We'll only become safer when we encourage families and mentors to enter and stay in the lives of our children.

Chapter 3

The Everydayness of Firearms

Fourteen-year-old Michael Carneal was said to have particularly liked the scene in the 1995 film *The Basketball Diaries* where the character played by Leonardo DiCaprio dreams that he enters his high school, pulls a shotgun out from under his coat and opens fire.

Perhaps that's what inspired Michael when he walked into Heath High School in Paducah, Kentucky, on the morning of December 1, 1997, carrying a package wrapped in an old blanket which he claimed contained a poster for his science project. But inside were three spare ammo clips and four guns bound together with duct tape—two shotguns and two rifles. He never got to use them since he opened fire with a semiautomatic .22 pistol hitting eight students at random in a crowded hallway, killing three.

"Only the first three shots could have been aimed," said a student who witnessed the shooting. "After that, it was just as fast as he could pull the trigger." Another student said, "I heard gunshots, about 10 in a row, just bang, bang, bang, bang, bang. People were just laying on the ground. People were screaming, running out of the hall."[1]

Carneal's school shoot-up took place only weeks after 16-year-old Luke Woodham's high school shooting spree in Pearl, Mississippi, where in the crowded school commons before classes, he shot nine students with a rifle, killing two girls. This, after he stabbed his mother to death earlier in the day. Three months later, on March 24, 1998, in an incident that electrified the nation, 11-year-old Andrew Golden and 13-year-old Mitchell Johnson pulled a fire alarm at the Westside Middle School in Jonesboro, Arkansas, ran outside and waited in the woods behind the school while their classmates filed out. They then opened fire with rifles, killing four students and one teacher and wounding 11 others.

Exactly one month later, on April 24, 1998, 14-year-old Andrew Wurth walked into Nick's Place, a banquet hall in the tiny northwestern Pennsylvania town of Edinboro, where a graduation dance for the James W. Parker Middle School was being held. He appeared to shoot indiscriminately as he killed the dance organizer, popular teacher and businessman John Gillette. Two pupils and another teacher were wounded.

The following month, on May 21, 1998, 15-year-old Kipland Kinkel sauntered into his crowded high school cafeteria in Springfield, Oregon, wearing a trenchcoat and pulled out a semiautomatic weapon. Calmly and methodically, he walked around as he fired, killing two students and causing 22 others to be injured. He had just come from home where he had shot to death his two parents.

These were five small town school gun shooting sprees in a little over a six-month period.

GUNS AS A WAY OF LIFE

At first glance, you might draw the conclusion that there are no lessons to be learned from the Pearl, Mississippi; Paducah, Kentucky; Jonesboro, Arkansas; Edinboro, Pennsylvania; and Springfield, Oregon cases. They're inexplicable acts without a readily apparent motive or reason. Unlike adult criminals, who appear to commit crimes for some motive, however reprehensible—be it revenge or money, for example—crimes by children such as these don't seem to have a hard and fast reason.

Mitchell Johnson, the 13-year-old Jonesboro shooter, was said to have fallen into despair and anger at rejection by a 13-year-old potential girlfriend. But every 13-year-old boy who gets rejected by a little girl doesn't start mowing down his classmates with semiautomatic weapons. Luke Woodham of Pearl, Mississippi, may have been chubby and bespectacled and picked on by classmates, and David Carneal of Paducah, Kentucky, may have been small and picked on also, but every slighted adolescent doesn't go into homicidal rage. Edinboro's Andrew Wurth had left hints that he was angry and depressed, but had never committed any crimes. The boys generally didn't have a prior criminal history, though Mitchell Johnson had been accused of previously improperly touching a younger girl. Most had generally nice parents. Only one—Kipland Kinkel—had been accused of torturing animals, normally a bellwether sign of a growing adolescent sociopath. None of these small-town boys were reported to use alcohol or narcotics, and none belonged to a gang.

Mitchell Johnson and Andrew Golden were surrounded by guns from early childhood and raised in an area where an inordinately high number of families were gun hobbyists. Guns were a way of life for them. Yet, to be fair, they appeared to have a number of other interests. Although Johnson and Golden appeared to have calculated a well-thought-out vicious scheme when they showed up in G.I. Joe cartoon character army fatigues and first pulled a school fire alarm to bring their fellow students out into the open and into their line of fire, once arrested, they reverted back to little boys. They cried for their mothers and just wanted to go back home. As stated previously in this book, generally speaking, the causes of youth violent crime are typically children (1) raising themselves without parents or role models enough in their lives, (2) compounded by poverty while (3) being bombarded by media violence. But not every delinquent child fits that mold. The bottom line is that, to the untrained eye, none of the kids in these three incidents appeared to be walking time bombs ready to go off. One common thread cannot be identified.

Yet, after each incident, particularly in the aftermath of the Jonesboro shootings, legal experts filled the airwaves scrambling to give reasons and find trends.

"There's not one answer," says Mark Soler of the Youth Law Center in Washington, D.C. "Anyone who says there's a single cause or a single remedy is ignoring the complexity of this problem."

Yet, perhaps whatever the varied reasons are for each individual case, they're not all that different from the sorts of problems, disappointments and confusions that have always been faced by adolescent boys. The only difference is that now, in the middle of trying to sort out these typical growing-pain difficulties, there are just so many guns out there at hand. Every time they feel relatively normal anger and frustration, they now have the means to act on it rather than just kick a chair or shove somebody.

"Without access to these guns, kids might break a couple of windows," Geoffrey Canada, a respected youth expert argued in the April 6, 1998, edition of Newsweek. "It would be a pain, but it wouldn't be mass murder."

It's true, there will never be any way to absolutely prevent unstable, emotionally distraught or mentally ill people from performing seemingly random acts of violence. Nor can we keep them out of the hands of the professional organized criminal.

The problem is that there are so many guns out there—192 million owned by private American citizens alone, more than one for every adult.[2] This means that just having so many around and available in such unprecedented numbers means that there has developed a matter-of-factness, an "everydayness" to them. As never before, children—not just mentally ill or criminal types—take them for granted, play with them, use them against each other and use them against themselves. Because they are there.

When I asked a 15-year-old from a tough urban neighborhood of Hartford, Connecticut, how many of the kids in his neighborhood had guns, he replied, "Everybody. Not everybody uses them, but everybody's got them. Just to make them seem bigger, better, badder. A lot of frightened kids will use them if they have to. It's all about survival."

Another 15-year-old from the same neighborhood told me, "You can buy guns like candy whether you're 12, 13 or 14. If it comes down to it, some kids will definitely use it. If you've got a gun, some people will say, 'Oh, you've got a gun. It's cool. Whatever.' "

It is not surprising to learn that the rate of children killed by guns in the United States is 12 times that of all other industrialized countries combined.[3]

"If you have a country saturated with guns—available to people when they are intoxicated, angry or depressed—it's not unusual guns will be used more often," says Dr. Rebecca Peters, a gun violence expert at Johns Hopkins University.

Peters said this in the wake of a study released in 1998 by the Centers for Disease Control and Prevention which reported that the United States has the highest rate of gun deaths—murders, suicides and accidents—among the world's 36 richest nations. The study found that gun-related deaths were five to six times higher in the Americas than in Europe or Australia or New Zealand and 95 times higher than in Asia. The United States had 14.24 per 100,000 people while the rate for second-ranked Brazil was 12.95; Mexico was 12.69, Estonia was 12.26 and Argentina was in fifth place with 8.93. Toward the bottom of the list was England and Wales with 0.41 per 100,000; Taiwan with 0.37 and South Korea with 0.12.[4]

In interviews with scores of youngsters from inner cities, I was told again and again that hearing gunshots in their neighborhoods is pretty much a typical daily experience not even worthy of a great deal of notice. It was clear that they were almost inured to it. I asked them what that was like because certainly if gunshots rang out any place that I had ever lived, it would be a memorable, shocking and fearful incident. Almost without exception, they claimed they were almost immune to feeling anything about it unless it was personal to them.

Fourteen-year-old Jamie told me: "I see people get shot. I see people get killed. I see people use drugs. It's like a normal way of life. I'd be scared to get shot. But I wouldn't be scared to just see it."

Fifteen-year-old Ronny told me: "If I hear shots it don't mean nothin' as long as it's not on my street. If it's on my block, I'd be scared."

Ineka has a similar view that gunfire is okay as long as it is not too close to home: "It goes on so much you get used to it. But sometimes it's scary because it could be one of your friends or family who's being shot at."

"The only time I get afraid is when it's close to home," said 15-year-old Tyrell. "I never know if it will come through my window or whatever."

In four of the five states where these schoolyard shootings took place—Arkansas, Kentucky, Mississippi and Oregon—the law allows children to carry rifles at any age. Perhaps that's why Mississippi ranks fourth in the nation in firearm fatalities; Arkansas ranks sixth and Kentucky ranks 27th. Nearly half the homes in the South have a gun while nation wide it's not much better—one in three, according to a report on the NBC Nightly News on March 27, 1998. In fact, when Kipland Kinkel either killed or injured 24 of his fellow students in his Oregon high school on that terrible morning of May 21, 1998, he was living in a state where 53 percent of all the households have guns. And all the guns in his possession that morning—a .22 caliber semiautomatic rifle, a Glock pistol and a .22-caliber handgun—were legal for a 15-year-old to own in Oregon.

It is worth noting a detailed list of the weapons and ammunition that was found on these two children, 11-year-old Andrew Golden and 13-year-old Mitchell Johnson, when they were arrested fleeing the scene of the school murders in Jonesboro, Arkansas.

On his person, Andrew Golden alone (not including a similar amount of weapons and ammunition found both on Mitchell Johnson and within the van they had traveled) was found with:

- *In left front top pocket*
  - two speed-loader clips
  - with .357-magnum shells
  - one .380-caliber shell
- *In left front lower pocket*
  - 49 .380-caliber shells
  - 16 .38-caliber special shells
  - 26 .357-magnum shells
  - six .30-caliber shells
  - two .38-caliber rat shot

- *In middle front pocket*
  - 34 .357 shells
- *In back pocket of vest*
  - three 30-shot clips
- *From upper top pocket of vest*
  - seven .357-magnum shells
- *From middle front pocket of vest*
  - 19 .44-caliber shells
- *Ammunition from pants pockets and from guns*
  - 38 .357-magnum shells
  - one .380-caliber shell
  - 22 .30-caliber shells
  - one .380-caliber clip loaded with four shells
- *Other items found on Golden*
  - one universal .30-caliber carbine unloaded
  - one Davis Industries .38 special two-shot Derringer, loaded
  - one FIE .380-caliber semiautomatic pistol, loaded with six shells
  - one Ruger Security Six .357-caliber revolver
  - one pocketknife
  - one holster

This astounding arsenal on this 11-year-old's person doesn't include the numerous handguns and rifles found on his partner, Mitchell Johnson, or the numerous items found in the van they were using including a crossbow, knives and a machete.

If firearms weren't available and kids were stuck with slingshots and water balloons and pea shooters, these events would have had an entirely different outcome. Since children aren't always the best at negotiating conflicts (hence a long tradition of schoolyard shoving matches and fights), they may just use what they have at hand. Nowadays, that means guns. In early March of 1998, a 7-year-old at an inner-city elementary school in Indianapolis tried to shoot a classmate with his brother's .25-caliber handgun, but it jammed. It was probably just what he had at hand. If he had no access to guns, a slap or a punch might have filled the gap.

A number of young kids I spoke with told me that guns were so common in their neighborhood that they noticed an emerging trend. It used to be that youths in their neighborhoods would do most of their shootings under the cover of night. But, increasingly, guns had become so common that the time of day had become irrelevant.

"Oh, it's all through the day," said 15-year-old Ronny. "It's like before, people would say we're gonna do a drive-by (shooting) at nighttime. They don't care no more. They do not care at all."

These five school shooting cases in late 1997 and early 1998 simply gained the most notoriety. But, within the previous five years, according to a list compiled and presented by the *New York Times* on March 27, 1998, there were numerous other instances where at least two people were killed or wounded on school property:

- A 16-year-old shot and killed two people and wounded two others at a Bethel, Alaska, high school on February 19, 1997.
- A 14-year-old shot and killed three people and wounded one other at a Moses Lake, Washington, junior high school on February 2, 1996.
- A 17-year old shot and killed two people and wounded one other at a Lynnville, Tennessee, high school on November 15, 1995.
- A 16-year old shot and killed two people and wounded one other at a Blackville, South Carolina, high school on October 12, 1995.
- A 13-year-old shot and killed one person and wounded one other at a Redlands, California, grade school on January 23, 1995.
- A 17-year-old shot and killed one person and wounded one other at an Amityville, New York, high school on February 1, 1993.
- A 17-year-old shot and killed two people at a Grayson, Kentucky, high school on January 18, 1993.[5]

Yet again, it's hard to draw a pattern or confirm a trend since a report released by the U.S. Department of Education less than a week before the Jonesboro shootings confirmed that school violence is generally uncommon in America's classrooms. Almost half of all public schools reported no crimes at all, neither serious nor minor. But 20 percent reported at least one serious incident a year such as a robbery.

The Department of Education released another report on May 8, 1998, which revealed that 6,000 public school students were expelled the previous year for bringing a firearm with them to class. Education Secretary Richard W. Riley said it was "a clear indication that our nation's public schools are cracking down on students who bring guns." But, because the report was the first of its kind, there was no way of telling whether this number had risen or fallen.[6]

That's why it's important to examine this chapter's most significant statistic—that gun homicides by children tripled from 1983 to 1993, while homicides involving all other weapons declined. Additionally, children themselves were the victims of gun homicides four times more often in 1994 than in 1984, while their victimization by other weapons remained flat.[7]

It's important to note that:

- Teenage boys are more likely to die from gunshot wounds than from all natural causes combined. These gun homicides offset the declining number of childhood deaths due to accidents (primarily automobile accidents), which went down 26 percent from 1987 to 1995.
- Between 1980 and 1994, the percentage of juveniles killed by the following weapons were:

—Guns	49 percent
—Knife/blunt object	15 percent
—Personal (including hands, fists, feet)	19 percent
—Other (including fire, asphyxiation, drugs, strangulation, drowning, poisons, explosions	10 percent
—Unknown	7 percent

- Firearm-related deaths, including unintentional shootings, homicides and suicides, went up 32 percent and account for 27 percent of all deaths from injury among children and teenagers, according to the National Center for Injury Prevention and Control.
- Guns claimed the lives of 88 percent of the 15- to 19-year-olds killed in 1991. From 1985 to 1991, 97 percent of the increase was attributed to guns, according to the Centers for Disease Control and Prevention.
- Arrests of males ages 15–19 on weapons charges doubled since 1983. This is in great contrast to that of grown-ups. Between 1985 and 1994, the adult arrest rate for weapons violations increased 26 percent while juvenile arrests soared 103 percent.[8]

"We've got to get guns out of the hands of these kids—it's an epidemic," says Alfred Blumstein, one of the nation's leading criminologists.[9]

Blumstein's use of the word "epidemic" may not have just been semantically descriptive. In 1998, a survey appearing in Annals of Internal Medicine found that 87 percent of surgeons and 94 percent of internists across the country believed it was time to consider gunshot wounds a public health epidemic—just like AIDS, alcoholism and tobacco use.[10]

Blumstein theorizes that the skyrocketing of the use of guns by youths began in the early to mid-1980s with the growing use of crack cocaine. Crack involves more street transactions than a number of other drugs. Juveniles were recruited by the illicit drug industry because they work for less than adults and are willing to take more risks. In fact, they have little sense of the consequences. They had been given firearms both as protection and as a means to resolve disagreements. Sadly, this use of guns eventually trickled down to kids who weren't involved with drugs since children seem to be tightly networked and then want to carry them for both status and protection. It's what Blumstein refers to as the community disorganization effect—drugs affecting the lives of entire communities that have no connection with them.

Virtually every urban youth from a tough neighborhood whom I spoke with told me the same thing. They said that the reason they and their friends carried guns was not to go out and aggressively use them, but rather as a defensive means of self-preservation.

Fifteen-year-old Ineka claims:

> There's so much stuff going on in the street, you need protection. I know people who don't want to shoot somebody on purpose, but if they had to, if their life depended on it, they would. . . . People these days think, "Why you get mad at me if I shot him? He'd-a shot me if he had the chance."

Fifteen-year-old Alan told me, "It's all about who gets who first. If you see the person first, you've got to shoot him first. That's how everybody's got to see it. That's how everybody does see it. A lot of people see it either you kill or get killed, know what I mean."

Another teenager, Alvarez, had a similar take on this: "Maybe they join a gang because they can't fight. They want somebody to watch their back . . . to make them look big and bad."

Ironically, even though it may have been the crack distributors who originally armed the children to work in the drug world, these guns were rarely used to enforce drug deals or fight drug market turf battles. Instead, once armed, even the drug gangs found themselves using their guns more

often for such petty reasons as "disrespecting gang colors, stepping in front of another person, flashing gang hand signs, or driving through a rival neighborhood."[11]

"Somebody says there's no reason to be shooting," says Alan. "There's always a reason. Nobody runs up and shoots for no reason. They don't care. They can always come up with some reason."

Ineka added:

> 'Cause in my project, you've got all people havin' rough times, sellin' drugs and all . . . the people are angry. Then somebody'll be sayin' their project is better than our project and everybody has to fight. Near where I live, some people be sayin' that the weed [marijuana] is better at their project. So the other project started pullin' in the business we used to get. So we started beefin' with 'em to get back our business.

A 1996 study by Decker and Van Winkle found most gang violence, including homicides, to be retaliatory or situationally spontaneous. "Whatever the 'purpose' of violence, it often leads to retaliation and revenge creating a feedback loop where each killing requires a new killing," read their report.[12] Drug dealing was not the chief reason for killing.

"Anything can start it," said 16-year-old Malvern. "The project where I live will get into a beef with another project. Anything can happen. They won't like a person and will beat him up. Then he gets his boys and retaliates."

Ronny told me that his neighborhood also doesn't have a lot of formal gangs but that the boys on his street will band together just the same. He told me the story about a friend of his who was killed and its inevitable aftermath: "He had a beef with these kids from another area and they drove up on him and shot him a lot of times," said Ronny. "A month later, one of the dudes he had a beef with who did this to him got killed."

Studies have borne this out. Firearms were involved in only 10 percent of all gang drug cases in a Los Angeles study while drugs were involved in only 10 percent of all violent gang crimes in Boston. A Chicago study found that only 8 of 258 gang-related homicides were related to drugs.[13]

Daniel Webster, an assistant professor of public health at Johns Hopkins University, expounds further on this destruction of the community brought on by the guns that followed the drugs:

People say it's really the breakup of the community that's behind the violence. But, in my mind, it's the other way around. It used to be that community elders would keep the young folks in line. But when 12- and 15-year-olds started carrying guns, it really tore down a lot of societal controls in those communities that controlled youth behavior.[14]

John Silva, director of safety and security for public schools in Cambridge, Massachusetts, notes that now:

Good kids have guns . . . there's so much fear. Good kids who want to go to school and do the right thing—they're afraid of the gangs and the drug dealers; they want to protect themselves and their families. Good kids, bad kids—the categories don't apply anymore.[15]

Once guns became part of the ordinary, day-to-day life of many children, they began to be treated with a matter-of-fact attitude. For some juveniles, when faced with a typical schoolyard confrontation, guns were put into use just because they were so readily available. After all, a survey by the Centers for Disease Control and Prevention taken in 1990, before gun carrying by kids had reached its peak, revealed that 135,000 students in grades 9 through 12 had carried a weapon at least once in the previous month. Additionally, 270,000 students had actually carried a gun into school at least once. The 1995 Youth Risk Behavior Study revealed that 10 percent of all high school students said that in the previous 30 days, they had carried a weapon on school property. This is half the overall number of students (20 percent) who reported carrying a weapon anywhere in the previous month.[16]

Finally, on June 21, 1998, just at the end of the school year, it was revealed by the PRIDE organization that nearly 1 million students had carried a gun to school that very year. The remarkable thing is that this number was, in fact, encouraging since PRIDE further revealed that this number had actually fallen 36 percent in the previous five years.

Having more weapons around than ever, combined with what Blumstein refers to as the typical "recklessness and bravado" for which teenagers are known, turns what "would have been fist fights with outcomes no more serious than a bloody nose into shootings with much more lethal consequences because guns are present."

Guns can distance and remove the killer from the killing. A young person who might have trouble killing someone with his bare hands, a knife or a club can fire into someone without it being so "up-close and personal." It emotionally distances him from the brutality.

DEATH AS A FUN GAME

Some people question whether all kids even realize the seriousness and finality of death. Having seen so many tens of thousands of murders on television and in films and listened to murders being romanticized in music, children really may not get the actual devastation of it. Perhaps this helped create fantasies in the mind of the Edinboro, Pennsylvania, school dance killer Andrew Wurth, nicknamed Satan because he was a fan of rocker Marilyn Manson.

Molly Baldwin, the remarkable youth organizer in Chelsea, Massachusetts, has counseled thousands of youths and isn't so sure that many of the young killers don't think it's just a game:

> They kill people. "I've got a gun, it's cool, and boom, I'm shooting, and boom." I don't think most of them even get what's going on. Like it's a real gun. Death is real. It's not pretend. . . . He stood there in the middle of the street and shot him over and over again and laughed. I think he didn't even realize the bullet even got him. He thought the bullet was somewhere else. It was a game, it was a movie, it was a picture.

This is the only explanation (and it's only my conjecture) I can come up with for those five brutal schoolground killings by 11-year-old Andrew Golden and 13-year-old Mitchell Johnson in Jonesboro, Arkansas, in March 1998. Perhaps it wasn't so much that they were evil but, rather, that they "just didn't get it." Maybe they did think that it was just some kind of entertainment and that there would be no consequences—no finality to death. There didn't seem to be any particular well-thought-out plan as to what they would do after they shot the other children. They had a van, $5 in cash and some food. Did they think that they'd merely drive off, live off the $5 for the next few years since they were to young to work, get their own place to live? Or did they even get that far in their thinking? Did they even weigh the consequences, come up with a scheme as to what to do after the shooting?

"I don't think that kids understand the value of human life," theorized Kevin Dwyer of the National Association of School Psychologists on the March 27, 1998, broadcast of the *NBC Nightly News*. "I don't think they understand death. I don't think they understand the permanency of it." On that same broadcast, which was just after the Jonesboro shootings, adolescent therapist Paul Davely said, "It may have felt like it was a game acting out the vision or fantasy they had in their head of how that game was supposed to go."

It's doubtful that they did initially understand the grave seriousness of their actions. This is so because, once arrested and in jail, Andrew Golden just kept requesting that he be allowed to see his mother and go home. Both boys were said to have asked if they could trade their first jailhouse lunch of corn bread, white beans and chicken for a pizza. They didn't seem to "get it." It had to be explained to them how bad their actions were, and at that point, it was said that they belatedly became full of remorse and contrition.

There's also a line of reasoning which flies right in the face of the old adage that "guns don't kill people; people kill people." This is that having a weapon itself, particularly in the hands of someone of an immature age, is a stimulant to aggression. One might feel cool and macho when they hold the gun and watch the fear in the face of someone else. The gun motivates the juvenile to shoot. In effect, the finger doesn't pull the trigger; the trigger pulls the finger.

Just having them around causes shootings, and not just the intentional kind against another person. Again and again, like a video played at a dizzying pace in fast forward, we see an endless procession of accidental shootings.

In early December 1997, a seven-year-old boy in Altoona, Pennsylvania, found a key to his parents' locked gun cabinet, pulled out the only loaded rifle and accidentally shot his two-year-old playmate Karissa Miller with a single bullet to the abdomen. She died instantly.

Later that month, on Christmas Eve, a 14-year-old boy pulled the trigger of a handgun that belonged to his mother. He had thought the gun was empty. As a result, he accidentally shot in the throat his 12-year-old friend, Brian Crowell, who was speaking on the telephone at the time.

At Brian's funeral, he was eulogized as a cheerful presence, a "kid on the go" who had just been nominated as Student of the Month at his middle school and also as a lover of "wheels"—all kinds including dirt bikes, Rollerblades and skateboards. But there in St. Margaret's Church in Saugus, Massachusetts, his uncle, Thomas Mauriello, said that although he would "never suggest that the constitutional right to bear arms be compromised," he also argued that guns be handled "in a safe and responsible manner, because when you fail to do so, tragedy and suffering is the result."[17]

The eloquent warning of Brian's uncle was not heeded by enough people. Two weeks later, it happened again in another part of Brian's state. Two 18-year-old twin brothers who lived in a small town, Kyle and

Shannon St. Jacques, were visiting a 17-year-old female friend. While they were watching television, she brought out a box with five firearms she said belonged to her boyfriend. They were, in fact, licensed and legally owned. The brothers were reported to be looking at the guns, which they knew nothing about, and the girl was even checking them out to see if they were loaded. The girl examined all the weapons emptying them of clips, but failed to notice that a bullet remained in the chamber of one of them.

No one was sure exactly what happened then, but they heard a bang and saw a flash. It was unclear whose gun went off. But Shannon saw his twin—his other half with whom he ran track, played music and from whom he was inseparable—slip away. Kyle St. Jacques died approximately two and a half hours later. And so did his plans for entering college as a business administration major the following autumn.

His father said of the twins, "They were each other's shadow, they were that close. They did everything together."

Since no one was really sure whose gun had gone off, the haunting specter that Shannon may have killed his own twin brother haunted him.

The brothers had never used guns and, in fact, their father had never even let them play with toy guns as young children because "I didn't want them to think they were cool." Regardless, the grief-stricken Shannon made a tearful public plea about gun safety. "Guns shouldn't be used by people who don't know what they're doing. Don't touch a gun if you don't know what you're doing."[18]

LOCKING UP GUNS

When, as previously noted, Michael Carneal entered his Paducah, Kentucky, high school so heavily armed, it was considered unusual particularly in light of the fact that, just like the St. Jacques boy, he was never known to have fired a gun. The firearms Michael brought to school on that sad December morning were said to have been stolen from the garage of a neighbor. Also stolen were the firearms Luke Woodham used to shoot his classmates in Pearl, Mississippi.

In Jonesboro, Arkansas, the boys, using a hammer and propane torch, attempted to steal the firearms of 11-year-old Andrew Golden's father but those weapons were, admirably, in a locked, steel gun safe. Still, they found three handguns. They fared much better at the home of Andrew's grandfather, whose guns were not secured. They emerged with four more handguns and three high-powered rifles.

A few weeks after the Jonesboro killings, when 14-year-old Andrew Wurst shot up his middle school dance in Edinboro, Pennsylvania, wounding several students and killing a popular teacher, the gun he used was borrowed from his unknowing father.

In all four of these highly publicized cases, the guns were stolen. This particular part is not unusual. Slightly more than half of all privately owned firearms are stored unlocked. Sixteen percent are stored unlocked and loaded.[19]

This is the most heartbreaking part, according to Suzette Wilson, mother of Brittany, one of the little girls killed in Jonesboro. At a White House ceremony on July 8, 1998, she said:

> What happened in Jonesboro could have been prevented. Two children who should never have had unsupervised access to firearms were able to put together a sort of arsenal. I don't care how many guns people own. But to every gun owner in America I want to say, "Please, please, for the sake of the children, lock up your guns. Don't let your gun become an instrument of murder. Don't let what happened in Jonesboro happen to your town."

In a CNN interview on March 25, 1998, right after the Jonesboro, Arkansas, shooting spree, Congresswoman Carolyn McCarthy, whose husband was killed and son grievously injured during the shooting rampage by Colin Ferguson aboard a Long Island, New York, commuter train, stated, "Most guns that come into the schools today are guns that are owned by their parents, but they're not locked and they're not put away safely and children have access to these guns."

McCarthy advocates a growing proposal—that parents who leave their guns unlocked should be penalized if their children use them illegally. This appears to emulate the antitobacco lawsuits where the supplier is held liable for the acts of the user. This is very different from the laws which are in effect in 42 states (though rarely enforced) which simply make parents responsible for the crimes of their children. These child access prevention laws simply make parents responsible for their own actions—allowing their own guns to fall in the hands of their children through their own negligence in not safely storing them. By mid-1998, 16 states had such laws in effect.

One such state is North Carolina. On April 27, 1998, when a little Greensboro boy was shot to death on his sixth birthday by a four-year-old playmate, his godmother was charged with failing to secure a weapon. The .38-caliber pistol was found in the unattended purse of his godmother.

I represented a teenager, whom I'll call Randy, from a very good home in the suburbs, who was a good student and had never had a run-in with the police. His father had a gun collection and was always careful to keep it under lock and key. One day, he neglected to lock one gun. Randy and a school friend discovered this and looked the gun over. His friend asked if he could borrow the gun to do some target shooting in the nearby woods. Randy said no, that he couldn't lend out one of his father's possessions and, besides, his father didn't allow him to touch his guns. But the friend persisted and Randy eventually gave in. The friend did do some target practice, and the police, hearing the noise, came and took it away from him. They learned who had provided it to him. Randy was charged. When I got to the court to represent him, I was told that they would seek to incarcerate him.

Now, I realized that Randy did an irresponsible thing. Someone could have been hurt as a result of his friend's borrowing the gun for target practice. No young person should have any role in putting guns out there. Punishment was not unreasonable. But I believed it would be wrong to pull a good student who had never been in trouble and did not have a bad attitude away from school and from a loving, nondysfunctional home just for the sake of scoring a political point. It would be pointlessly spending government funds when they could be used through other programs to really fight youth crime. Fortunately, Randy, ultimately, didn't go to jail nor did he receive a criminal record, but he did suffer alternative punishments. Perhaps, our modern-day goal and anthem should be to lock up guns, not children.

GUN SUICIDES

Possibly the most disturbing rise in shootings which aren't intentionally against another person is the meteoric surge in juvenile suicides. Overall there was a 14 percent rise in suicides in the United States among all age groups between 1979 and 1994. But for youths younger than the age of 15, the rise was a shocking 112 percent.[20] For every two youths under age 19 murdered in 1994, one youth committed suicide.[21] Almost inevitably, those youthful suicides are performed with a gun. Between 1980 and 1994, firearms-related suicides accounted for 96 percent of the overall rise in youth suicides.[22]

Inevitably, someone will say, "So what? If someone wanted to commit suicide and guns weren't available, they'd still commit suicide. They'd just find some other way to do it. In the case of a suicide, it's not the gun that kills the child. It's the child that kills the child." This line of reasoning might almost sound logical. Only it isn't true.

Most teen suicides are impulsive, with little or no planning, and 70 percent occur within the victims' homes. In fact, the risk of suicide is five times greater if one is living in a house with a gun than if the house has no gun.[23]

"A lot of teenage firearm deaths are suicides, and typically it [involved] a gun that was right in the home," according to Susan P. Baker of the Johns Hopkins School of Public Health who led a study on juvenile injury deaths. Baker went on to say that suicides often occur after "a fight with a girlfriend, despondence over grades. The records show crises that might be temporary" if a gun weren't at hand.[24]

It brings to mind *Crimes of the Heart*, the Pulitzer Prize-winning play later made into a film, in which a character commits suicide and leaves a suicide note which reads, "I had a bad day." In the play, it's an almost whimsical line of black comedy. But in real life, it's all too true.

One of the problems with attempting suicide on an impulse during what may be only a temporary dark moment is that a great many suicide attempts aren't successful—that is, unless a gun is used. Emergency room data verified that, nationally, gun suicide attempts are almost always fatal. In fact, according to the Centers for Disease Control, one study in Oregon showed that from 1988 to 1993 78.2 percent of all suicide attempts with firearms were fatal, but only 0.4 percent of suicide attempts by drug overdose were fatal.[25] Guns are just so much more lethal. A teenager or child, hit with a momentary despondence, may not have the wherewithal to figure out a proper combination of something to ingest or have the will to stab him- or herself or face the terror of crashing a car or jumping off a roof. Pulling a trigger if a gun is at hand is the easiest of all the horrible choices. So the argument can be made: It's not just people who kill themselves. Guns kill people.

In a live Internet conference with journalist Steve Roberts of *U.S. News and World Report* on March 15, 1994, hosted by U.S. News Online on CompuServe, a person wrote in that "Guns are inanimate objects. How can they commit crimes?" Roberts answered, "That's the oldest argument on the books . . . guns are operated by people . . . but they do a lot more damage than knives or fists."[26]

In fairness, though, an argument was made by Mike Males in his 1996 book *Scapegoat Generation*, that although some say the teen suicide rate has tripled since the 1950s, a lot of the reported rise in teen suicides can be attributed to the fact that, after 1960, coroners started recording teen firearm deaths more accurately. They no longer just labeled so many of them "accidents."[27]

YOU SHOOT WHO YOU KNOW

If so much of this shooting is done on momentary impulse with guns just happening to be around, it's easy to figure out who are the likely victims in those cases which don't involve suicide. It is, of course, the people you know in your life. Of all juveniles murdered between 1980 and 1994:

- 24 percent were killed by a parent
- 4 percent were killed by another family member
- 36 percent were killed by an acquaintance
- 11 percent were killed by a stranger

It's unknown who killed the remaining 25 percent.

So, to sum it up, 64 percent of juvenile homicide victims were killed by someone they knew, while only 11 percent were killed by strangers (and the rest had unknown killers). But it is important to keep in mind that only about half the female victims of violent crime by an intimate (a husband, ex-husband, boyfriend or ex-boyfriend) ever report the incident because they consider it a "private or personal matter." So, the number of incidents is probably much greater than even these statistics indicate.[28]

Families and friends kill each other—because they are there. In the heat of day-to-day life, the sad truth is that people often lash out at those around them. Guns increase the chances of that murder attempt being successful because, as established above, guns have been proven to be so much more lethal. If a gun weren't in the vicinity at the moment of emotional outburst, perhaps a still unfortunate slap or punch or thrown piece of crockery would be the result. As unfortunate as that would still be, at least the victim would still be alive. According to Handgun Control, Inc., the family gun is 43 times more likely to kill you or someone you know than to kill in self-defense. The one thing that rings through loudly and resoundingly after sifting through the above statistics and studies on the epidemic of shootings and gun suicides enveloping our communities is a disturbing and overall despair.

Attorney Steven Weymouth, who represents hundreds of kids in court, says:

> I think a lot of the kids are surrounded by helplessness. You know, they see lousy housing opportunities, they have lousy educational experiences, they have a mother or a father who doesn't care too much about them or who is not available, they have turf issues to worry about, they have diseases to worry about. I think a lot of kids figure that if they have to rely on their own, they have to become armed and become hateful and become feelingless because they might have to kill to survive. If you have to kill to survive, you can't be feeling all guilty and queasy about it. You have to go out and do it. People survive that way and, unfortunately, that's the way it is. People support themselves that way. It becomes easier to do and there's less and less remorse.

A Harris poll showed that an astounding 35 percent of children ages 6 to 12 fear their lives will be cut short by gun violence.[29] It was reported that a disquieting new pastime of young kids in many neighborhoods is to plan their own funerals. They speak among themselves of the music they'd like and what they'd like to wear at their own wake.

One tough, urban 15-year-old I spoke with, Ronny, told me of his near-apocalyptic worldview. He said:

> The guys who kill in my neighborhood . . . it's like they just don't care. The way society is now. It's like the world's about to end. Yeah, I think it's about to end. Like all this El Niño weather stuff is part of it. If the world's got to end, it's got to end. I wouldn't want to die by myself. But if the world's gonna die with me. . . ."

It's that despair and fear which makes many young people pick up guns themselves to ill-advisedly try to gain that power over their own lives.

GANGS AND GUNS

Tom Myers, a supervising correctional officer in Erie County, Pennsylvania, has worked tirelessly with young people for years in an effort to see that they don't join the ranks of the incarcerated men he watches over. He says:

What they tell me is that for them to survive in the wild kingdom, they need protection such as belonging to a gang or carrying a gun. . . . To the youth, the gang represents a safe haven for the weak and the outcast. When I was growing up in the 60s and the 70s, boys would have a fist fight and that would end it. We knew if we became involved with any more serious crimes, we would be punished by our parents. As children growing up, we respected our parents for taking care of us and showed appreciation by doing the right things.

Many of today's youth cry out for help and attention the only way they know how, by being violent and resorting to serious crimes. They have been let down by their role models and decided to give in to peer pressure.

Eric Rodriguez, who was profiled in the previous chapter, spent his juvenile years committing unlawful activity and now works with youth gangs. He believes that gangs with guns also came into existence because of this combination of despair and fear:

Gangs are a phenomena that actually starts with good intentions. People join gangs because they're trying to meet very basic needs that nobody can fault anybody to look for. They're looking for people to love them, genuinely and unconditionally. They're looking for people to protect them. They want to feel protected and safe. They want camaraderie, they want to be included. That's it. That's why gangs are around if you really break it down.

People, they come together. Here's a group who says, "Look, we don't care what you're dealing with, man. Come hang with us. You're all right with us. We'll protect you. We'll watch your back. We'll make sure nothing happens to you. We'll be your friends. We'll be here through thick and thin with you. Everybody else is going to cast you out. We won't. . . ."

Those are basic needs that everybody in this world tries to have met, regardless. So people make bad decisions on how they get met, and that's because they don't see the other options and opportunities. And, in fact, there are no opportunities for people out there.

Fifteen-year-old Alan from Hartford, Connecticut, explained his banding together with other young urban toughs by way of a rather sophisticated analogy:

It makes you stronger. That's your power. It's like you, Mr. Elikann, with your book. You can't publish it and get it out yourself. You'll get a publisher, someone to print it up, someone to truck it over to bookstores and get it out to the people. It's the same thing here. Out in the street you can't do it all by yourself either. That's why they all tight like that here.

Saroeum Phoung, also profiled in the previous chapter, illustrates the fact that this hopeful joining of gangs and arming of themselves in order to fulfill their needs is, ultimately, a sad disappointment. Saroeum recalls his memories of belonging to a very violent gang and how it soured for him:

> I guess gangs suck, you know. For a young person like me who has no one to look up to, who has no one to really understand or to talk to about a lot of issues I'm facing during that time, I guess you turn to gangs. You don't really care if you die or not, but when you're actually in there for a while, you start to do some time in jail, you see your friends get killed, you see your friends get stabbed, you get hit, and you can feel all those feelings, and then you know how it feels. A lot of people, they're in too deep and then they never get out.
>
> And then as every generation grows out of it, the next is getting younger because a lot of young folks who are out there, they watch what happens in the street. So the more they see and the older they get, they could be seven years old and they see their older brothers out there doing gang bangs, doing drive-by shootings, smoking cigarettes, drinking beer and everything already. They see that it's all right to join a gang and it's all right for me to die young. I lived to the fullest and its all right to be in a gang when you're seven years old.

Part of the allure may just be the material rewards initially offered to these impoverished youths. Fifteen-year-old Tyrell says, "They get you bribed. Gang life? Yo. It's like, 'I get you this, this, this, this and this. You just gotta represent us. You know what I'm sayin'? You gotta be down.' That's life."

It's clear that gang membership has been soaring across the nation, but with so many cities lacking the capacity to compute gang membership, estimates fall all over the place.

- A 1995 Justice Department survey reported an estimated 23,388 gangs with nearly 665,000 members.
- Depending on which of the myriad surveys you believe, the number of estimated gang members in 1993 represented a 51.9 percent or a 122.7 percent increase over 1991, just two years earlier.
- During that two-year period, the number of gang crime incidents represented either an 843 percent or 1,152 percent increase.
- Nearly twice as many teenagers reported gangs in their schools in 1995 as in 1989, according to a survey disclosed in 1998 by the Bureau of Justice Statistics and the National Center for Justice Statistics. This survey found that gangs and violence went hand-in-hand.

In 1995, 7.5 percent of all students who reported gangs in their schools also reported that they'd been victimized by violent crime there, compared to 2.7 percent of students who reported no gangs in their schools.[30]

It's frequently hard to tell whether particular criminal activity can be attributed to gang activity or just a few random youths together at the moment. Some are comprised of a few friends who often hang out together when they get into trouble, while others have very rigid and sophisticated structures.

"They're in the process of growing into Mafias," says Notre Dame University law Professor G. Robert Blakey, who wrote the federal Racketeer Influenced and Corrupt Organization Act (RICO). Although when he wrote the statute in 1970, he had traditional mobsters and white-collar criminals in mind, he now believes the RICO statute should apply to youth gangs. "The Mafia started out as a street gang."[31]

Clearly gangs have evolved from our 1950s street corner image of hubcap-stealing hoods or the leather-jacketed, cigarette-smoking *West Side Story* hooligans singing, "Gee, Officer Krumpke."

It used to be that gangs were still pretty homogeneous groups made up of youths from the same neighborhood. Essentially, a particular ethnic group on a particular city block—Asian, Hispanic, white or African-American—would stick together to protect their community turf. But since the 1970s, the goals became more economic (primarily narcotics) and certain gangs branched out from their neighborhoods. Chapters of California's Crips and the Bloods sprang up throughout the country, and the Latin Kings from New York made inroads into the neighboring states.

Today, abandoning the traditional bats and blackjacks and sticks and knives in favor of semiautomatic weapons, their kill ration has jumped straight up. In a fascinating revelation, a study found that Chicago gang homicides increased during a three-year period in which there was no increase in street gang assaults, indicating that the lethality of weapons accounted for the greater number of homicides.[32] In other words, the same number of assaults resulted in more deaths because the assaults were done with a firearm rather than a fist, a shove or a stick.

In one instance I was told about by 15-year-old Tyrell, his neighborhood body count got so high during a gang war that almost everyone dropped their gang colors and left the gang life:

What made me get out of the gang? Everybody just dropped their colors because too many beefs was going on and stuff like that and I was like, man, I'm not about to lose my life over something stupid like that. At that point, that's when the Baby Loves and the Solids had a beef and everyone was just dying. Too much for me. Everyone was dropping their colors. I wasn't about to get popped.

Additionally, gangs aren't just teenagers leading each other. Ten percent of all youth gang members, usually in leadership positions, are adults.[33]

"People assume that gangs mean teenagers and juveniles," said Kenneth E. New, chief of the FBI's Safe Streets/Gangs Unit. "But that's just not true. When you have a Black Gangster Disciple Nation, the leaders are all adults. Hoover's no spring chicken."[34]

New was referring to 47-year-old Larry Hoover who was convicted of running what was considered to be a 30,000-member Chicago youth gang which conducted a $100-million-a-year drug enterprise. I was involved in a similar case involving dozens of federal indictments in the early 1990s where 39-year-old Darryl Whiting was convicted in federal court of running a very violent juvenile drug gang centered at the Orchard Hill Projects in Dorchester, Massachusetts.

Law enforcement is clearly cracking down on these increasingly lethal gangs with guns. In addition to using the above-mentioned tough RICO statutes, different localities are coming up with different approaches. Currently, if officials in the Massachusetts correctional system even suspect an inmate is a gang member, perhaps because the inmate speaks with someone who is suspected of being a gang member, they are sent without a hearing to the state's maximum security prison and held in 23-hour-a-day lockup until they are judged to have successfully completed a gang program. In Los Angeles in 1997, a controversial and constitutionally questionable injunction was used against the 18th Street Gang which forbade them from speaking to each other on the street even if they were related, blocking sidewalks, informing others that the police were coming or even using vulgar language. Many in the public, so disgusted with gangs, loved the injunction.

"Anything they try will help," said one man in the gang's neighborhood. "There have been a lot of drugs, a lot of trouble. It was better just to stay inside."

Unfortunately, many of these gang and gun suppression methods don't work. For example, a similar 1993 California injunction against a

San Fernando Valley gang failed to make a dent in crime in the area and was reported to have possibly caused crime to increase in nearby neighborhoods.

"They're very popular because what they offer in their advertising is a cheap, easy way to reduce violent crime," said Allan Parachini, author of that report. "Who could be against that? . . . The problem is people want so much for it to work that they don't want to listen to a contrarian view that uses irrefutable statistics, the LAPD's own statistics."[35]

A U.S. Justice Department study confirmed this, citing a number of other studies that both providing opportunities for the young and having community programs intervene in the lives of young people were the most effective strategies against gangs. It read, "Suppression strategies [tough prosecutions and laws] were not reported to be particularly effective, except in conjunction with other approaches." The study didn't say that the suppression strategy was never effective, just not as effective.[36]

Another Justice Department study, entitled *Prosecuting Gangs: A National Assessment*, was compiled by conducting a survey of local prosecutors across the country—those on the front lines of fighting crime. The study announced its chief finding: Ultimately, however, prosecutors believed that early intervention with children and youths and more effective services designed to strengthen families were necessary to prevent gang violence and crime.[37]

THE EFFECTIVENESS OF GUN CRIME PREVENTION

It is clear that a variety of gun prevention programs aimed at taking guns out of the hands of young people are critical. Certainly, a violent, dedicated criminal will almost always be able to gain possession of a gun. But so many children are shot through accidents, impulsive suicides or intentional shootings by another child who just happens to have a gun at hand but who wouldn't go looking for one if it weren't there. These high body count numbers can move and are moving downward wherever programs are in place. For example, the community-based Kansas City [Missouri] Gun Experiment was striking in cutting a homicide rate in half within six months while not causing crime to increase in any of the surrounding areas. Similar programs have recently worked in Detroit; Prince George's County, Maryland; and Boston.

This is true in spite of the fact that removing guns from the hands of young people will ultimately only have minor, though still positive, results. Youths will continue to cause destruction in their communities until there are enough role models in their lives to bring them morality, opportunity and motivation. A comprehensive study of gun-toting juveniles both in and out of prison concludes:

> From the viewpoint of public policy, it matters less, perhaps, where these juveniles get their guns than where they get the idea that it is acceptable to kill. It may be convenient to think that the problems of juvenile violence could be magically solved by cracking down or getting tough, but this is unlikely. The problem before us is not so much getting guns out of the hands of juveniles, as it is reducing the motivations for juveniles to arm themselves in the first place.[38]

Still, every avenue must be pursued in lowering the gun-inflicted body count of American children. This is so because the results from a diversity of methods are positive:

- Programs throughout Massachusetts contributed to a 41 percent reduction in gun injuries. The now-legendary Boston Gun Project smashed all preconceptions that there were so many guns out there that youths would either steal them or get them through other states with more lenient gun laws. First, their research told them that kids like new and semiautomatic guns; they shy away from guns stolen in burglaries; and since a large number of guns originated in their home state which had rigorous record keeping, a great many guns could be traced. They also learned that since most youths who carry guns carry them for protection, if the authorities could make the area safer and reduce the climate of fear, fewer kids would carry guns. Amazingly, it worked.
- When Virginia and Maryland instituted a "one gun a month law" which prohibited people from buying a number of guns at once, homicides committed by juveniles in Washington, D.C., dropped by 63 percent, a drop related to no other recognizable factors. Before the passage of this law, Virginia was the chief supplier of guns seized in homicides in Massachusetts. After the law went into effect, murder weapons seized in Massachusetts that could be traced back to Virginia declined by 72 percent. No doubt this contributed to the fact that, immediately afterward, Boston had a two

and one-half year period when not a single minor was shot to death.

- A study in the *Journal of the American Medical Association* in October 1997 revealed that laws making gun owners criminally liable if someone is hurt because a child gains unsupervised access to their gun reduced unintentional shootings by 23 percent. These safe-storage laws also produced modest declines in suicides and homicides.
- In fact, all gun deaths of juveniles declined 9.4 percent from 1994 to 1995.
- Weapons violations arrests of juveniles were down 16 percent from 1993 to 1995.
- Police background checks across the country since the Brady Bill went into effect in 1994 stopped about 242,000 sales out of 10.4 million attempted handgun purchases. Most of those thwarted were felons, but others were fugitives, subjects of restraining orders, the mentally disabled or drug addicts. There can be no doubt that the number of lives saved by this dramatic number was large.
- As New York City's violent crime rate has dramatically plunged so has the number of gun permit applications granted by the New York Police Department. This resulted in a 20 percent decline in the number of licensed handguns in New York from 1992 to 1997.[39]

Other methods which have had some levels of success in reducing juvenile gun deaths are childproofing of guns which have safety switches on them and pressure sensitive grips which make it difficult for the younger child to fire them. Trigger locks which come with a key are also similarly effective. A $12 trigger lock would have saved the life of his son, says Marc Mathieu. His 12-year-old son, Ross, was killed when Ross's friend showed him a .25 Beretta which had been lying on a closet shelf of the friend's father. The boys unloaded the clip but didn't realize a bullet remained in the chamber. The gun in the friend's hand was just six inches away when it released a bullet which entered Ross just under the left eye and exited the back of his neck. It killed him instantly. Today Marc Mathieu helps spearhead a trigger lock distribution program raising money to buy trigger locks which the local police departments give away for free.

"I always stress, I am not pro-gun, I am not anti-gun," says Mathieu. "People have a right to own guns and I support that right. But I have a right to know those guns are secure when kids are around them. If you're in the house, fine, unlock the gun if you're going to be around because in that sense, you are the lock. If you're not, lock it up."[40]

Ninety percent of all unintentional shooting deaths of juveniles are done within a home—50 percent in the victim's own home and 40 percent in the home of a relative or friend. In fact, kids are killed in gun accidents at home at a rate 23 times greater than those killed in schools.[41]

In the 1990s, under pressure from gun control groups, eight of the major gun manufacturers voluntarily agreed to sell safety locks with every handgun.

Guns in and of themselves are inherently dangerous to kids and that's why harsh punishment alone of children who use them will be selling us short. "Instead of banning guns, we banish kids," one recent op-ed piece declared in disgust.[42] In reality, we neither have to ban guns nor kids.

Until we make an effort to intervene in the lives of many of today's lost children, we can lock up as many as we can hold and we can pass endless gun laws, and it still won't work. Criminal justice researchers James D. Wright and Joseph Sheley say much the same thing in their declaration that:

> Until we rectify the conditions that breed hostility, estrangement, futility and hopelessness, whatever else we do will come to little or nothing. . . . Widespread joblessness and few opportunities for upward mobility are the heart of the problem. Stricter gun control laws, more aggressive enforcement of existing laws, a crackdown on drug traffic, police task forces aimed at juvenile gangs, metal detectors at the doors of schools, periodic searches of lockers and shakedowns of students, and other similar measures are inconsequential compared to the true need: the economic, social, and moral resurrection of the inner city.[43]

We'll never be able to eliminate all incidents of children killing other children. If you could at least make guns more difficult to come by, you'd still have some of the extremely hardened violent youths and the psychopaths gaining possession of them. But you'd eliminate a huge number of the child gun deaths by the soaring number of juveniles attempting suicide on sudden impulse, children killed by accident and kids casually lifting a gun to fire in a schoolyard dispute when a shove or punch might have been substituted if the gun weren't there.

"It is better to prevent another crime from occurring than to punish the criminal after another victim is harmed," says Attorney General Janet Reno.[44]

We cannot ignore the previously stated fact that the skyrocketing of murders committed by juveniles from the mid-1980s to the mid-1990s was attributable entirely to guns. Gun homicides tripled while the rate of homicides by all other methods stayed flat.

But pulling guns out of the equation will still only accomplish a small fraction of what could be accomplished by instilling in our children, through family or community, a vision of what they can achieve and a sense of morality.

Chapter 4

Adult Trials and Prisons for Juveniles

In the 1960s, the juvenile justice system of Massachusetts was under fire, known throughout the country as a "mess." State legislative investigations, the federal government and a variety of children's advocacy groups all united in denouncing a mismanaged system which abused children, deprived them of adequate rehabilitation programs to help those who could benefit and, essentially, ultimately released juveniles into the unsuspecting public more dangerous than when they went in.

In response, a bipartisan group of politicians, led by the Republican governor and the heads of the Democratic legislature, passed a new law that electrified juvenile justice professionals across the country. Among other things, in 1972, they abandoned the old way of incarcerating serious juvenile offenders in large reform school-type settings in favor of small, community-based programs where kids learned job skills, received individualized treatment and worked. Remarkably, the new system was cheaper. A study by the National Council on Crime and Delinquency found that states which eventually adopted the Massachusetts-style community-based programs found them less than a third as costly to operate as the large state training schools.[1]

The Massachusetts program was wildly successful. Crime by children nose-dived. By 1985, Massachusetts ranked 46th in its juvenile crime rate compared to the other 49 states and the District of Columbia.[2]

"Massachusetts is a national model," said Phillip Kassel, once an attorney in the state of Washington who is now based in Massachusetts where he frequently works on youth issues. "When I was in Washington,

I saw juvenile correctional administrators traveling to Massachusetts to get ideas on how to reform their heavily institutionalized system there." In fact, it was so successful that, in a 1991 report issued by the National Council on Crime and Delinquency (NCCD) entitled *Unlocking Juvenile Corrections: Evaluating the Massachusetts Department of Youth Services*, it concluded that:

> Public officials will face the imperatives of either investing massive amounts of taxpayers' dollars into expanding state training schools, with little guarantee of reducing youth crime—or they can explore the path pioneered by Massachusetts. Given the documented and persistent failures of large training schools to enhance public safety or protect child welfare, it is not surprising that many jurisdictions are implementing the principles embodied in the Massachusetts . . . approach.[3]

The towering proof of the effectiveness of Massachusetts' emphasis on small, community-based programs is that the NCCD report made a comparison between the recidivism rates of Massachusetts juvenile offenders once released and those of California, which kept its youth locked up for longer and longer periods of time in large reform schools with no treatment. The reincarceration rate of California was 62 percent. Massachusetts' rate was a significantly lower 23 percent. Again, California politicians, in an attempt to appear tough on crime, were, ironically, actually soft on it.

One of the hallmarks of Massachusetts juvenile law was that even when a young person was charged with a murder, a judge would make a determination if there was any way this juvenile could be rehabilitated. After a hearing, known as a transfer hearing, the judge would then decide whether to try the youth as an adult or a juvenile and whether to send him to juvenile or adult incarceration. Perhaps that helped contribute to the fact that the system worked so well that, by 1995, the Massachusetts juvenile arrest rate for murder was less than half the national average.

LEGISLATION BY ANECDOTE

That very year, though, something happened which made it all come crashing down. As mentioned in previous chapters of this book, on July 23, 1995, 42-year-old Janet Downing was brutally stabbed and slashed to death in her home in a working-class neighborhood of Somerville, Massachusetts. The suspect was Eddie O'Brien, a seemingly happy-go-lucky 15-year-old kid from across the street who had never been in any kind of trouble and was best friends with one of Downing's children.

Prior to trial and after comprehensive evaluations, the judge ruled that O'Brien be tried as an juvenile, thereby making him eligible for release after 20 years if convicted. That decision was successfully appealed by the prosecution and O'Brien was later tried as an adult, convicted and given a sentence of life without possibility of parole. But the horrific crime so outraged the media and the public that a bill was hastily passed through the state legislature which, among other things, automatically transferred any child accused of murder to adult trials and, hence, adult prison. It gave discretion to prosecutors, not judges, to charge most serious juvenile crimes as subject to adult sentences.

This system which worked so extremely well in comparison to other states in keeping youth crime down and the public safe that it attracted the attention of the rest of the nation was jettisoned because politicians jumped on this one incident which was, without a doubt, vicious and depraved. Certainly, even one murder is too many. But, if you have a system where the murder rate is driven to record lows, why abandon it?

According to Steven Weymouth of the Youth Advocacy Project in Roxbury, Massachusetts, it was unnecessary to tamper with what worked:

> There was hysteria in this country about increased juvenile crime . . . . Boston mobilized itself and did tremendous things to fight that down and did a really good job doing it. That didn't happen across the rest of the country. The legislatures, inflamed and emboldened by public improper perception, generated by the media, continued to pass legislation that continued to treat kids more harshly and more harshly.
>
> In 1994, in Massachusetts, in spite of all the hoopla, there were only 14 juveniles charged with either first or second degree murder. That's all across the state in one entire year. That shows, one, how good the mobilization efforts were across the state to reduce crime, and, two, it was never really that big of a problem in Massachusetts. . . . That's a very small number, it seems to me. It isn't necessary for the legislature to do major league tinkering . . . which is what it did.

Boston Globe columnist Eileen McNamara had the very same thing in mind when, in an October 11, 1997, column about that district attorney entitled "Political Capital from a Tragedy," she wrote, "We have had enough of legislating by hysteria in this state."[4]

TRANSFERS TO ADULT COURTS AND PRISONS

Massachusetts was not alone in letting one case dictate what the law should be. Pennsylvania Governor Tom Ridge used Jan License as a "poster girl" for his 1994 campaign, in which he vowed to change the existing juvenile law. She related in television commercials how she had been cruelly raped at knifepoint by a teenager in her home in a suburb of Philadelphia.

In fact, juvenile violent crime rates were already plunging by the mid-1990s. Indeed, across the country, 95 percent of all juvenile arrests are for nonviolent crimes. Additionally, most homicidal kids were transferred anyway to adult courts by judges without having to make such transfer automatic and beyond the judge's discretion. Between 1985 and 1994, the number of juvenile cases transferred to adult courts across the country through a judge's discretionary decision (judicial waiver) increased by a whopping 72 percent. So it wasn't as if new legislation were needed to do what the judges would not, because the judges were doing it.[5]

Still, politicians, not just in Massachusetts but across the nation, have been filing legislation at a dizzying rate to pull youths out of the juvenile system. As one state legislator phrased it, he would not allow criminals to "hide behind youth."

- From 1992 through 1995, 48 states passed laws making it easier for juveniles to be tried as adults.
- Since 1992, 49 of the 51 state legislatures (including the District of Columbia) have made substantive changes in their laws regarding juveniles to increase their eligibility for being tried in adult courts and jailed in adult facilities.
- From 1984 to 1990, prior to the time the real push began to send youths to adult prison, the number of juveniles entering adult prisons increased by 30 percent. At almost the same time, from 1983 to 1995, the number of youths held in juvenile facilities also rose 47 percent.
- Today, over the course of a year, more than 65,000 children are held in adult jails and that's not even counting police station lock-ups.[6] There are now approximately 200,000 children prosecuted in adult courts every year.

The way legislators have composed the laws, there are three different basic methods by which young people can find themselves in adult court or adult prison. Of course, there are variations on these several basic routes. They are:

1. *Judicial Waiver:* The juvenile court judge has the discretion to waive juvenile court jurisdiction and send the case over to adult court. Frequently, the judge's decision is based on the standard of whether the child is capable of being rehabilitated. In that case, where there is deemed to be hope for the child, the child may remain in juvenile court instead of being transferred.
2. *Prosecutor Discretion:* The prosecutor has the choice to charge the case at his or her discretion whether the case stays in juvenile court or is transferred over to adult court.
3. *Automatic Transfer (or Legislative Exclusion):* The state statute will automatically transfer juveniles charged with certain crimes and/or with a particular background to adult court. In this case, there is absolutely no discretion on the part of judges or prosecutors.

In most cases, the result is that it is the prosecutor who makes the decision whether to transfer the case to adult court. This is, of course, true under the second method—prosecutorial discretion. But it is often also true under the third method—automatic transfer—since, in that case, the prosecutor may have the discretion to charge a kid with something over which only the adult court has jurisdiction.

This "gives unbridled power and discretion to the district attorney's office," according to Steven Weymouth. "So the decision about—is the judge limited to a commitment to 21 years in DYS [Department of Youth Services] or life in a state prison—is now a decision not to be made by a judge at a transfer hearing, but made by the district attorney in the charge. It's a charging decision. You know how overcharging they can be." In essence, the prosecutor also gets to be the sentencer because determination of the charge may also determine the sentence.

Depending on how the legislation is written up, some sentences are called graduated sentences. This means they may first be served by the youth in a juvenile facility until he reaches a certain age and then he is transferred over to an adult facility. For example, a 13-year-old may spend the first five years of his sentence in a rehabilitative-type youth facility. Then, on his 18th birthday, he packs up his things and is taken over to the adult big house to serve the rest of his sentence with the older criminals. A "blended sentence" allows the court to impose juvenile and/or adult correctional punishments on particular young offenders. This answers the fears raised by some, such as Sean Hannity, the conservative cohost of the Fox News Channel's *Hannity and Colmes* show, who on November 21, 1997, said:

> But with the present juvenile laws as they're written, let's say they try him as a juvenile. He can only be held until he's 21. What happens if he's not ready to go back out in society? We're sending out another predator to go out once again and commit these horrible heinous crimes on society. We've got to change the rules some way.[7]

This overwhelming trend toward harshness against juveniles is reflective of a national frustration and anger.

Americans are "shocked by the brutality and viciousness of crimes that are being committed by 13 and 14 and 15 year olds," says Congressman George Gekas of Pennsylvania. "And they're equally shocked when they see a system that treats these juveniles as something less than the predators they seem to be."[8]

Congresswoman Sue Myrick agrees when she reflects on her days as the mayor of Charlotte, North Carolina: "I attended more funerals of more 13, 14 and 15 year old children than I care to remember. Senseless murders. And young people who did these things that I would talk to afterwards had absolutely no remorse for their actions."[9]

In many states, not only have rapid and sweeping changes been made to make criminal laws harsher against young people, but they've been doing it once a year. For example, a particular state will pass a new law one year and then the following year will up the ante and, whatever the penalties were, they'll make them that much harsher. There's political capital in constantly increasing the number of new laws being piled on top of one another—and in increasing the rhetoric. The words "predator" and "superpredator" are now almost terms of art and way behind the curve. In 1995, when a bill was introduced to the state legislature in Michigan, it called for the establishment of a "Punk Prison" for young people found guilty of violent crimes.

As fear grows, many of these bills are targeting younger and younger youths. No longer are they just going after the older teens and ignoring the younger children. In Colorado, for example, in the late 1990s, some people were surprised when the minimum age for a child to be tried and sentenced in adult court was lowered from age 14 to age 12 only after a proposal to lower the age to 10 failed to succeed. But a closer examination revealed that this was not at all unusual.

- In six states—Illinois, Mississippi, New Hampshire, New York, North Carolina and Wyoming—a child as young as 13 can be tried in adult court.
- In three states—Colorado, Missouri and Montana—a child as young as 12 can be tried in adult court.
- In three states—Indiana, South Dakota and Vermont—a child as young as 10 can be tried in adult court.
- In 20 states, there is no minimum age limit for exclusion from adult court.[10]

This may be at least partly due to the fact that more of these younger children are getting arrested:

- The number of children under the age of 16 (as opposed to those juveniles aged 16 or older) who were waived into adult court doubled from 1984 to 1995.
- Between 1985 and 1994, juvenile court cases involving offenders age 12 or younger increased 32 percent.
- The Violent Crime Index arrest rate increased 91 percent for juveniles age 12 or younger between 1980 and 1995. This was a greater increase than for juveniles above the age of 12. However, since that time, as the overall juvenile crime rate began to drop, the crime rate of these youngest criminals encouragingly declined more than that of any other age group.[11]

Still, most juveniles transferred into adult court are older teens. This is so despite the fact that, statistically, someone who is arrested for the first time in his late teens has a much better chance of breaking out of his world of crime than someone who begins his history of being arrested in his earlier teens or even his preteen years. However, these very youngest offenders are more amenable to services, sanctions and rehabilitation if, after that first young arrest, professionals quickly intervene to turn their lives around. Without those efforts to move in and intercede with help, these youngest arrestees have very high rearrest rates. If anything, this is an argument for not transferring the youngest offenders to adult jurisdiction and adult prison where they'll get the least help in turning their lives around.

MINORITIES LEAD THE WAY

In addition to the youngest children leading the pack in terms of both arrests and increased transfers to adult court, minorities also lead the way. Nonwhite juveniles are disproportionately more likely to be involved in the juvenile justice system than whites. For example, 15 percent of Americans ages 10 to 17 were African-Americans in 1991, yet they represented:

- 26 percent of all arrests of juveniles
- 49 percent of juveniles arrested for violent crimes
- 32 percent of delinquency referrals to juvenile court
- 52 percent of all juvenile cases waived into adult court
- By 1994, 1.9 percent of all minority juvenile cases were being waived into adult court, compared to 1.2 percent for whites.
- Among white juveniles between 1985 to 1994, most were waived into adult court for offenses against people. Among African-Americans, most were transferred for drug offenses.
- Minority youth outnumber white youth in public custody facilities 2 to 1.[12]

The explanation for this is not as simple as the assumption that young African-Americans committed more crimes, therefore more of them wound up in prison. In fact, they committed the same number of crimes commensurate with their 15 percent of the population figures. Every step of the way, they're treated more harshly than their white counterparts. Place an African-American offender next to a white offender charged with the same crime and having the same criminal history record, and the African-American is more likely to be sentenced to incarceration or for a longer period of incarceration.

Nowhere was this more apparent than in the war on drugs. African-Americans use drugs at the same rate as whites per their percentage of the population. In other words, they represent approximately 13 percent of the population and approximately 13 percent of all drug users. Yet they comprise 35 percent of all arrests for drug possession, 55 percent of all convictions and 74 percent of all prison sentences.[13] In many areas, the arrest rates for African-Americans were even higher. For example, in Baltimore, 13 white youths were arrested for selling drugs one year while at the same time an astounding 1,304 African-American youths were arrested for the same charge. This is a ratio of 100 to 1.[14]

By the early 1990s Alfred Blumstein, a leading criminologist, who had previously stated he saw no evidence of racism in the number of imprisoned citizens, affirmed he saw potential racial disproportion in the number of African-Americans arrested for drugs.[15]

One older inmate, Voy Cooks, says this is simply racism:

> The quickest route to an American penitentiary is to be born a black male. I think that's by design. It's racism at work. And how better to perpetuate it than to target black youth. . . . It begins with the screening process with the arresting officer who is empowered with the decision on whether or not he wants to make the arrest. And that's a huge decision because, after you arrest, you can't "unarrest."
>
> I think you see a disproportionate number of youths with black and brown faces entering prison gates. I think it's because their lives are less valuable and it's more acceptable. If this were an influx of white youth, it would be declared a national emergency.

It is not just African-American or Hispanic youths. One teenage Cambodian immigrant I spoke with in Revere, Massachusetts, whom I'll call Sary Somphon, is a student who does community outreach work with other Cambodian youths. He tells me he himself is constantly rousted by the police in what he believes to be acts of discrimination. Somphon says:

> We were sitting on a bench near the beach and there were a lot of people sitting in that place. Then a cop comes and he just chases out my friends and I and not the other people. That's why I think they just pick on us because we're Asians. . . .
>
> Once I got assaulted by some people and I told a cop. The cop wouldn't do anything. He thought I was part of a gang, too. He thinks it's a gang fight. . . .
>
> Another time, one friend did something wrong and got into trouble with the police and they came to the park where we hung out and nobody knew anything about it. They asked why we were near some of the stolen stuff. When we still said we didn't know anything about it, they said, "Yeah, right." They arrested everybody. We got taken to the station. Handcuffs. The way they'd talk, they'd ask us a question and like they didn't prefer the truth. They kept saying, "Yeah, right." Of course they had to throw the case out, but it made me feel terrible.

Somphon always managed to behave himself, but another of his 16-year-old Cambodian neighbors, whom I'll call Arn Bani, told me this discrimination drove him to unfortunately react with wrongheaded violence. He told me he and his friends had to do this every time someone called them racist names such as "gooks." He said:

> It's like no other way for us. That's the way to deal with it. If you don't deal with it that way, it's like we're too low, like we don't know how to fight. Like people always pick on us. So, in order to have people not pick on us, we have to do that. To show people how strong we are.

Some of this can be attributed to outright racism. But there are also other, subtle forces at play here. Court officials sometimes take minority youths out of their homes and communities for what they perceive to be their protection—away from gangs, away from what they suppose to be less intact families and away because there might be fewer community-based alternatives in the inner city.

Joe Clark, the African-American former New Jersey high school principal, who was the subject of the 1989 motion picture *Lean on Me* which chronicled his successful but unorthodox methods to turn around his tough urban school, attributed the number of minority youth crimes to one main thing. On the July 11, 1998, edition of the Fox News Channel's "Beyond the News" program, he argued:

> In my experience in education and corrections, it always comes back to the family. Most of the inner-city youth specifically do not have family structures. As a result, they are led astray by errant forces. . . . In the inner city, there are killings every day. Paducah, Kentucky—that's abnormal. It's normal in the inner city where black Americans are killing one another at the rate of 15,000 a year and no one does anything about it. It's related to the family structure.[16]

The issue of racism cuts both ways. A sad fact is that most racist or hate crimes against minorities are not caused by bona fide hate groups such as the Ku Klux Klan or Aryan Nation. In studies done by Northeastern University criminal justice experts Jack Levin and Jack McDevitt, authors of *Hate Crimes,* they determined that the majority of hate crimes in the country are carried out by young white males. They may be in groups of threes or more out for a good time at night and for someone to strike.[17]

FEMALES: MORE CRIME, STILL LESS JAIL

Violent crime is still, by and large, the province of boys rather than girls. Boys, to use one example, commit murder across the United States

10 times more often than girls. The reasons for this aren't entirely clear. Although some have argued that males have a slight genetic predisposition toward violence, this theory of biological hard-wiring remains controversial. Much more acceptable is the belief that culturally boys learn to be violent. Television, video games, films, their peers and even society have traditionally let them know that it is acceptable to fight to resolve differences. Even good parents turn their heads at playful roughhousing. Boys are given toy guns and toy soldiers. Girls, on the other hand, are culturally led to believe that such aggressive displays are socially unacceptable. They're shown other outlets for expressing their feelings.

But in the 1990s, all that seemed to be changing. The trends took a sharp turn and female juveniles, while still behind male juveniles in arrests, were now breathing down their necks. There was a revival of girls participating in untypical masculine behavior of carrying guns, fighting other girls and joining gangs. The rate of increase in their arrests now greatly outpaced that of boys.

- Between 1989 and 1993, the number of arrests involving female juveniles increased by 23 percent, compared with an 11 percent increase in arrests of male juveniles.
- The female proportion of all juvenile arrests grew from 21 percent to 24 percent between 1983 and 1993.
- The most common violent offenses for which females are arrested are robbery and aggravated assault. The arrest rates of females for those crimes rose 43 percent and 62 percent respectively between 1989 and 1993.
- Almost a third of all committed females are now juveniles[18]

Female juvenile crime, particularly female violent crime, is now growing by leaps and bounds, increasing at a much faster rate than that of males. Is it that the bombardment of violence in our culture is so overwhelming that it's starting to seep into female culture, also? Or are young girls today less shy, more assertive, more inclined to express themselves and less deferential to the boys? Is the glass ceiling being raised ever so slightly to allow females to have better access to guns and more of a role in crimes or gangs where once they were kept out? Some researchers have argued that the increase is not as dramatic as it appears to be since the absolute numbers of girls arrested for violent crimes are still so very small that any numerical change will cause a much greater percentage change. Still, it can't be assumed that girls become involved in violence for the same reasons boys do.

The reasons for increased acts of violent crime by females are numerous and complex and there is still little research in this area. But research does exist showing females as increasingly the victims of violence and abuse. It is believed that there is a link here between their victimization and their own increasing aggression. In a 1994 article by Dr. Ruth H. Wells in the *Corrections Compendium* entitled "America's Delinquent Daughters Have Nowhere to Turn," she points out that adolescent females are disproportionately the victims of homicides, four times more likely than adolescent males to be the object of physical or verbal abuse, and make up three-quarters of all sexual abuse victims.[19]

The theory is that females are becoming more aggressively violent in response to their own increasing role as victims of violence. The majority of female offenders have been abuse victims. In other words, an abused female could become a violent juvenile offender.

Years ago, young females in crisis might have internalized their problems and become severely depressed, even became runaways. One young girl from a poor urban area told me:

> They got problems in they life and they think they can't handle it. They think they at the end of they rope and they think they can't go on. Mostly a lot of girls. Mostly they's a lot of girls gettin' pregnant, as you know, at a young age and most of the fathers are young and they, you know, not men yet. So they don't know the responsibility of having a child. So they always leave them and then the girl be like, "I don't know what to do." Then they got problems. Most of the time, they mothers not there for them. They done got into an argument, ran away or whatever. So, they figure why live any longer? I might as well kill myself. I got no one there for me.

Today, more young females are inclined to just lash out. One of the differences between girls and boys is that girls tend to fight people they know even more often. It is much rarer that they commit violence against a stranger. It is not at all uncommon that we learn the victim contributed to and is partially responsible for the aggression which ultimately harmed them. Often the attack against the victim is a retaliatory response to a rising series of insults, conflicts and threats.

Fourteen-year-old Twanda explained to me she won't hesitate to fight another girl who she believes has personally slighted her. It is part of the growing honor culture where being "disrespected" will not be tolerated by young people.

> I ain't gonna let a girl get in my face, talkin' about me and stuff, cause she now in my personal space. I'm not gonna let a boy do the same thing either. . . . Most girls, when they fight, they just don't fight with they fist or whatever. They always got, like, a blade or something on them to help them fight. They aren't sure of themselves especially if they got to fight a boy.

When I spoke to her, Twanda was in a day reporting program where she could sleep at home, but was undergoing a rigorous seven-day-a-week, 10-hours-a-day education, community service and life skills program. She had been sentenced there for fighting.

> Kimberly and Adrianne and me. We all live in the same building. We all friends. We see each other every day. So Kim and Adrianne got into a fight about "he say/she say" stuff about a boy. So Kim came and said to me that this is what Adrianne was sayin' about you all the time. She say this and that. And Adrianne would do things that nobody else would notice, but since they were being done to us, we would notice. So one day we was comin' home from school, all of us together, and we just confronted her. Kim wanted to fight her. So she said, "Come on. Let's go get 'er." She went and pulled her ponytail and dropped her on the floor. I was supposed to fight her too, but, at first, I didn't want to go do it. But I didn't want to make Kim look like dumb or whatever. I had to stick up to my word. So I went over there and got her. The reason I'm not in that much trouble is because it was only a fight like that. And plus, we didn't really hurt her that bad. If we had really got her the way we wanted to, we would of been locked up somewhere.
>
> I'm not too much for fightin'. I was gonna let things pass. I could just not talk to her or whatever. The only thing was I said I was gonna do it, so I gotta do it. You see what I'm sayin'?

In the past, female juveniles were rarely jailed for violent crimes. Typically, females in custody were there for simple status offenses or, even if they had done nothing wrong, for what the authorities felt was their own good. They might be in custody if they were abused or neglected or (and here was a real double standard) to control their sexual behavior. Today, things are different. In Massachusetts, where the number of females in juvenile custody more than doubled between 1992 and 1996, Barbara Morton, a regional director of the Department of Youth Services there, says, "The socialization of girls is changing. They feel they don't have to be submissive."[20]

Regardless of the reasons, young females still make out better at every stage of the process than young boys in what can only be viewed as the last vestiges of an era where authorities would chivalrously go easy on them for the mere reason that they're little girls. For example:

- Females who are brought to the attention of the juvenile authorities for violent acts are less likely to be formally charged than males.
- If convicted of a violent offense, female juveniles are more likely than their male counterparts to be placed on probation rather than the much more restrictive punishments such as jail or being placed in a juvenile facility. Even prior to adjudication, girls are less likely to be held in custody.'
- Juvenile males were five times more likely to have their cases transferred to adult court than the juvenile females.[21]

Now, when female juveniles are in custody, they tend to be offered fewer educational and rehabilitative programs than the boys simply because there are fewer of them. However, as stated, the trends are all moving in one direction. If they continue, females youths could eventually catch up to the boys in terms of arrests, imprisonment and transfer of their cases to adult prison.

NONVIOLENT OFFENDERS JAILED MOST

Finally, it's interesting to note that most juveniles whose cases are transferred to adult court are not charged with a violent offense. Historically, more juveniles have been waived into adult court for property offenses than for any other crimes. Since 1992, property offenses no longer lead, but the situation still exists where more juveniles are transferred to adult prison for nonviolent crimes. For example, in 1994, 56 percent of all cases transferred were for nonviolent offenses and 44 percent for violent offenses.[22]

Studies done by the Youth Law Center based in San Francisco and Washington, D.C., revealed that:

- In Boise, Idaho, jail records show that of all the children held there during a three-year period, 42 percent were there on traffic offenses and 17 percent for status offenses.

- In a study in northern Kentucky, jail records revealed that most children were held in jail on minor property offenses or status offenses. (Status offenses in this instance are offenses which would not be a crime except for the age status of the person charged. These would include such things as underage drinking or breaking a curfew set for minors.)
- In southeastern Ohio, many children were incarcerated for status offenses such as truancy.[23]

"These children are not 'superpredators' by any stretch of the imagination," according to Mark I. Soler, renowned head of the Youth Law Center, during testimony before the Judiciary Committee of the United States Senate on the Violent Juvenile and Repeat Offender Act of 1997. "The overwhelming number are kids in rural areas who are involved in some kind of adolescent misbehavior and get thrown into the local lockup."[24]

In 1997, the United States Congress passed H.R. 3. The bill advocated a sweeping change in that, for the first time, 13-, 14- and 15-year-olds who commit certain federal offenses would be tried as adults and serve time in adult prisons even for nonviolent offenses. It would give federal prosecutors "unreviewable discretion" to do this. This bill, titled the Violent Youth Crime Act, was previously titled the Violent Youth Predator Act, but was changed after fierce debate. Yet with such a previous title, it's easy to understand why politicians blocked any crime prevention from being included in the bill.

"The essence of what we're doing today is to try to fix a juvenile justice system so the very bad are removed from society because they commit the most heinous of crimes we have here," said Representative Bill McCollum of Florida, the chief architect of the bill, on the day of its passage through the House of Representatives. "We need to be tough with them."[25]

But it was this failure to include crime prevention which caused the bill to stall in October 1998 when the House was unable to reconcile H.R. 3 with the Senate version of the bill.

Yet even when the bill had originally passed, the vote was considered to be largely symbolic because so few juveniles are ever charged with federal crimes. The last year for which figures were available, prior to the vote, was 1994, where only 200 youths 18 or younger were tried on federal charges. Still, it gave politicians a chance to crow. "Our youngest career criminals are getting away with the most heinous crimes over and over again," said Florida Congressman Porter Goss. "Wake up."[26]

But where the new federal juvenile laws may have their greatest impact is, ironically, not on the federal courts, but, rather, on the state courts. It will offer billions in incentive grants to states which will transform their juvenile systems into the harsher federal model. To get this money, the state must change to meet four conditions. They must: (1) try all 15-years-olds as adults for serious violent crimes; (2) impose increasing penalties for repeat offenders on all offenses including such things as vandalism; (3) require that open criminal records be established for minors having committed a second offense and make those records public; (4) allow judges to issue orders against parents of convicted minors who don't properly supervise them.

The Senate version of H.R. 3 goes even further, including placing many more nonviolent offenses under federal jurisdiction. These offenders will then be mixed in with the older, violent federal prisoners.

Even in instances where the children in adult prisons will be kept segregated from adult prisoners, they'll still frequently walk past each other. According to attorney Gerald Lefcourt in an aptly titled commentary, "Congress Confronts the Baby Boomerang: Bad Ideas from People Old Enough to Know Better," in the January/February 1998 edition of *Champion* magazine, "These adults are hardly the strong male role models too often absent from the lives of our most disadvantaged youths. They are a distinctive type of 'strong role model'—the dangerous type."[27]

ABANDONING THE OLD WAY

This entire trend of harsh, no-nonsense treatment toward youthful offenders represents a sea change in the way America has long traditionally treated its delinquents. The juvenile system of *parens patriae,* where the court acts as a kind of well-meaning parent or kindly uncle looking after the best interests of the child, is being dismantled. It was a view that said we should rehabilitate, not just punish, the child. Since most children aren't evil and can therefore be redeemed, the court's emphasis was less on punishment and more on helping steer the wayward child back on the right path. It fostered the belief that since many young people do have the ability to change for the better, rehabilitation will make us safer since the delinquent won't commit future bad acts.

It was back in 1825 that a group of citizens set up the New York House of Refuge because they were alarmed about what was happening to children being made into criminals in adult jails. This argument couldn't have been summed up better at the time than by John Pintard, one of the reformers, who declared, "The present plan of promiscuous intercourse [makes] little devils into great ones and at the expiration of their terms turns out accomplished villains."[28]

This new concept of the youth prison emphasizing work, moral training and education caught on throughout the country. But within a few decades, many of these youth prisons were themselves violent and cruel with an inordinate use of solitary confinement and corporal punishment. The prisons were marked by riots and escapes.

But in 1899, beginning in Chicago, specialized juvenile courts were initiated to try to right these abuses. Judges were given wide latitude to not only deal with lawbreaking children, but to help others, also. They could remove children from terrible family situations and even supervise them in the community. The idea was to look at what could be done to save the child along with protecting society.

But many today hold the view that this system needs to be taken apart because it is a throwback to an earlier era when kids committed different kinds of crimes such as vandalism, petty thefts, truancy and schoolyard fist fights. They weren't doing the sorts of high profile murders with sophisticated assault weapons that young people are perceived to be doing now.

Criminologist Bart Lubow, who himself is not in favor of the widespread trend of transferring juveniles to adult courts and prisons, still was able to sum up the growing mood as "a crisis of confidence, since the very notion that has been its cornerstone, that children are different from adults and therefore need to be treated differently, is in question."[29]

"The thinking behind the juvenile court, that everything be done in the best interest of the child, is from a bygone era," according to Patricia L. West, head of the Virginia Department of Juvenile Justice.[30]

This perception is, of course, not true. According to a U.S. Justice Department report released in 1997, "Although homicide and forcible rape cases attract a substantial amount of public attention, they account for a small fraction of personal offense cases referred to juvenile court in 1994 (2%)."[31] Still that does indeed remain the perception, and in fact, the rate of other, lesser kinds of violent crimes had been going up for a while until around 1995, according to the report.

"We've got to quit coddling these violent kids like nothing is going on," says Senator Orrin Hatch of Utah with typical political rhetoric. "Getting some of these do-gooder liberals to do what is right is real tough. We'd all like to rehabilitate these kids. But, by gosh, we are in a different age."[32]

Los Angeles District Attorney Gil Garcetti, who has backed legislation in California to automatically transfer juveniles to adult court for a number of serious crimes, subscribes to this misguided point of view. "I'm not interested in legislating out childhood," says Garcetti. "My concern is that juvenile crime has been rising unacceptably fast, and kids learn that they can get away with it because there is no real punishment for the first few crimes."[33]

Many judges who deal specifically with children disagree. Chicago Juvenile Court Judge William Hibbler believes that approach goes against logic. "There is a crisis [but] children don't stop being children because they commit a crime," he argues, "and calling for an end to the juvenile court is the same as saying we should do away with grammar schools and junior high schools and just put everyone in college."[34]

New York State Supreme Court Justice in charge of youth courts Michael Corriero argues, "Don't get me wrong. I put 15-year-olds away for life. But they're saying, 'We're expecting this incredible bubble of youth violence, so let's build more jails, let's increase sentences.' " If that's true, he said, "the answer is not to increase sentences. The answer is to stop crime before it happens."[35]

It's an age where, in April 1997, two teenagers in a rural area of Franklin, New Jersey, ordered two cheese pizzas from a pay telephone with the intent of killing whoever showed up to deliver that pizza at a desolate abandoned house. Four pizzerias refused to deliver either because of the especially remote location or because the boys just sounded like they were pranksters. The fifth place they called agreed to come and the pizza restaurant owner along with an employee took the two-mile drive there. When they showed up at the address, they rolled down the window of their Grand Am to hand over the food. They were shot eight times in the face and neck. The two victims were dragged out and their corpses were left next to the pizzas on the ground. The two killers, 18-year-old Tommy Koskovich and 17-year-old Jay Vreeland, didn't bother to rob them or even take the pizzas. They were said to have killed just for the thrill of it.

"I don't know what they had on their minds," said Police Chief Pete Wahaly.

"They were looking for a victim," said the local county prosecutor. "There is no rational answer for this irrational act."[36]

It's an age where, in 1993, a 10-year-old Chicago boy beat 83-year-old Anna Gilvis with her own cane, slit her throat and drowned her in a toilet bowl. He was placed on probation and put in his grandmother's custody.

Until around the 1940s, only about 10 states gave discretion for judges to try primarily older juveniles as adults in certain circumstances. But beginning in the 1970s and accelerating in the 1990s, state after state began to enact statutes sending more and more children to adult courts and prisons.

It is clear that the trend toward treating juvenile offenders more harshly, abandoning rehabilitation and education for them and transferring them to adult courts and prisons, is popular among certain segments of the population, especially politicians. But the bottom line question is—is it working? Are we members of the American public being made safer?

JUVENILES IN ADULT PRISONS ENDANGER THE PUBLIC

There haven't been many studies conducted so far, but those that are available are unanimous in the unequivocal conclusion at which they arrive: they compare young offenders who were sent to adult prison against young offenders with the same criminal background who got to remain in juvenile facilities for the same crime. Every single study shows that the juveniles who are sent to adult prison, once they are released, have startlingly higher recidivism rates than those sent to juvenile facilities. This means that, once released, they tend to endanger the public more and get rearrested shortly thereafter:

- There was a Florida study released in 1996 which found that not only did the youths who were transferred to adult prison tend to get rearrested more often once released, but for more serious and dangerous crimes. Interestingly, Florida transfers more of its young offenders to the adult system than all other states combined.
- A study of New York and New Jersey prisons found that those youngsters sent to adult prison had a recidivism rate 29 percent higher than those eventually released from juvenile facilities. Studies in Minnesota, Nevada and New York yielded similar results.

- Another study was done comparing three states—Idaho, Wyoming and Montana. Idaho enacted a statute for automatic transfer of juveniles into the adult system. Following this, Idaho's violent youth crime rate went up. During this same time, the violent youth crime rates of Wyoming and Montana—the states that kept juveniles in juvenile courts and facilities—actually dropped.
- Another recent study showed that while Connecticut has the highest juvenile-to-adult transfer rate, and Colorado the lowest, their juvenile crime rates have remained the same.
- In 1978, California rewrote its laws, doubling the percentage of juveniles incarcerated there than in the rest of the country. They did this by increasing the number of juveniles transferred to adult prison and also by just increasing the number of juveniles jailed in youth facilities. By the end of the decade, California's youth recidivism rate had nevertheless shot upward.[37]

A chorus of corrections officials and experts who have studied the results of these and similar studies have concluded that the increasingly popular transfers to adult jurisdiction are endangering all of us. They argue that some realize the effect of sending kids to schools for crime when they need treatment.

"Ultimately, you are going to release all these people back into the community, and the juvenile justice system does a better job of reclaiming them," said Professor Charles Frazier of the University of Florida, one of the coauthors of the report chronicling the failure of Florida's system of trying youngsters as adults.[38]

Violence researcher Jeffrey Fagan gave a reason for this. "They're prisonized," says Fagan. "Developmentally, their identities are very firmly and concretely molded as criminal offenders. And what they don't learn because they're locked up are the skills needed to become a family member, husband, neighbor or worker."[39]

Older inmate Voy Cooks sees the problem as:

> I think that those who profit from this sort of prison bonanza have done a terrible thing to our youth in assigning labels to them because, sadly, a lot of youth who are coming through the prison gates clearly bought into those labels. They refer to themselves as thugs and gangsters which by definition have negative connotations. But they somehow wear those labels as badges of honor. If you continually call a person a thug, they transform into a thug. I interact with a lot of young

people who come through here. I know many of their mothers and fathers. And it saddens me that no one has tried to tap into their potential.

President Ronald Reagan's director of the National Institute of Corrections and former head of the California Youth Authority, Allen Breed, who also spent a lifetime fighting crime on the front lines, drew the same conclusion. According to Breed, "The environment of a prison setting causes violent behavior to be intensified, thus causing youth to be far more dangerous upon release than are juveniles retained in the juvenile system."[40]

Attorney Gerald Lefcourt came to a similar conclusion when he expressed his fears that, under the proposed new federal laws transferring more and more children to adult facilities:

Children who commit even nonviolent offenses (e.g., theft or drug possession) will find themselves "mixed" in prison with older, stronger adults: murderers, rapists and robbers. These adults are hardly the strong male role models too often absent from the lives of our disadvantaged youths. They are a distinctive type of "strong role model"—the dangerous type.

Ten states alone account for the vast majority of juveniles age 17 or younger admitted to adult prisons.[41] It may not be by accident that most of these states have rather high juvenile crime rates and high juvenile recidivism rates.

Take, for instance, our neighbor Canada, next door. Canadian juveniles can only be transferred to adult prisons at the discretion of a judge. American judges transfer 11 times more juveniles to adult courts than do Canadian judges. But when you consider that most American transfers aren't done by judges—they're done automatically by statute or by discretion of the prosecutor—the ratio of American transfers is significantly greater than 11 to 1.

This statistic is significant when you consider that, while the juvenile property crime arrest rate in Canada is actually similar to that of the United States, the Canadian juvenile violent crime rate is half the U.S. rate.[42] This means that based on the fact that we're transferring children to adult prisons in rates that dramatically dwarf Canadian rates and yet their violent juvenile crime rate is half that of the United States, sending kids to adult prison is not the significant element that makes a country safer from youth crime. Other, more important factors are at play.

Take a look also at Germany, a large, industrialized country with no death penalty and considerably shorter prison sentences. According to a 1998 Justice Department report by Professor Floyd Feeney of the University of California at Davis entitled *German and American Prosecutions*, in Germany no one under the age of 18 is ever tried as an adult. Additionally, there is a special court system and rules for those between the ages of 18 and 20. While the United States has twice as many homicides and rapes committed by its youths than Germany, they have similar youth rates of robbery, aggravated assault, other serious thefts and drug cases. Again, our rules don't make us safer. But not only is it not making us safer, it may actually be creating more crimes by making the youth incarcerated in adult prison more violent.

"If you incapacitate the children in the same way we incapacitate adults, the result is going to be no benefit to the individual and thus the society, because the kids are going to learn how to be better criminals and they won't learn how to survive and be productive citizens," notes attorney Phillip Kassel.

Allen Breed, former head of the California Youth Authority and director of the National Institute of Corrections during the Reagan Administration, says, "The environment of a prison setting causes violent behavior to be intensified, thus causing youths to be far more dangerous upon release than are juveniles retained in the juvenile system. . . . No juvenile will benefit from the prison experience, and many will be hurt both physically and emotionally."[43]

With so many studies and criminal experts such as corrections officials and police officers (who are truly on the front lines of fighting crime) proving that sending young people into adult prisons makes them more dangerous to the public, why are so many politicians in favor of juvenile transfer to adult jurisdiction? "[L]egislators pursue the incorrect but intuitively appealing notion that treating more kids as adults will increase public safety," says Robert G. Schwartz, executive director of the Juvenile Law Center.[44]

Gil Kerlikowske, former police commissioner of Buffalo, New York, takes a more cynical view: "the preventive programs are getting lost because everyone [in politics] is trying to grow hair on his chest in this election year."[45]

After all, if the national recidivism rate of adults in prison is around 65 percent, meaning that 65 percent of adult offenders gets rearrested for new crimes shortly after their release, why would we think it would help to keep the public safer to throw children into that unsuccessful mix?

Rebecca Young of Citizens for Juvenile Justice makes that point when she comments:

> If you look at what we think generally about the adult prison system for adults, nobody's saying, "We have a great adult prison system in this country. So boy, let's put those kids in too because it works so well." I mean, I think it's no surprise that it's not successful with kids. It's not successful with adults either.

No one can testify more powerfully to this than Ada Vera, the mother of one inmate, a former honor student from a very close-knit family who got into trouble and was sent to prison. There, he was forced to choose between two gangs, one of which he had to join for protection.

> Finally he decided he was going to get out of the gang. But he was in prison so he had to go through what the gang calls a "termination." He was terminated. They broke his jaw. They wired his jaw shut for, at least, a month. Although he asked for termination and was given termination by his so-called gang member friends, the prison system would not let him forget that he was a gang member. They continued to segregate him (in the designated special gang section). He spoke out against gangs and tried to talk to other young men who were going into the prison system. . . .
>
> He came out. One day I said to him, "Why can't you change your life?" This is what a mother tells her son. He said to me, "Mom, you don't understand the prison system. You just don't understand it. I can't even begin to explain it to you. But I am now ruthless." He said, "I am ruthless." To me, that was a stab in my heart to hear my son, who I knew in a certain way, say, "I am ruthless."
>
> He got into drugs because he couldn't handle being here. He couldn't sit at home, he couldn't eat, he couldn't sit at the table. He was nervous all the time, because he had spent two and a half years mostly in the hole, in isolation. He said he couldn't be home, he couldn't be at anyone's house. He was always fidgeting, running around. . . . Hated cops, of course. We couldn't get him to sit down and have a dinner like a family anymore, like he used to.
>
> If the prison system is going to destroy our children in that manner, for them to come out and be somebody different than when they went in, then I feel as families, we should come together and fight . . . because if not, then we'll lose our children to the prison system and they will come out, basically, a time bomb.

Sending the young people to adult prison who really don't need to be there or are in for nonviolent offenses ultimately further endangers the public by doing nothing with them while inside the prison walls except for turning them over to their violence instructors—older, hardened violent adults. They come out more violent than ever, then they prey upon the public. Or, as Ada Vera, phrases it, they become "a time bomb."

THE MYTH OF DETERRENCE

The question arises whether, at the very least, the threat of adult prison will deter some juveniles from committing crimes. Will juveniles who, let's say, are thinking of murdering somebody, hear that someone else got a harsh sentence for such a deed, and reconsider the wisdom of committing such an act? Judge Thomas Knopf of Jefferson County, Missouri, says he doesn't at all mind certain laws in his state which take away a judge's discretion on whether to transfer a child offender to adult court. These laws which automatically transfer children are necessary because, "We need to send a message," says Judge Knopf.

It's the most popular phrase in law enforcement—"We need to send a message." The question, though, is whether children are getting the message. Most youths who commit bad acts aren't thinking of the consequences and, in the rare instance when they do, simply assume they won't get caught. Very few kids would say to themselves, "I'm going to commit this crime and I'll most likely get caught. But I'll do it anyway."

According to Molly Baldwin:

> Most young people don't choose not to do crimes because they're scared of going to prison. Never have, probably never will, because they don't think about it. . . . Well, first of all, adolescence is the time of momentary existence. If you merge adolescent development on top of this, and if then you're acting out, too, it gets really crazy. It's the time of momentary existence. "Not me. I'll live forever, I don't care." It's not a group that tends to think about futuristic things, anyway. The deterrent doesn't happen, any way it goes. . . . The point is, how do you help young people get to the point where they understand consequences to choices? Again, it's about accountability and responsibility.

Fifteen-year-old Tyrell said much the same thing when I asked him whether his fellow youthful lawbreakers in his inner-city neighborhood ever thought about whether they might get caught and whether they might go to prison. He said:

> Most young people . . . it's like they don't even care. They just go out there and kill somebody. They don't realize what the consequences are

until that consequence happens. They just think "Oh, this kid disrespected me. I gotta do what I gotta do to earn my respect. I'm gonna
go shoot 'im or kick his ass or whatever." They don't think "I could go
to jail" or something like that.

Richard Mendel of the American Youth Policy Forum also argues, cor-
rectly, that:

> For deterrence to work, would-be offenders must be rational in their
> decision making and determined to avoid prison. Most crimes are
> committed in the heat of the moment, however, often under the influ-
> ence of drugs or alcohol. In many inner-city communities, impulsive
> behavior and a predisposition to violence are the norm, and they may
> be the immediate, automatic response to any tense situation.[46]

Mendel could have been speaking of the same youths that Rosa, a 14-
year-old inner-city resident, was telling me about. She tried to describe the
kinds of kids in her neighborhood who do shootings right out in the open
in broad daylight: ". . . right in front of the police or anything. They'll just
pass by and shoot. I don't think they're afraid. Nobody afraid of nothing.
I don't know why. They'll just shoot you wherever you are and kill you."

Maybe this is why automatic transfer has not been shown to have a
deterrent effect. For example, Idaho's juvenile violent crime rate went up
after their automatic transfer statute was implemented. During the same
period, the juvenile violent crime rates in two neighboring states without
automatic transfer decreased.[47]

The previously stated fact that some of the states that have the most
automatic transfers of youths to adult prisons (such as Florida) do not
have lowest violent youth crime rate—in fact, they're among the highest—
gives support to the view that children aren't deterred by the threat of
adult trials.[48] That is, if they're even aware of the high juvenile transfer
rate, since a lot of children who get into trouble are not among the most
aware or best-read citizens who would be well versed in the law.

If the concept of deterrence works, then why, after Luke Woodham
shot and killed others at his school in Pearl, Mississippi, in late 1997 and
faced a life sentence, did that do nothing within the next six months to
stop the subsequent school killings in Paducah, Kentucky; Jonesboro,
Arkansas; Edinboro, Pennsylvania, and Springfield, Oregon? Each additional time the school killings occurred, the suffering, remorse and immediate loss of freedom of the young perpetrators was highly publicized
and became known to Americans old and young. After some of the
killings, it would be immediately announced that those children would

be tried as adults. But to the impulsive perpetrators of each successive school shooting spree, it was irrelevant. It didn't even appear to be up for consideration.

One courageous politician who intelligently made this connection was Oregon Governor John Kitzhaber. On the very day in 1998 that 15-year-old Kipland Kinkel shot to death his parents, then entered his Springfield, Oregon, high school cafeteria, shot to death two students and injured 22 others, Kitzhaber said: "All of us should look at how we have failed as a society and how this could happen in the heart of Oregon. It has been a priority to build prison cells and prison beds—after the fact. These actions in no way prevent juvenile violence."[49] If every politician in America shared the view of Governor Kitzhaber, crime in this country would plummet.

But regardless of whether the adult transfer laws deter or discourage juveniles from committing crimes, it is clear that, if they are on the wrong path, adult prisons don't do them any good and make them more dangerous. Attorney Phillip Kassel states:

> Locking up a kid and not providing any kind of rehabilitative program is tantamount to basically giving up on them. And the younger the kid, the less justified that is. . . . If you incapacitate the children in the same way we incapacitate adults, the result is going to be no benefit to the individual, and thus the society, because the kids are going to learn how to be better criminals and they won't learn how to survive and be productive citizens. . . . It's just going to fuel the whole problem.

The bottom line is that the use of rehabilitative programs in juvenile facilities—as opposed to the lack of rehabilitation in adult facilities—has been proven to be less expensive and to keep the public safer because of the lower recidivism rates.

Gerald Lefcourt agrees with this. He says, "An important reason juvenile violence is dropping is because local communities are attacking the problem with a smart, cost-effective mix of proactive enforcement and prevention, consistent with the character and traditions of the particular local community."

Since these prevention and enforcement programs ultimately save more money than courts and incarceration and victimization expenses, it is not a matter that the money is not there to do more of this. It is a matter of understanding and motivation. Maybe this is so because, as Molly Baldwin explains, " Locking up kids doesn't teach them lessons. I mean they get locked up and either they're back out on the street the next day or they go away. But there isn't a whole lot of work with them in the context of the world they live in and how you make changes. What's the lesson?"

Indeed, some juveniles who weren't rescued in time have become so dangerous that they must, unfortunately, be incarcerated for long periods of time in order to protect the public. But it is clear and well documented that automatically transferring youths to adult trials and prisons, without first having a hearing to determine whether they can be salvaged, is costly and will further endanger the public. When laws are passed to automatically require that such actions be taken without thinking or consideration beforehand, it appears to support Mark Kappelhoff's view: "I think the whole thing that is going on is extreme and shows how far politicians will go for political purposes. This is no longer a war on crime, but a war on children."[50]

These same politicians are, ironically, big spenders, only with a lesser rate of return. For the price of locking up one nonviolent juvenile, which can be as high as $80,000 a year in some states, you could pay for three others to attend an Ivy League college.

- In 1995, for the first time ever, more money was spent building new prisons than new university structures in the United States. "So we're spending more on building prisons than we are on universities, even though we have 10 times as many college students as prison inmates," wrote columnist David Nyhan. "This is brain-dead public policy."
- In 1995, state bonds across the country allocated to university construction decreased by $954 million (to $2.5 billion) while state bond expenditures for prison construction increased $926 million (to $2.6 billion). This is an almost a dollar-for-dollar amount.
- From 1987 to 1995, spending on state prisons rose 30 percent while higher education spending fell 18 percent, according to the Justice Policy Institute.
- California has built 21 prisons in what's been called the largest prison construction effort in the world, but added only one college in the past two decades.
- Since 1990, California's once world-class universities have laid off 10,000 professors and other employees while, at the same time, 10,000 prison guards have been hired. The portion of the state budget which went to its universities dropped from 12.5 percent

to 8 percent while correction's share rose from 4.5 to 9.4 percent, an identical amount.[51]

"Prisons are built when we plan for young people to fail," says Vincent Schiraldi. "while universities are built when we plan for young people to succeed."[52]

JUVENILE COURTS ARE TOUGHER

Many politicians don't know that, ironically, if they really want to be harsher on youthful offenders, they might have them remain under juvenile jurisdiction rather than transfer them to adult courts. Juveniles tried as adults are less likely to be convicted than their counterparts tried for the same offenses in juvenile court and therefore less likely to receive either punishment or treatment.[53] The reason for this is that often even the relatively bad crimes a child commits pale in comparison to the ones committed by the adult criminals he stands next to in adult court. So they give the child in adult court a break or find him not guilty. Or the adult courts are so busy that the child defendant is given very little attention, is ignored and left alone as he slips through the cracks. "Quite frequently they walk," says Dean Louis McHardy, who runs the National Council of Juvenile and Family Court Judges.[54]

This is different from well-run juvenile courts, where they are able to concentrate and spend more time on a young person's case. They generally don't treat a violent youthful defendant too leniently because, unlike the adult courts, a youthful defendant is not a rare novelty. They don't let things slide and give a lot of slack to a young offender merely because of his age and the fact that he may have a lesser criminal history than the grown men he stands beside.

Additionally, in juvenile courts there's less foot-dragging and delays of justice. Punishment, while longer and harsher, is also swifter in juvenile court. One typical study showed that accused youths who were transferred to adult court were held an average of 246 days before they were ultimately sentenced. In juvenile court, the average time between arrest and sentencing was a speedier 98 days.[55] The practice of transferring juveniles to adult courts robs the public of their age-old cry for swift and tough justice.

Additionally, when they are found guilty, they don't necessarily get longer sentences in adult court. Again, stacked up against their fellow defendants who are adults, they are treated with leniency. More often than not, adult courts pay less attention to children and give them something of a free pass.

In studies in both Ohio and Illinois, it was discovered that children given "adult time for adult crime" were almost always released earlier than their counterparts serving time for the same offenses in juvenile facilities as long as it was a nonmurder case.

JUVENILE COMPETENCY

Another issue which is not always clear is whether young children charged with a crime have the developmental maturity and capacity to really understand what is going on in the legal process and to help with their own defense or, particularly in the case of the very youngest offenders, whether they understand what they did was actually wrong in the way that an adult would understand it. Do they understand things like Miranda rights, plea bargaining and whether, in their own particular cases, it would be better to have a trial or to plead guilty?

Garry Cantrell is a criminal defense attorney who represented an 11-year-old in Texas who was convicted of sexually assaulting a three-year-old. Cantrell said, on the June 17, 1998, edition of *ABC World News Tonight*, "An 11-year-old is not all that helpful with his defense. . . . Using everyday terminology became a struggle. I spent fully half an hour going over what the term 'likely' meant."[56]

Historically, defendants in general have been found legally incompetent to stand trial only for reasons of severe mental illness or retardation. Immaturity has never been a standard. This may be because, in the past, even when juveniles were transferred to adult court, they were almost always in the upper age brackets, such as 16 or 17. So it was never an issue. But now, as more and more 11- and 12-year-olds are transferred, the question comes up—do they always have an idea what exactly is going on? Do they really know what they're doing (1) as they're committing the crime and (2) when it comes time to aid in their legal defense?

Never was this question brought more clearly into focus than in August 1998 when two innocent seven-year-old and eight-year-old boys were charged with the murder of an 11-year-old girl named Ryan Harris in the neighborhood of Englewood on Chicago's South Side. No one could remember when anyone so young had been suspected of murder. One attorney said, "There is no direction. There's no precedence for this."

According to the police story, Ryan was riding her bicycle through the neighborhood along with the eight-year-old boy when they encountered the seven-year-old in an alley. They began throwing rocks, one of which fractured her skull, knocking her off her bike. They are said to allegedly have dragged her away, molested her, stuffed her panties in her mouth and leaves up her nose, and smothered her. All this, with the goal of stealing her shiny blue Road Warrior bicycle.

Neighbors who knew the two boys, particularly the eight-year-old who had an excellent academic reputation and was described as shy, found it impossible to believe that these boys, who were more interested in cartoons and candy, could have done this abominable act. A local store clerk who often sold them candy said, "There's no way they'd do anything like that. They don't steal soap out of the stores." Their minister, the Reverend Paul Jakes said, "It is very inconceivable to us that these young, tiny children—50 or 60 pounds—would actually have committed such a hideous crime."

The first issue which came up was whether these children had any idea what they were alleged to have done. When brought into court, they sat and drew pictures, ate Skittles and cried. One of their attorneys, Andre Grant, remarked, "My client is eight years old. He is behaving like he's eight years old. He has absolutely no idea what is going on." The eight-year-old was right. Five weeks later, in a major embarrassment to the Chicago Police Department in front of the entire country, the case was dropped after it was discovered that the arrests were a mistake.

The police had rushed to file the charges without any physical evidence. Weeks later, when they finally got around to doing such tests as the one where they found sperm on the victim's underwear, the case fell apart. But why were the little seven- and eight-year-old boys arrested in the first place?

The reason was that, although the police had initially suspected an adult of the crime, the two boys were questioned after someone reported a possible rock throwing incident at the time. The police began to suspect something when the little boys gave contradictory accounts and kept changing their stories. It was a classic case of children being incompetent to aid in their own defense.

The eight-year-old told a story about having seen the victim, Ryan Harris, get into a car with a man who also took her bike. But at the same time, he spoke of seeing the Harris body earlier after having been led to it by the seven-year-old. The seven-year-old, though, said he had seen the body, but that he'd seen another boy take away the bike which was lying next to the victim. Then he said it was the eight-year-old who had led him to the body, only to change his story shortly thereafter to say that it was actually two much older boys who had led him to the body. In later interviews, the police heard even more embellished versions of the story including one where the seven-year-old admitted to throwing a rock at the girl. Although a bloody brick was found at the scene, and neither boy had talked about a brick, the police theorized that, since they believed it was "impossible" that the seven-year-old had delivered the fatal blow on his own, he must have somehow done it with the eight-year-old's help. The police ignored a plethora of evidence pointing to an adult sex crime and information from eyewitnesses who had seen a neighborhood adult with Ryan Harris at the time of her death.

Although it is believed that the seven- and eight-year-olds may have seen the body before it was discovered, it was their unclear contradictory storytelling that led to their being named as the chief murder suspects. Thankfully, they were exonerated within a few weeks. But it is frightening to think that, if other evidence hadn't surfaced, they might have been convicted of the murder just based on their confused, inconsistent stories. Their stories would have been viewed, as they were by the Chicago police, as a pack of lies which couldn't be reconciled. They would have been just too little and incompetent to save themselves. This incident is a clarion call to why charging very young children—in particular charging them as adults where they can then receive either a life sentence or the death penalty—is fraught with danger. Incapable of understanding what is going on, they could often be easily and unfairly convicted. How often has this happened in other cases where the child suspects haven't been so lucky?

There is undoubtedly a point when a child is too young to understand the nature of his offense. Ages two or three, of course. Ages seven and eight, quite possibly. In Illinois, where this crime was committed, children that age could not be held in a penal facility while awaiting trial. There was an argument whether these two would be held awaiting trial in, at the very least, a mental health facility. The judge ultimately ruled that they should wait at home in the care of their families, on electronic monitoring bracelets.

But the following week in Pawtucket, Rhode Island, prosecutors seemed to have an easier time making up their minds when four-year-old Luis Omar Trinidad drowned in a foot-deep inflatable pool while playing with four boys all between four and six years old. They were playing "Mortal Kombat," a game based on the video game and motion picture of the same name.

Rhode Island Attorney General Jeff R. Pine said of the Trinidad case, "It would be totally inappropriate for any kind of charges to be rendered against a four-year-old and a six-year-old who clearly don't have the cognitive development or the competency to be part of the legal system."[57]

The Rhode Island authorities came to their conclusion by looking at the age and determining that the other children in the pool were just too young to be able to form the necessary legal intent. But still the tougher questions come when children are slightly older. Do they understand what is going on?

Dan Bagdade is an attorney who represented 12-year-old Nathaniel Abrahams who was tried in Michigan as an adult for murder. He reported on the June 17, 1998 ABC World News Tonight, "I have spoken to Nate repeatedly about the court proceedings specifically and Nate still does not understand what is happening."[58]

Nate's confession was thrown out by a judge because it was clear that he had no idea what it meant to waive his right to an attorney at the time he gave the police an interview. Although they may have read him his Miranda rights, he wouldn't have actually understood them. He also didn't seem to understand the gravity of the proceedings. "He tells me repeatedly that he wants to go home," said Bagdade. " 'When can I go home?' He tells the same thing to his mother."

Not every child is rescued when a confession they cannot understand is bullied, manipulated and tricked out of them. There can be no such case more egregious than that of Lacresha Murray, an 11-year-old African-American girl from Austin, Texas, convicted of criminally negligent homicide in the 1996 death of two-and-a-half-year-old Jayla Belton. Lacresha is currently serving a 25 year prison sentence.

The sole evidence was a signed confession extracted from Lacresha, who is learning disabled and has an I.Q. of 77. She was kept away from her family for four days, denied a lawyer and was threatened and misled by police for hours after denying 39 times that she knew anything about the homicide.

There was evidence that the victim Jayla had long been a victim of child abuse, though prosecutors ignored this. Jayla had been dropped off at the small home of Lacresha, where she lived with her three siblings and her grandparents. Jayla's mother and her boyfriend were told not to leave

Jayla there because the primary caretaker, Lacresha's grandmother, was away for the day. According to the Murrays and other people who were at the house that day, Jayla was lethargic and slept a lot, vomiting and sweating profusely. Lacresha noticed that Jayla was shaking and she and her grandfather, who is confined to a wheelchair, brought her to the hospital where Jayla was pronounced dead. Though she died of a ruptured liver, she also had broken ribs, more than 30 bruises, and was severely malnourished. Since the medical examiner told the police that no one could survive more than 15 minutes with a ruptured liver, they zeroed in on the last person to be with her at that time. Lacresha had carried her into the hospital in her arms.

Despite the fact that approximately 20 police officers and forensic experts entered the Murray home, not one iota of evidence was found—no blood or any other bodily fluid—none of the many people who were in the Murray house when Jayla was there heard anything or noticed any incident, though they did state that they had noticed Jayla's ill symptoms that day. Later, medical experts would say that the number and extent of injuries Jayla suffered were rarely caused by a single incident.

The interrogation of Lacresha Murray was such a travesty that a complete transcript of it is now available on the Internet by groups supporting Lacresha. Before the interrogation, police intentionally tried to circumvent the juvenile law designed to protect children from roughshod police tactics, which would have required the police to bring Lacresha before a magistrate to have her rights explained to her and to have a lawyer appointed for her defense. Instead, as the police testified, they phoned a prosecutor and learned that if they didn't take Lacresha into custody or bring her to the police station, but instead, kept her at a state child services office and did not notify anyone there that she was a suspect in a capital murder case, then they wouldn't have to follow the law.

The police read the isolated 11-year-old what must have been incomprehensible rights and asked, "You've heard them before on TV shows probably, huh?"

They then threatened, cajoled and lied to Lacresha. Though she told them 39 times that she had nothing to do with Jayla's death, they repeatedly told her that if she told them the "truth," she could go home. She was told that her family had already admitted she had beaten the child. She was told that a doctor with "over 20 years of experience" had said that the baby must have died at the exact moment that Lacresha had seen her shaking. The police still got nowhere. Then they repeatedly asked her if it was "possible" that she may have dropped the baby while carrying it to the hospital and then accidentally kicked it, and told her "that's perfectly all right . . . it happens all the time." They continued to say that she couldn't leave until she told the "truth." Still, she denied any role. Eventually, she said "maybe." This despite the fact that such numerous and extensive injuries could not have resulted from such actions.

The police typed up a confession and asked her if she could read. She said, "Not well, but I try hard." She asked them what the word "home-a-seed" meant and one of the officers corrected her on the pronunciation of homicide. Lacresha asked, "What's that?"

No one answered.

One of the police officers asked her if she was being forced to sign the statement. She answered, "Yeah." But when the police officer forcefully asked her, "What?!" she changed her answer to, "No."

There was no other evidence. Just the confession which was not supported by the facts which she was tricked into signing and most certainly did not understand. The child will now languish in prison for 25 years.

It is a popular trend today to say that lawbreakers should no longer be able to hide behind their age like a shield. If you're going to do serious crimes, you must now take responsibility for them and can no longer use childhood as its own excuse. But Alan Colmes argued persuasively to the contrary on the November 21, 1997, broadcast of the *Hannity and Colmes* program on the Fox News Channel:

> We say that if you're a child . . . if you're 11 years old, you can't make decisions about drinking, about sex . . . you can't even drive a car. If we think that kids that age aren't responsible to do these very basic things, how can we say they're responsible for their actions in making decisions that might lead them to an adult prison?[59]

In other words, a parent says to his or her little 12-year-old boy that he can't stay up late or vote or just have cake and ice cream for dinner or never have to do homework again because he's too little to make those sorts of decisions in a responsible, well-thought-out manner. Obviously, a child doesn't have good mature judgment and needs some guidance on these issues from older and wiser adults in his life. The reason you don't allow little children to enter the military or begin full-time jobs or run for Congress is that you know that their cognitive and intellectual development is not as sharp and experienced as that of an adult.

So, some have asked whether we can hold children to two different standards. When it comes to rights and privileges such as voting and driving and deciding whether they want to go to school, we tell children they in no way have the judgment or ability to be able to take responsibility for such decisions. On the other hand, if they do something bad, we essentially say to them, "You knew good and well what you were doing and you are going to take full responsibility for your actions."

Taking responsibility for actions is an important lesson no matter what the age. Occasionally, though, it's questionable whether a child is aware of the consequences of his actions and, as a result, his situation.

In Chapter 2 of this book, the case of a six-year-old boy in Richmond, California, was noted. Looking for a Big Wheels tricycle to steal, the boy and others entered an apartment, heard a one-month-old baby making noise, knocked over the crib and kicked the baby, grievously injuring it.

In a PBS documentary, "Little Criminals," which aired on December 2, 1998, as part of the *Frontline* series, videotapes of the police interview of the six-year-old were aired. He appeared to have no understanding of what went on or of what it meant to have a court case and attorneys.

"I'm still not convinced that these kids knew the gravity of what they were doing," said Richmond Police Captain Ray Howard. "To this day, I still don't believe they knew how bad this situation was in terms of what they did to that infant and what they did to themselves."[60]

The six-year-old was kept in a youth detention home with teenagers, where he cried every night he was locked in his room. Eventually, a judge ruled that, at least for the time being, he was incompetent so couldn't be tried. He couldn't understand what it meant to have a lawyer, to be prosecuted, to gather evidence or to have a standard of proof beyond a reasonable doubt. He was sent to a group home, but the prosecutor has vowed to have a trial for him in the future if he eventually becomes competent. The prosecutor said it is irrelevant how old a person is. They must take responsibility.

Historically, this goes against the grain of all cultures. Catholics have recognized the age of seven as the "age of reason" when one may first take Communion and participate in religious studies and certain observances. Similarly, both Islamic and Jewish cultures bestow certain rights and responsibilities on children around the age of seven, though neither Islam nor Judaism set the age of majority until 13. Even then, theologians of these three religions and most others argue whether children, even of that age, truly understand the nature of sin.

This issue of murder by very young children is something of a red herring since the number of children under the age of 10 who commit such acts is almost statistically nonexistent. There were 17 such incidents in 1996 and 13 the year before.[61]

It is a difficult question at what stage a child becomes competent and knowledgeable about what he did and how to help defend himself in a legal arena. It is clear, however, that today there is little interest in exploring this question. There is now very little patience for youthful offenders, who are usually expected to answer for their offenses just as any adult whether they have the legal capacity to or not. This is wrong. This doesn't mean that very young children should not be held responsible for their actions. But many very young children don't have any more criminal intent or understanding than would a retarded or mentally ill person who is not held criminally liable for a crime. They don't have the level of reasoning that an older youth would have.

JUVENILE RECORDS

Along those same lines, there's an increasing intolerance toward letting citizens bury their sometimes long-ago youthful bad acts. It was long traditional that offenses committed as a juvenile would not come back to haunt you for the rest of your life. In order to encourage a fresh start upon reaching adulthood, juvenile records could be expunged or sealed so that they could never be used against you. This way, if you were once punished for a teenage prank or childhood act of shoplifting or fighting, the punishment would not continue forever.

It went along with a theory of fairness and redemption—that if you mess up and get punished for it, you learn a lesson, then you move on to a wiser and better life. Eternal punishment neither is just nor does it serve any purpose. If anything, as the theory went, keeping juvenile records open will help create more crime. Kids who once got in trouble will be prevented from getting certain jobs in the future or be blocked from getting into college. Keeping their childhood criminal records alive could make them unemployable, bitter and angry—a great prescription for encouraging criminal behavior.

One of my clients had, years earlier, as a teenager, a drinking problem. At that time, he had stolen some things from a neighbor's house. He was caught and admitted his guilt. Eventually, in a truly exemplary fashion, he had turned his life around. He got help for his drinking, worked his way through college, married a woman who became a corporate executive and he became a homeowner. In his late 20s, he wished to embark on a career in a financial investment corporation.

We checked into it, speaking to a number of high level corporate officers in various stock brokerage houses and financial services companies. We were told that if his juvenile record of theft was discovered, he could forget about ever being hired by a reputable large financial corporation. As it was explained, while the crime may be relatively small and long ago, there are so many applicants that, if a hiring executive compares them all and is looking for something to distinguish one over the other, why would he or she bother to hire the one with the checkered past? Also, the fact that these are companies which handle large amounts of other people's money would, obviously, make them less than enthusiastic about hiring an admitted and convicted thief. This, despite the fact that it was a childhood act of so long ago.

What was the faulty message here—that, if as a child you do something wrong, you should have to pay for it forever and be prevented from being able to work toward a future of contribution to society? The question here has much greater implications than ruining the life of an individual. Forget about that unemployable person for the moment. The larger issue is, if we prevent people from entering society as good taxpayers and make them embittered, discouraged and angry, will it cost us good citizens so much more in terms of money and public safety? These people will pay less taxes, if any, and cost us more in terms of their alcoholism, drug use and cost of imprisoning them. It will endanger us all.

Fortunately for my client, I managed to get his teenage record sealed. But increasingly, that will not be happening. States are more and more enacting laws which make juvenile offender records available. Between 1992 and 1995 alone, 40 states in some manner modified their juvenile court records' confidentiality procedures to make them more open. The records are not just available to prosecutors and adult courts, but also to schools, various state agencies, victims and law enforcement groups. Federal legislation has been proposed blocking funds to states that don't open up their juvenile records even if the young person was never convicted of the accusation. By 1995, 40 states authorized fingerprinting of juveniles. There is a serious push to eliminating the separate record keeping of juvenile records and adult records and just combining them with no distinction.[62]

The argument against destroying or sealing juvenile records is effectively summed up by T. Markus Funk in an article published in *Reason* magazine:

> Supporters say expungement is an enlightened practice which merely forgives youthful transgressions. But expungement is actually an astonishingly counterproductive policy that benefits only young criminals. The practice prevents society from acting on the simple fact that those who have committed crimes in the past are likely to commit crimes in the future and hence should be treated differently from true first-time offenders. By making it virtually impossible to collect meaningful data on juvenile delinquents, expungement also makes it difficult to evaluate crime prevention and rehabilitation programs.[63]

Funk goes on to argue that even beyond the world of criminal justice, wiping out juvenile records is not good. He states, "Employers, for instance, can't know whether potential employees are prone to stealing or other criminal behaviors." On the contrary, the majority of juvenile offenders never commit a crime as an adult.

David Kopel in his 1995 book, *Guns: Who Should Have Them*, argues that only juvenile records of felonious violence should follow the child forever:

> Unfortunately, many criminals who, in their early twenties, are facing their third or fourth violent felony conviction are treated as first-time offenders because their previous felonies were committed while they were juveniles. Changing the repeat offender laws so that violent armed felonies committed by juveniles would be counted toward habitual criminal status for adult offenders is a sensible approach toward concentrating criminal justice resources on the thugs who have shown a repeated willingness to commit violent crimes.
>
> In addition, juvenile records involving violent felonies should be disclosed to school administrators when the juvenile enrolls at a school. The privacy interests of the juvenile criminal are outweighed by the rights of teachers and other school personnel to know whom they are dealing with.[64]

But a 1998 poll commissioned by the Justice Policy Institute and Youth Law Center found that the public, by an overwhelming 70 percent, believes that juvenile arrest records should not be made available to colleges to which they apply for admission later on.

Even with juvenile records being expunged and sealed, it is difficult in these times of greater media access to keep anything private. A case in point was that of Gina Grant who, in 1990, as a 14-year-old girl in Columbia, South Carolina, used a candlestick to kill her alcoholic, abusive mother. She spent six months in a juvenile detention facility and then was released to relatives. With a sealed record, it was believed that no one would find out about her case in the future. Within the next few years, her development and growth was striking. She became an honor student, exceptional athlete and became involved in a number of projects to help the community. She was accepted to Harvard on early admission. This very success proved to be her undoing. It was a 1995 newspaper article about youths who had made enormous contributions despite great adversity (but didn't mention the murder of her mother) which caused someone to expose her. Both the newspaper and Harvard were notified. Harvard rescinded her admission, giving as its reason that she had not mentioned the murder in her application as they believed she was required. The national media swarmed over the story. Again, the two sides of the issue are defined as (1) encouraging those who once did something wrong to bury the past, better their lives and therefore give a benefit to society, or (2) notify people that there might be someone potentially dangerous in their midst and not let them be treated as a first offender if they get in trouble again.

The fact of that matter is that most youngsters who get into trouble with the law as juveniles don't get in trouble as adults. Should most of them be punished in perpetuity and be blocked forever in making valuable contributions to society? On the other hand, there are strong arguments stating that, yes, unfortunately, the privacy interests of so many who have turned their lives around must be sacrificed in order to protect us from killers or violent offenders in our midst of whom we can never become aware of because of confidential juvenile records. Some suggest a compromise of eliminating the right to juvenile criminal record confidentiality only in cases of extremely violent crimes such as rapes and murders.

CURFEWS

Another, increasingly fashionable weapon against youth crime is the use of curfews. This means, for example, that a person below the age of 18 might not be allowed out of his home between the hours of 11 p.m. and 6 a.m. There may be exceptions to this which include children accompanied by an adult, going to and from work, responding to an emergency, being married or attending a bona fide supervised school, religious or recreational activity. Depending on the particular law of the locale where they live, offenders may be arrested, booked and held in jail; brought to special curfew violation centers; or even brought home.

More than 1,000 localities enforce juvenile curfew laws. Of the 200 largest cities in the United States, over 160 of them have such laws.[65]

Are these laws effective? One would hope so because they not only place limitations on the liberty of the 0.2 of 1 percent of minors who commit serious crimes, but also on the remaining 99.8 percent who generally always do the right thing. In other words, every child is a suspect. At first blush it seems that there is an irrefutable logic to curfews. After all, if you keep kids home during the night, they won't be out breaking the law. Right?

Not quite. The fact is that it has long been acknowledged that most juvenile crime doesn't even happen during the curfew hours. Only one in six violent juvenile crimes occurs during the curfew hours—about 17 percent. Most violent youth crime happens between 2 and 6 p.m. with the high point being around 3 in the afternoon.

According to the Justice Department:

> A greater proportion of all violent juvenile crime occurs between 2 and 6 p.m. on those days when school is in session than during an entire year's curfew periods. The relative level of violent behavior is even more discrepant when it is recognized that the after school period is limited to half the number of days on which the curfew is applied and that the after school period is four hours long compared to the 6–8 hour curfew period.[66]

In fact, 80 percent of juvenile crime occurs between 9 a.m. and 10 p.m.[67] Perhaps this is why all the resources and efforts made on behalf of this politically popular idea are misplaced. The proliferation of juvenile curfew laws have offered no panacea. They divert money and energy from more effective youth crime-fighting techniques. In all fairness, it is not that a nighttime curfew will have absolutely no effect on crime—just very little. Keeping kids inside the house at almost any other hours would be more potent. But there are so many methods which would do so much more than making it illegal for citizens who are breaking no law other than simply being outside.

Curfews just don't do much. According to records compiled by Vincent Schiraldi of the Justice Policy Institute:

- In Detroit, to combat the fearsome "Devil's Night" where, every Halloween, youths set fire to buildings and commit vandalism, curfews were put into play. In the ensuing five years, incidents of arson doubled.
- When San Francisco dropped its juvenile curfew law in 1990, youth crimes in those hours dropped 16 percent.
- When Phoenix imposed a curfew, while at the same time starting a policy where juvenile recreation centers were kept open much later, youth crime declined 55 percent. But when the rec center hours were cut back to much earlier, youth crime once again rose.
- In New Orleans, new juvenile curfew laws were credited with bringing down the youth crime rate. But what wasn't always noted is that these laws came into effect at the same time that the number of youth recreation centers tripled, 1,300 additional youth jobs were added and money was poured into a volunteer program. Ironically, as the curfew laws became less often enforced, the city's homicide rate dropped.
- When the Center on Juvenile and Criminal Justice issued their findings in June 1998 of the first comprehensive academic study of juvenile curfews, it determined that, for the entire state of California, there was no category of crime (misdemeanors, violent crime, property crime, etc.) which significantly declined where a youth curfew existed. Also, counties with strict curfews had no decrease in youth crime when compared to counties without strict curfews.[68]

This is not to mention widespread complaints of selective enforcement of the law. For example, in the above-mentioned New Orleans instance, African-American youths were stopped by the police for alleged curfew violations 19 times more than white youths. In the California study it was revealed that, in the four largest counties, Latino and African-American youths were arrested for curfew violations at rates several times that of whites (in Ventura County, it was seven or eight times higher).

Perhaps the reason why curfews are not that effective is that they fail to address the root causes of why at-risk kids are out at night. Instead, energy and resources should be put into giving kids a place to go at night such as recreation centers, sheltering them from abuse and shoring up families in crisis. It is also sad to acknowledge that some kids are safer getting out of the house at night. The streets may be preferable to remaining inside with an abusive or drunken parent. It is a surprise to many that 90 percent of all unintentional shooting deaths of youths occur inside a home. Fifty percent of those are killed inside their own home, while 40 percent are killed in the home of a relative or friend.[69]

When individual curfew laws have been challenged in court, the decisions have been split, but more often than not, the laws are upheld. When the laws have been knocked down, it is because they are overly broad or they don't demonstrate that the curfew achieves its stated goal of reducing youth crime.

A curfew in Washington, D.C., was declared unconstitutional in 1996, when the United States District Court ruled:

> This court would be remiss in putting its imprimatur on a law that impacts on thousands of law-abiding citizens based upon a mere assumption that a majority of the district's parents require the city government to second-guess their parenting decisions.[70]

Curfews are indeed part of an onslaught by politicians to substitute the government's judgment for decisions that were once the domain of parents.

ABUSE OF CHILDREN IN PRISON

As stated earlier, it is my belief that there are children who have been raised in such abusive situations without adult role models that, by the time they are in their midteens, they may have already been made into extremely violent, sociopathic killers who must be incarcerated to protect the public. It is unfortunate that children, who start out so pure and innocent, are treated so badly and turned into something they weren't, are the ones who must be punished as a result of the crimes previously committed against them. Yet, unfortunately, if that child has been raised to be so heartless and dangerous, regretfully the public must now be protected against that child. But the motives are suspect of many who want all juvenile records to follow people forever, who want all children to serve time alongside hardened older criminals, who want to abandon all crime prevention efforts and want to abandon all the particular programs that have proven over time to change for the better the lives of troubled young people. Frequently, it is just a politician's feel-good simplistic solution in a cynical attempt to garner votes. It is easier to spout a simple slogan than to work on the complex causes of crime.

But there is such frustration and anger with violent youth crime that politicians tap into it and try to exploit it. There's very little sympathy with the fact that juveniles incarcerated in adult facilities are at far greater risk of physical danger and abuse than their counterparts in juvenile facilities. These youths are:

- Eight times more likely to commit suicide
- Five times more likely to be sexually assaulted
- Two times more likely to be beaten by staff
- 50 percent more likely to be attacked with a weapon.[71]

In spite of this, 36 states currently disperse young inmates with adult inmates.[72] As Rebecca Young, of Citizens for Juvenile Justice, argues, even if you have no sympathy for the young people, it's in your own selfish interest to keep juvenile offenders out of these abusive prison situations:

> There are a lot of concerns about both the physical safety of the young person while they're in the facility and then I think again, going back to the public safety issue, what does this mean for the broader community. I don't really want to have someone living next door to me who was sent to an adult prison when they were 14 and gang-raped. That's not a good idea . . . not a good idea for them and not a good idea for the rest of us. So I think the protections, they're partly about basic human rights, but they're also about public safety.

In other words, sending children to adult prison will make the rest of us less safe. But still, lest we forget, permitting brutality and depravity against children is in and of itself wrong.

In fact, in November 1998, Amnesty International issued a report condemning the entire youth criminal justice policy of the United States, claiming that an increasing number of children in U.S. courts and prisons are subject to beatings, excessive detention, solitary confinement and other abuses. This was just two weeks after the Justice Department filed suit against Louisiana for failing to provide adequate care for the 1,750 children in its correctional centers.

Amnesty International noted numerous cases of abuse including South Carolina guards who would punch, choke, kick and spray chemicals at children; guards in Kentucky who use stun guns and pepper spray against children; and guards in Arizona, who, after continuously placing one child in solitary confinement, forced him to do push-ups when he said he was too ill. He died during the forced push-ups.

In general, Amnesty International deplored the practice of trying children as adults, placing them in adult facilities, sentencing juveniles to life in prison without parole and executing children as violations of both human rights as well as some international treaties.

Take the case of Rodney Hulin, for example. Sixteen-year-old Rodney Hulin, Jr. of Beaumont, Texas, was convicted of arson and sentenced to eight years in adult prison. Within days of his transfer to the Clemens Unit in Brazoria County, he was raped and sodomized. He asked to be moved into protective custody, but this was denied because, according to the warden, it didn't meet "emergency grievance criteria." For the next few weeks, Rodney was repeatedly beaten, raped, robbed and forced to perform oral sex on the older inmates. Each time, the warden shook his head at Rodney's request to be placed by himself in a cell where the other inmates couldn't get to him. After 75 days there, Rodney hanged himself. He remained in a coma for four months before he died. In one of his last letters before he died, he wrote to his father, "Dad, I'm scared, scared that I will die in here."

Testifying before Congress, his father said, "Sending young children to adult prisons will not make our streets any safer. Sending children to be beaten, raped and robbed does not deter crime."[73]

Rodney Hulin Jr. was no isolated case. In his own testimony before the Senate Youth Violence Subcommittee of the Judiciary Committee of the U.S. Senate on the Violent Juvenile and Repeat Offender Act of 1997, Mark I. Soler of the Youth Law Center, told the stories of:

- 17-year-old Christopher Peterman who was placed in a Boise, Idaho, jail for failing to pay $73 in traffic fines. Over a 14-hour period, he was tortured and finally murdered by other, adult prisoners in his cell. Another 17-year-old, Frederick Yellen, was beaten unconscious in the same cell only days earlier, but obviously there was no learning curve for the jail staff here.
- A small 15-year-old boy in Portland, Maine, with no prior record who was put in a cell with an older, violent prisoner and sexually molested within minutes.
- In southeastern Ohio, a straight-A 15-year-old high school girl who played in the band and was sexually innocent, ran away from home one night, but voluntarily returned the next day. A county court judge put her in the county jail to "teach her a les-

son." On her fourth night in jail, she was sexually assaulted by a jailer.

- In Glenn County, in northern California, 15-year-old Kathy Robbins was put in jail for violating the town curfew by being outside after 10 p.m. on a Saturday night. Kept in jail for a week, isolated from everyone, she hung herself.[74]

Attorney Phillip Kassel tells of a juvenile detention facility in the state of Washington where a youth suspected of wrongdoing can be taken. Once brought there, a prosecutor has three days to decide whether to file formal charges and another three days to hold a hearing. So the prosecutors are able to get in six days of punishment (three of them in solitary confinement) before a hearing can even be held to determine whether the child needed to be held. According to Kassel:

> I remember very specifically a young girl who had no prior involvement with the courts, a real sweet girl from a very nice family, who was hanging out with some other kids, smoking cigarettes in an abandoned building. She was charged with trespassing and locked up for six days, the first three days in solitary confinement. I spoke to a number of kids who, for acting-out behavior, were strapped by their wrists and ankles to the bare wire frames of a cot and left that way overnight. They were unstrapped in the morning or uncuffed, and there were deep indentations from the wires of the frame on the body.

These children weren't superpredators. They were just adolescents doing adolescent things, albeit regrettably bad behavior. But, the bottom line is that this sort of abuse of children is not at all effective in lowering our nation's serious violent juvenile crime rate.

THE DEATH PENALTY FOR CHILDREN

The go-after-and-beat-up-on-children atmosphere is similarly exhibited in the increasing calls for the death penalty for children—another ineffective measure in the real fight against crime.

The United States is one of only six countries in the world that now execute juveniles. It shares that distinction with Iran, Nigeria, Pakistan, Saudi Arabia and Yemen. To underscore the isolation of the United States in its giving the death penalty to juveniles, it is noted that between 1979 and 1995, only 14 children were executed worldwide. Nine of these executions took place in the United States and the remaining five in the rest of the world— specifically in Bangladesh, Barbados, Pakistan and Rwanda. Incidentally, those four countries have since abandoned the death penalty by signing or ratifying the United Nations Convention on the Rights of the Child.

The practice of executing adults for crimes they committed as children is prohibited by the International Covenant on Rights. However, the U.S. government, when ratifying the treaty, filed what is known as a "reservation" against the provision banning these executions. A 1998 report by Amnesty International recommended that the United States join most of the rest of the world community by signing all such treaties protecting the rights of juvenile offenders without reservation.

By early 1998, there were 63 juvenile offenders sitting on death row. Texas and Florida led the rest of the country in children sentenced to death.[75] Ironically and not surprisingly, these states have some of the worst crime rates in the country. This extremely expensive method is not working for them and is ultimately a diversion from real crime fighting.

Although only about 2 percent of Americans given the death penalty are children, calls for it by politicians are increasing. Former governor Pete Wilson of California suggested the death penalty for those as young as 14, while in Texas, in 1998, state legislator Jim Pitts proposed as part of a larger crime bill package that offenders as young as 11 years old be killed. This despite the fact that the United States Supreme Court said, in both the 1982 case of *Eddings v. Oklahoma* and the 1988 case of *Thompson v. Oklahoma*, that the death penalty cannot be applied to those under the age of 16.[76]

Death penalty opponent Steven Hawkins, interviewed for the December 2, 1997, showing of the *NBC Nightly News*, argued, "And when we say that a 16- or a 17-year-old child is irredeemable, that they're human waste, we as a society have really failed, not the child." Hawkins' viewpoint was countered by Louisiana prosecutor Roger Jordan, who said, "There comes a point when you have to judge people by their actions, not just their age."

Jordan had successfully prosecuted and gotten the death penalty for 16-year-old Shareef Cousin in a very controversial case wrought with accusations of prosecutorial misconduct which illustrates the inherent weaknesses in so many of these death penalty cases against children. "Capital cases are so political that winning becomes far more important for the average D.A.," attorney Denise LeBoeuf says.

In 1996, Cousin was convicted of shooting to death a man in the French Quarter of New Orleans during a robbery. Among very questionable evidence are the facts that:

- He was convicted almost solely on the testimony of an eyewitness who told the jury, "I will never forget that face as long as I live. I'm absolutely positive that was the one." What the jury didn't know was that three days after the slaying, this eyewitness told the police in a formal taped interview that she didn't think she could identify the killer because, "It was dark and I did not have my contacts nor my glasses." It was not until a few days after the trial that the defense team received from an anonymous sender a copy of the initial statement.
- In that statement, never seen by the jury, the eyewitness told the police that what she could make out was that the killer was shorter than the victim. (Cousin is actually four inches taller.) She also testified the killer was wearing boots although police couldn't find any at his home and Cousin says he never owned any.
- Cousin's alibi was that he was playing basketball in the city's recreational department league at the time of the slaying. There is even a videotape of the game which the jury never saw. His coach says he gave Cousin a ride home afterward and is positive he could not have done the killing since the game ended at 10:30 p.m., he dropped him off at home at 10:45 p.m. and the killing took place at 10:23 p.m.
- The accounts of two referees who also told the D.A.'s investigators that the game ended at 10:30 p.m. were never shared with the defense. Additionally, three boys who were subpoenaed by the defense to testify at the trial that they also got a ride home with Cousin and their coach were taken by the District Attorney to his office and the defense counsel could not find them. Thus, their testimony was never heard.
- Not a shred of evidence, other than the questionable eyewitness account, existed against Cousin—no blood, no gun, no fingerprints, no DNA.[77]

In the spring of 1998, Cousin's very flawed conviction was overturned and he was granted a new trial. If the prosecutor Roger Jordan had not had his successful conviction overturned, he might have succeeded in killing an innocent child.

The execution of innocent children can happen. But the spirited quest of politicians in their cynical quest for votes (and as we all know, kids are easy targets since they can't vote) will endanger the children and for no purpose since the death penalty certainly won't act as a deterrent.

Texas State Representative Jim Pitts, who proposed his state's bill to execute 11-year-olds, argued on the *Today* show on April 20, 1998, that he believes letting children know they will be put to death will serve as such a deterrent. Pitts said, "We've got to send a message to these kids that, 'No, you're not going to get out of jail when you're 18. You're going to be accountable for the crime you've committed'."[78]

But deterrence in this instance is essentially a myth. If a child actually did kill someone, it is unlikely that he first did a careful cost-benefit analysis and said to himself, "I'll only commit this murder because, if I'm caught, I'll go to jail for years or receive a life sentence. Now, on the other hand, if this was a death penalty state I'd never do this crime." The fallacy of this way of thinking is that, even more than older criminals, children commit most bad acts on impulse or without a clear, thought-out strategy. So they're not even thinking of the consequences. However, during those rare times when they do think of the consequences, they merely assume they won't get caught. They typically wouldn't do the criminal act if they were reasonably certain they would get caught. There may be a number of reasons why someone is for the child death penalty, but the idea that it will act as a deterrent is stupid. No thought or research could have gone into that idea. Even a number of pro-death penalty activists who have seen the numerous studies concede it is not a deterrent, yet advocate the death penalty for other reasons.

The execution of children diverts funds and energy from real crime fighting and the most important objective of all, which is preventing crimes in the first place.

FEWER ADULT PRISONS, FEWER CRIMES

The one thing which rings loud and clear is the pervasive anger of the American public. When Maine prosecutors wanted to rework their state's law, making it easier to try youths in adult courts, Vito Caiazzo III was behind them. His son's face had been slashed with a beer bottle by another youth and had required 80 stitches. Now the assailant would be released what Caiazzo believed was too soon. "These kids can do what they want and get away with anything short of murder," said Caiazzo.[79]

Still, many criminal justice experts, including David B. Kopel, head of the libertarian conservative Independence Institute in Colorado, believe that transferring young people to adult courts and prisons should not be inflexibly automatic. He wrote in his 1995 book, *Guns: Who Should Have Them*:

> Referral of a juvenile case to adult court should be up to the judge, not the prosecutor. Some juveniles who have perpetrated awful violent crimes can still be reached and rehabilitated through the juvenile system. Even for murder, waiver should not be automatic; a 15-year-old girl who shoots her stepfather to stop his violent sexual abuse is different than a 15-year-old boy who shoots a stranger simply to watch him die.[80]

Kopel goes on to say that one of the most difficult decisions is always to determine which young people can be saved and which can't, and how one can best intervene in the life of a particular young person who is headed on the wrong path. This is because there are a great number of young people who get into trouble only once or twice and then spontaneously stop their lives of crime. Spending enormous amounts of public money on them may not be the best use of resources.

Again, it's hard to determine which kids are your best bets for saving. But Kopel goes on to cite the already well-established fact that children who begin their lives of crime earlier at, let's say, the age of 12 or 13, tend to become much more ingrained in the crime world than those who first get into trouble in their later teens.

Eighty percent of children who eventually become criminals exhibit very strong signs of antisocial behavior by the age of 11. Two-thirds of antisocial kids will get arrested by the time they're 15.[81] Also, those who get into trouble once or twice are much more amenable to rehabilitation than those who are already in their third or fourth encounter with the criminal justice system. Kopel concludes, "In the long run, programs which help prevent people from becoming criminals in the first place will pay for themselves many times over in juvenile justice savings, as well in the savings of young lives."[82]

Rebecca Young, of Citizens for Juvenile Justice, agrees that when you automatically transfer children to the adult system, "you're no longer looking at the individual juvenile offender and his or her background and characteristics. You're just looking at the offense."

She says individual young offenders should be looked at on a case-by-case basis. Young says she believes there are some kids who would be tough to rehabilitate and that if placed in the same programs with young people who have the potential to be helped, they might diminish the effectiveness of such programs. But she goes on to say:

> I don't think that necessarily says, oh, so in that case, if there's nothing we can do with them in the juvenile system, we should just say to hell with them. There's nothing we can do and just sort of admit defeat, put them in the adult system and say, whatever happens. It's not our problem any more. They either committed an offense that was so outrageous or they're just so far gone there's nothing we can do and let them fend for themselves.

Young believes that even for these children, there is a middle ground.

But, if a teenager commits a heinous crime and does need to be incarcerated, adult prison is not a place where the young person can learn to be a better person. Nothing will be done with him there to educate him or train him for work or get him away from a life lived among generally ignorant, violent criminals. Ricardo Garcia, who entered adult prison at the age of 18 for an 8- to 15-year sentence, now lectures youth groups who come to visit his prison. He tells them, "You are nothing but a number. A piece of property. This is a warehouse."

Steve Weymouth of the Youth Advocacy Project believes that many youthful offenders are still young enough to save. He says:

> So if you take kids who could still be salvageable and put them in an institution where the emphasis is on punishment, as opposed to an institution where the emphasis is on programs, intervention and rehabilitation, i.e., the juvenile system, you're going to lose the kid. I don't think they learn the necessary skills to keep them away from trouble and they sort of continue to offend and continue to reoffend.

Missouri is one of the few states bucking the trend. They are getting tougher on young offenders not by transferring them to adult courts and prison, but by committing ever younger offenders to their juvenile program jurisdiction and keeping them there longer. They extended the age from 18 to 21. Additionally, they now have dual jurisdiction where they can give a juvenile both a juvenile and adult sentence. The way it works is that a juvenile will get his juvenile sentence, but have a suspended adult sentence hanging over his head. If he successfully completes his juvenile sentence, he is free. If, on the other hand, he doesn't do a good job in the ju-

venile program, rather than be released at age 21, he then simply is transferred over to begin the adult portion of his sentence.

"If we can provide services . . . and turn them around, that's certainly
going to cost less to the state of Missouri than incarcerating them for many
years," says Vicky Weimholt of the Jefferson City, Missouri, Division of
Youth Services.[83] Colorado's Youth Offender System (YOS) works in a similar way. Youthful offenders can have their adult sentences suspended in
favor of two- to six-year terms in YOS. They start out with a short-term,
military-style boot camp, followed by a long-term program of rehabilitation and education, followed by a prerelease program of skills training and
planning. Once released, there's a final phase of intensive supervision.
Those who don't cut it simply have their adult sentences reinstated.

No responsible youth expert in the country, even those who believe
strongly that rehabilitation can ultimately turn around the life of even the
most dangerous youth, actually believes that violent juveniles should be
kept out of confinement and just left alone. Mark I. Soler, of the Youth Law
Center, when testifying before the Senate Judiciary Committee on their Violent Juvenile and Repeat Offender Act of 1997, said:

> First, I want to make it clear that this issue is not about whether juve-
> niles who commit violent crimes should be locked up and fully prose-
> cuted. They should. There is no real dispute on this. No responsible
> person—public official or children's advocate—thinks that public
> safety should be compromised by allowing violent young people to
> run around free.
>   The incarceration of children in adult jails is quite a different
> issue. . . .[84]

Youth worker Molly Baldwin says that:

> I don't think kids can murder people and you can have them walking
> around the streets. You've got to do something. . . . But I'm convinced
> that locking them up and putting them in an adult prison is crazy.
> How do you begin to say that somebody 14 years old is a grown per-
> son? You know most 14-year-olds haven't even made developmental
> shifts to full-blown abstract thinking. We have partnered with young
> people who have been very violent and helped them make shifts, so in
> some arenas it's possible.

I asked Baldwin if it really is not too late to turn around the life of a juvenile who has been raised in circumstances so bad that by the time
they're 12 or 15 they're extremely violent.

"Yeah, absolutely," she replied. "We've partnered with people who have done it. We've created situations where people have made tremendous changes."

"How do you do that?" I asked.

Baldwin replied: "The way you raise your children. You pay attention to them, you love them, you bother them, you build a relationship with them and you work over time to get enough rapport going so they can start to see and answer some questions about their life."

All children who have done bad things should not be painted with the same broad brush. Some children may be almost past the point of no return, but there are incredible stories of youths who have been given up on who then have turned their lives around and made great contributions.

Each young person in crisis should be looked at on a case-by-case basis. There should be no one-size-fits-all punishment. Therefore, there should never be an automatic transfer of a child to the adult system. A hearing before a judge should always happen first.

But children who enter the juvenile system get rearrested a lot less often once released than those their age who go into the adult system with similar backgrounds charged with similar crimes. So, yes, some extremely violent youths must be sentenced for long periods to protect the good members of the public. But for the most part, we send too many youths into the adult courts and adult prisons, where they learn to be better criminals from the older violent criminals.

It's regrettable that some victimized young people, who didn't start out behaving badly, are raised so poorly in such abusive situations without adequate adult supervision in their lives that they ultimately become victimizers. A grade school teacher I spoke with told me:

> I know kids who are victims, who, when they get to be nine or ten, will victimize other kids in some way. I'm not just talking about physical violence, but I'm also talking about sexual violence. Oftentimes, the victims who become victimizers are angry kids and they don't know what to do with their anger. I feel bad because, when we see this, we'll take care of the victim, but, for the victimizer, nothing is done. I mean giant red lights should go off and services should be provided for these little victimizers. But often, I hear adults just saying, "Oh, isn't that kid terrible. . . ." Yeah, but this is a child. You don't want to wait until they're an adult before you start dealing with them.

It's regrettable that now we often have to further punish these former victims by locking them up for long periods of time when they themselves were not the initial cause of their violent demeanor. But it would be naive to say that we don't ever have to do this in order to protect the public. Still, such cases are the few. For most of the children who are given up on and are sent into the crime schools that are adult prisons the result is a big spending program which ultimately endangers the public.

Chapter 5

Shame

The Little-Known Secret of Crime

Boy, if . . . if I had one day when I didn't have to be all confused, and didn't have to feel that I was ashamed of everything. . . . If I felt that I belonged someplace, you know, then. . . .

James Dean, *Rebel Without a Cause*

THERE ARE NO MOTIVELESS CRIMES

Toward the end of my previous book, *The Tough on Crime Myth: Real Solutions to Cut Crime,* I had a chapter entitled, "The Death of Conscience" where I discussed, among other things, the fear many Americans have today of what they consider to be a rising trend— the era of the motiveless crime. It seemed that in the past, whenever you heard of a terrible crime being committed, there was, at least, on some tortured, twisted level, a motive. A criminal would steal because he wanted money. A criminal would assault someone because they had gotten him angry or he needed them silenced.

Crime is always both tragic and inexcusable. But there is something almost more viscerally frightening about crimes—particularly random shootings and killings—without reason or purpose. It might be that someone just shoots into a crowd at a playground seemingly just for the heck of it. Yes, there have always been a few celebrated seemingly motiveless crimes committed by such criminals as a Jack the Ripper or a Son of Sam.

But these were perceived by us as true "crazies" or psychopaths. Our fear increases today because it seems that now there are these aimless, pointless crimes done by seemingly normal youths. That is what so many good citizens today find so much more frightening. We don't know whom to look out for and how to protect ourselves.

But there is an emerging theory that there is not, in fact, any motiveless crime. It's just that the reasons for the crime may be so insignificant compared to the extreme reaction such as killing, that the crime may only seem motiveless.

One of the chief proponents of this view is Dr. James Gilligan, one of the nation's leading experts on violence. He served for years as Director of Mental Health for the Massachusetts prison system and also as Medical Director for the state hospital for the criminally insane, and therefore spoke with thousands of violent criminals. He found a connecting thread through almost all of them. Almost without exception, they had been raised in brutal or abusive situations, lived with extremely deep shame and lashed out at others in a futile attempt to gain respect—to somehow make themselves feel alive.

This is why we hear about a teenager shooting someone because they were picked on, they perceived an insult to their gang, someone called them a name, stole their girlfriend or looked at them funny. Almost daily, we learn of crimes or reasons for crimes, that insinuate this desperate struggle to gain a tortured version of respect:

- After David Carneal shot and killed a number of his fellow students after randomly shooting into them at his high school in Paducah, Kentucky, in December 1997, some of the students told detectives that Carneal had been frequently teased. As a freshman, he was small, wore funny hats, was different and was often pushed around and ridiculed by members of the football team.
- After Kipland Kinkel shot and killed two of his fellow students and injured 22 others after shooting up his high school cafeteria in Springfield, Oregon, in May 1998, some friends speculated that he had been "embarrassed" the day before by being arrested and suspended from school for bringing a gun into the building. Others said he was angry about "insults" from seniors.
- In a case that shocked the nation in October of 1998, two young men in Wyoming, Aaron McKinney and Russell Henderson, were accused of savagely beating Matthew Shepard, a gay college stu-

dent, and roping him to a rough-hewn fence where they continued to beat and burn him there in frigid temperatures until he later died. McKinney claimed that one of the reasons for the killing was that Shepard had come on to him and others and had "embarrassed" him in front of his friends. The incident was not unlike the case several years earlier of Jonathan Schmitz who was accused of murdering Scott Amedure after Amedure announced on *The Jenny Jones Show* that he had a homosexual crush on Amedure. Schmitz claimed he was "humiliated."

- According to a taped police confession, 15-year-old Richard Rivera heard that 16-year-old Emir Quintana had called him a "punk." A friend handed Rivera a pistol and told him to "do what you have to do." Rivera shot and killed Quintana, a basketball standout who had never been in trouble before, right out on the basketball court. In late 1997 Rivera was convicted of first-degree murder.

- Earl Behringer was given the death penalty for killing a couple at a lovers' lane outside of Fort Worth, Texas, for a $15 robbery. On the day of his execution, he expressed his version of dignity and self-respect by declaring, "It's a good day to die. I walked in here like a man. I am leaving here a man."

- A teenager, Levar Leggett, shot a man he didn't know who happened to be walking down the street. The man got up and tried to run away, but was shot a second time in the back. Leggett then put the gun to the victim's head but the victim managed to knock the gun away. He survived. A codefendant told the police that Leggett shot up the stranger to "earn his stripes."

Former gang member turned responsible youth worker Saroeum Phoung used these very same kinds of terms in describing what his once violent behavior had done at the time for his self-esteem:

> Yeah, I think the reason I earned a lot of "respect" in the gang, and to a lot of different gangs, and to a lot of different people, was because of what I could do in a gang during that time. You know, people were shooting at me, I was chasing them around with a butcher knife, and people would say, "Oh, don't mess with him. He's crazy." So you know, a lot of people "looked up to me" and a lot of people had "respect" for me in many ways, because of the activities I did in the gang during that time.

During a conference on youth in Boston on November 6, 1997, Dr. Gilligan explained it this way:

The underlying universal cause of violence is—people become violent when they feel that they are being insulted or disrespected or treated as an inferior or being placed in an inferior position, treated with contempt or disdain or treated as unimportant or insignificant. And what I want to suggest is that the greater the gap that exists in a country that has the Horatio Alger myth and the myth of equality of opportunity . . . the greater the gap is between the rich and the poor, the more the people at the bottom of the social and economic structure cannot feel anything except inferior and looked down upon and treated as failures.

Dr. Gilligan's theory rings true. As a criminal defense attorney who has spent years of his time speaking to prisoners in prisons and criminals on the outside who are charged with crimes, the one line I hear out of the mouths of my clients, more than any other, is, "He disrespected me" or "He dissed me." It comes up again and again and again. It is almost a mantra of the American criminal—the complaint of being "dissed."

THE SIGNIFICANCE OF BEING "DISSED"

For example, I may be meeting with one of my clients in prison who has been thrown into the "hole"—solitary confinement as a punishment. I'll say something to the effect of, "You knew you were going to get thrown into solitary if you mouthed off at the guard and swore at him. Why'd you do it, then? It was a guaranteed 'no-win' situation for you. It wasn't as if when you refused to cooperate with him and do as he said and then cussed him out, that he was going to just say, 'All right, then' and walk away. But you knew this. So, why'd you do it?"

Inevitably, the answer will come back, "But he dissed me. I'm not taking that."

Criminals are fearful that, without this sense of self-respect and self-esteem, they'll lose their entire sense of themselves, lose their very souls and essentially experience a spiritual death. They'll risk anything, bring down any calamity on themselves and even cause their own destruction rather than lose their fragile dignity and sense of self. In other words, shame becomes the deadliest of emotions.

This is why so many acts of violence which initially appear motiveless may not in fact be so. They're just outsize responses to the very slightest perceived humiliations. Take, for example, the first three paragraphs of an article appearing in the January 24, 1996, issue of the *Boston Herald:*

Dirty looks were blamed for a back stabbing at the Forest Hills station yesterday after an eyeballer went to the hospital in an ambulance, police said.

"It was apparently an eyeball catching thing; sometimes a look is all it takes," said MBTA police Major Roger Ford, discussing why parolee Benjamin Espino, 21, allegedly stabbed Tyrone Douglass, about 21.

No other motive is apparent, but the investigation is continuing, police said.[1]

The eyeball thing is becoming a classic reason for fighting. One youth I spoke with whom I'll call Mark had been in trouble most of his life. He told me what happened one day when he was walking down the street and another kid he had never met before walked past him on the sidewalk:

This kid gave me a look. So I just kicked him in the head. You know, it was an up-and-down look. Like you're a piece of shit or whatever. I don't know why. He looked me down like I'm nothing. Sometimes, people give you looks that you don't really like, you know. Like you're a sucker.

When I asked Mark why he couldn't let a simple look like that go, he couldn't articulate it. He just kept saying, "I don't know."

In his book, *Violence: Our Deadly Epidemic and Its Causes*, Dr. James Gilligan tells the story of someone he calls Ross L. whom he was referred to after Ross L. cut his wrist in court to delay the sentencing in which he was to receive a life sentence without parole. Ross L. had been convicted of murder—he had run into a former high school classmate in a convenience store and accepted a ride back home with her. During the ride, he stabbed her to death and depravedly mutilated her eyes and cut out her tongue. The horrific crime was seemingly senseless in that he had not attempted to rob or rape her.

In his conversations with Ross L., Dr. Gilligan was struck by his seemingly total inhumanity, a complete lack of remorse and regret for the crime even though he didn't deny he had done the act. Instead, Ross L. acted the part of the aggrieved, much put-upon party, talking about how people had treated him unfairly his entire life.

But after listening to enough of his story trying to see if he could make any sense of the senseless, Dr. Gilligan began to piece together an explanation for his vicious debased acts. Ross L. in his childhood had been beaten up regularly by others and often called a "punk" or a "wimp." By the time he turned 13, he began taking street drugs and committing acts of violence himself. The one thing he could brag about, like so many other teenaged boys, was his ability to work on cars. But at the time of the murder, he didn't have the use of a car since he was unable to pay the mechanic who was rebuilding his engine.

When he accepted the ride on that cold winter night from his victim, a high school senior who had once been his classmate, it was, in his eyes, an admission that he lacked the money for a car and the mechanical ability to fix one. He was ashamed at having to depend on this girl for help. Additionally, he was enraged at women for his lack of success with them and his sexual frustration. In his mind, he may have killed her because, "I didn't like the way she was looking at me" and "I didn't want her talking about me." Hence, his going after the eyes and the tongue.

So, perhaps, this seemingly senseless murder may be logical to the murderer. As Gilligan puts it, "The emotional logic that underlies this particular crime, then, which I called the logic of shame, takes the form of magical thinking that says, 'If I kill this person in this way, I will kill shame.'. . ."[2]

Gilligan notes the signifance of Ross L. going after the victim's eyes and tongue as hints to his extreme sensitivity of being swallowed up by his terror of being humiliated. It is as if he wanted to blind the eyes of the one who had been watching his shame or cut out her tongue to prevent her from telling others about him. Gilligan concludes that, at the very least, the story of Ross L. infers:

> . . . the plausibility of looking further to see if there is evidence that it might be this fear which ultimately motivated not just this particular murder, but all aggressive apparently unprovoked violence. If Ross L. is at all typical of other murderers, then we would have to conclude that the most dangerous men on earth are those who are afraid that they are wimps. . . .

YOUNG, URBAN, VIOLENT "SUCKERS"

In a series of interviews I conducted with 14- and 15-year-olds who lived in violent urban neighborhoods and had themselves been in trouble with the law, every single one told me that the need for respect is a rigid, nonnegotiable demand and is worth risking death. Typical was 15-year-old Ineka who told me:

Nowadays kids want respect because if people don't respect you, then they'll run all over you. Then you can't get along in life. Because if people disrespect you, you're never going to get anywhere. If you stand up now, nobody'll be bullying you. I got a girl right now who wants to fight me 'cause her boyfriend told her I look good. I don't want him. But this is what ya gotta fight over with someone.

Alan feared the same loss of himself so much that he claimed it would be worth giving up his life rather than lose dignity. He said, "If they disrespect you and you don't do anything, it's possible for another person to take over your life. You don't want to live through that."

In an analogy quite sophisticated for an uneducated street kid, Alan made the connection between a youngster's need for respect and the larger world around him:

It's politics. When the U.S. gets disrespected by Iraq, we go to war. Just like that, it's basically politics in the streets. One kid is like a nation, you know what I'm sayin'? Without putting fear in the other guy, you can't be respected.

Only one juvenile I interviewed professed that she detected a weakness in their respect culture. Fourteen-year-old Denise told me:

Sometimes I won't fight you even if you call me a bitch. If I really sat down and thought about it, I think I would leave it alone because it's dumb. I know I'm not a female dog. Their reaction could be that they're not getting to me and they'll go to the next thing. Because people are going to try this all your life. They're going to say things to you, instigate, look at you wrong. . . .

Similar conclusions on shame as the underlying cause of violence were drawn by two physicians working at a large urban hospital. They conducted interviews with young African-American men between the ages of 18 and 25 who were admitted to surgical service because they had been either shot or stabbed. More than three-quarters of them identified with the concept of being a "sucker." They defined sucker as someone who is weak because they fail to retaliate violently whenever they are perceived to have been disrespected. They believed if you don't respond violently, you'll be taken advantage of in the future, lose your status in the community and be viewed as a "nobody."

In a stunning short paper entitled, *The Experience of Violent Injury for Young African-American Men: The Meaning of Being a "Sucker,"* the two doctors, John A. Rich and David A. Stone, quote one teenager who had been shot while in the middle of a gun battle give his definition of being a sucker:

> Like if someone walks up on you and starts pushing you, he's pretty much sayin' I don't respect you. Who are you? What are you gonna do? If you ain't doing nothing, he's gonna keep punkin' you, keep callin' you a sucker, showin' you no respect the whole time. . . . I got to get my respect. Cause if I don't go for mine, he's gonna try and take advantage of me and take what I got.

Another young victim told Rich and Stone:

> So nobody wants to be nobody. Everyone wants to be somebody. That's why they sell drugs and stuff. They get the gold. They get the car. They somebody. Now they respect you. Everybody looks at you. They get attention. Once you get disrespected, you're nobody now, you're a sucker.[3]

Dr. Rich and Dr. Stone came to the same premise as Dr. Gilligan— that violent behavior among young men may often be perceived to the untrained eye as senseless and simply an uncontrolled response to anger. But they too believe there is "an underlying logic to some violence." It is interesting that they use the same word as Gilligan—"logic"—to refer to seemingly illogical behavior.

THE AMERICAN TRADITION OF THE "HONOR CULTURE"

Criminologist James Wilson, in a speech at Claremont-McKenna College in California aired on C-SPAN on November 27, 1997, also spoke of this way of thinking—what he dubbed an "honor culture"—which has begun to permeate our society:

> Honor, now renamed respect, becomes the dominant value. And so people are shot and killed to get control of a pair of Reebok sneakers. They are shot and killed because they are dissed. They are shot and killed because they looked at somebody else the wrong way. This is not a unique American urban phenomenon. This is a phenomenon that has always existed throughout human history whenever unattached, unmarried men operated in an environment in which success depended on expropriating the available capital with no legal system to protect you.[4]

It is frequently asked why the United States has one of the highest rates of violent crime in the world, and the answer might be found in the roots of our "honor culture." It is acknowledged that the most violent area of the United States has always been the South. This is contrary to the mistaken belief that it is the industrial urban areas that produce the most violent crime. Even in the early to mid-1800s, for example, rural South Carolina had a murder rate four times higher than that of this country's most industrial state at the time, Massachusetts. This has persisted to present times. In the mid-1930s, when the government first began keeping crime statistics, it was found that the 10 states with the highest murder rates were either southern or southern border states. Today, Louisiana has the highest homicide rate and one of the highest rates of violent crime (note also that today Louisiana has the highest per-capita number of its citizens in prison than any other state, and its reliance on prisons alone, with little emphasis on crime prevention and other kinds of crime fighting, has proved disastrous). Wilson and others cite the tradition of violence in the South as having its roots in the large number of Scots and Irish who immigrated there first. These clans had hundreds of years, dating back to the Middle Ages, of blood feuds, border disputes and violent clashes over insults and slurs on one's good name. A man would have to kill to protect his honor and valor.

That emphasis on honor, brought to the New World primarily by way of the Old South, was, surprisingly, upheld, more than anywhere else, by the landed gentry and the supposedly more sophisticated new aristocracy. The concept of the southern "gentleman" was that of a courtly, polite, chivalrous, though heavily armed person who would stand up against slights and insults to the dignity and honor of his own good name and that of his women and his region. When one's honor was challenged, it was an affront to his manliness and would readily be answered at the risk of one's life. Hence, the excessive number of wealthy men with so much to lose risking it all in the all-too-popular tradition of duels.

They passed this culture of excessive violence onto their slaves in the brutality and torture which were often wreaked out against them. This didn't end with the demise of the slave system, as lynching and other forms of savagery continued as part of the heritage. The barbarous legacy of the medieval clans lives with us today in that the United States is still one of the most violent places on earth.

The one aspect of today's new "respect culture" which I had the most trouble understanding was the idea that you no longer have to show your physical prowess over your opponent. It used to be that a violent person might be proud of his size and strength, that he was the "biggest and the baddest" from a muscular point of view. I recall people saying machismo things like, "If you want to fight me, you'd better bring a gun." Or, if challenged to a fist fight, the traditional boastful response might have been, "Oh yeah, you and who else?"

Voy Cooks, an extremely articulate inmate now in his mid-40s, with whom I have had a longtime correspondence, spends a good deal of his time trying to counsel the younger violent ones who enter the prison gates. He also marvels at the disintegration of the old codes of combat. Cooks told me:

> I have seen groups of 10 guys jump on one other youth. Somehow, that's fashionable today. We never did that as kids. In my day, to maintain your honor, you had to fight with your fists. Two guys . . . it was a battle of the titans. You knock me down or pin me down . . . fight's over. You won. What happens today is, if you belong to a particular set, then you're loyal to anybody in that set. So, if one guy has a beef with another guy, the entire set has a beef with that guy. While I can understand the loyalty, it just doesn't look good. The only things that travel in packs are wolves. It doesn't take a lot of courage for 10 guys to beat up one guy.

I asked 15-year-old Frederick how one could brag about how tough they were over shooting someone. Wouldn't there be a perception that they weren't tough at all and that's why they needed a gun? Absolutely not, was his response, at least not in his community. He said:

> Fightin' . . . that's about played out. Nobody gets into no fights no more. That's how it is. I can't tell you why. Everyone know if you give a fair fight, the other fellow not goin' to be playin' it like that. You may wanna fight fair, but the person you're fightin' is gonna get a gun. So now both guys know they gotta have guns.

As stated, this craving not to be "dissed" is leaking into all aspects of our society. In a notoriously ugly incident, Golden State Warrior professional basketball player Latrell Sprewell didn't like his coach P.J. Carlesimo telling him how to pass the ball, so he leaped off the practice court and went for his throat. Twenty minutes later, he assaulted him again. Sprewell later explained that he did it after "a lot of verbal abuse by P.J."

While the nation was shocked that a professional athlete would physically assault a coach, it was merely another example of the increasingly popular tradition of young men lashing out physically at those who they believe malign them. Authorities at schools and workplaces now face the same retaliation as those who dispense schoolyard taunts. It is the transference of playground rules into the professional arena.

In typical macho bravado, Sprewell explained, "If I really went after P.J., he'd look a lot worse than he did on TV."

During the previous season, another young professional basketball player, Allen Iverson, who had ugly encounters with other players, management and the law explained, "I can't change and I don't want to. There is a certain way I carry myself and a certain way I expect to be treated."[5]

Another professional athlete who views things the same way is boxer Mike Tyson, now best known for biting off a piece of the ear of the boxing opponent who was beating him, Evander Holyfield. "Basically, I've been taken advantage of all my life," Tyson told a joint interview of several dozen sportswriters in Las Vegas on June 24, 1997. "I've been abused. I've been humiliated. I've been betrayed."

During this interview, Tyson began to speak about former heavyweight champion Sonny Liston, the predecessor with whom Tyson said he most identifies. Liston, a great fighter, is now too often thought of as a thug who broke legs and twisted arms at the beginning of his career and reportedly at the end. He died of a drug overdose in his home, which some believe may not have been self-inflicted.

Tyson explains his perception of Liston: "I just think he wanted people to respect and love him and it never happened. You can't make people respect and love you by craving it. You got to demand it. . . . I'm going to be respected as a man. I demand it. You have no choice. You can't be in my presence if you don't."[6]

It was just a few days after this interview that Mike Tyson bit off a piece of his opponent's ear.

Many of these attitudes are held by young, impoverished, urban, African-American males who feel they have to overcome their early-childhood experiences of being treated as inferior by a racist society along with the shame of early poverty and deprivation.

What the United States Supreme Court said in 1954 in the landmark decision of *Brown v. Board of Education* was: "To separate (black children) . . . solely because of their race generates a feeling of inferiority as to their status in the community that may affect their hearts and minds in a way unlikely ever to be undone."[7]

In his 1952 book, *Black Skin, White Masks,* the radical African writer and psychiatrist Frantz Fanon described growing up black in a white society as, "Shame, shame and self-contempt."[8]

Without dignity, money, education, position, all many are left with is their rigid, indefatigable sense of pride in not having to back down to anyone. If absolutely all they have is their pride and honor, the threat of the loss of that is worse than death. Many would rather lay down their life—totally do themselves in—than hand over their dignity.

Elijah Anderson, in his examinations of life among African-American youth in inner-city Philadelphia, wrote in a 1994 *Atlantic Monthly* article titled, "The Code of the Streets":

> To run away (from a fight) would likely leave one's self-esteem in tatters. Hence people often feel constrained not only to stand up and at least attempt to resist during an assault but also to "pay back"—to seek revenge—after a successful assault on their person. This may include getting a weapon or even getting relatives involved. Their very identity and self-respect, their honor is often intricately tied up in the way they perform on the streets during and after such encounters.[9]

While a middle-class successful citizen might have experiences where he or she faces some humiliation, it might not feel like the absolute death of their soul or spirit, something where they would risk their own life rather than back down. If a middle-class person who had been raised on a generous dose of positive reinforcement were to be "disrespected" or even assaulted, as bad as that experience might be, it probably would not feel like the end. That is because they might have other good things in their life to fall back on to keep them buoyed up—a fulfilling career, loving relationships, money, intellectual interests and material items. They could retreat and find solace in other aspects of their multifaceted lives. This is in contrast to the "dissed" young violent person who feels his only choice is between being disrespected, which signifies the loss of himself, or violently assaulting someone. For him, there is no middle ground.

MAINSTREAM AMERICA'S PERVASIVE NEED FOR RESPECT

But it is not just an urban male street culture which fosters this extremely perverted understanding of the otherwise positive virtues of self-respect, honor and human dignity. Nor is it particularly recent.

In 1947, Frank Sinatra knocked the *Daily Mirror* columnist Lee Mortimer to the floor with a punch in the head (and, ultimately, had to pay a $25,000 settlement for the action). Sinatra's initial explanation was, "He gave me a look. It was one of those 'Who do you amount to?' looks. I followed him out. I hit him. I'm all mixed up."[10]

Much deadlier was the case of Diane Zamora. Diane was a high school honor student living in Mansfield, Texas. She and her boyfriend, David Graham, made up one of the potentially great successful power couples. She had been admitted to the Naval Academy and he was admitted to the Air Force Academy. Her goal was to some day be an astronaut and she was off to a bright start. Their future was unlimited.

During the fall of 1995, in what was their senior year, David admitted to Diane that he had previously had sex one time with a sophomore at his high school. The incident occurred in the past and the sophomore was not a potential girlfriend or threat to their relationship. Yet, when Diane learned of this, she insisted the life of the sophomore be snuffed out. As she later said in a statement to the police, "I screamed at him, 'Kill her! Kill her!' "

David made up a pretense for getting the sophomore to go for a ride with him in a hatchback automobile. What she didn't know was that Diane Zamora was hidden in the back of the hatchback. The plan was to break the victim's neck and then tie weights around her to send her to the bottom of Joe Pool Lake. Together they assaulted her in the car at the side of the road. The victim was injured but managed to escape. She was hunted down by David Graham and shot to death with a Makarov 9-mm pistol.

Initially, the murder went unsolved. It was only the following year when both Graham and Zamora were at their respective service academies that Zamora began to confess to a number of people about the murders.

I covered the Zamora trial live in 1998 in my capacity as a commentator for the Court TV network. In separate trials, she and her boyfriend David Graham were eventually found guilty and sentenced to life in prison. One day during her trial, I spent several hours on the anchor set with a guest psychologist, Dr. Jane Greer of New York City, who had written a book about betrayal entitled, *How Could You Do This to Me?* I asked Dr. Greer a question that had me perplexed. I wanted to know why Diane Zamora had to take the extreme reaction of murdering this former, one-time, insignificant, alleged sex partner of her boyfriend who was not an apparent threat to her relationship. Or if Diane Zamora was truly angry at this sophomore, couldn't she have taken a less radical step such as yelling at her, writing her a nasty letter, even giving her what could have been a still absurdly excessive slap? Why the fanatical overreaction?

The gist of what Dr. Greer told me was that Diane was such a narcissist that the idea that another girl had had sex with her boyfriend was an unforgivable impossibility. It was as if a pristine, clean white wall had suddenly had a bit of red paint thrown at it and the only way to restore the purity was to quickly paint the red smudge over again with white to blot it out forever. It was an extreme and outrageous sense of honor.

Her boyfriend David Graham, in his confession to police, explained this very thing in language that almost seemed like the stilted writing of a bad romance novel. He said, "When this precious relationship was damaged by my thoughtless actions, the only thing that could satisfy her womanly vengeance was the life of the one that, for an instant, had taken her place."

As previously stated, shame is perhaps the deadliest emotion, yet it is not just within the province of urban young men, though it is certainly strong among this group. It is also responsible for violence, death and suicide among all groups from all backgrounds.

The playwright Arthur Miller once wrote, "I think the tragic feeling is evoked in all of us when we are in the presence of a character who is ready to lay down his life, if need be, to secure one thing—his sense of personal dignity."

Carolyn Chute grew up in grinding poverty in a rural area of Maine. She wrote a novel called *The Beans of Egypt, Maine,* about dirt-poor people living off the beaten track there and struggling to survive. In the dust jacket to that 1985 book, she commented, "This book was involuntarily researched. I have lived poverty. I didn't CHOOSE it. No one would choose humiliation, pain and rage."[11]

Shame is an intrinsic problem in American culture and if you listen carefully to its echoes, it is pervasive in American life. It is all too present all too often.

While preparing to write this chapter, I happened to be perusing an old copy of *Newsweek,* the April 14, 1997, issue. In article after article on completely diverse topics, the theme of shame kept coming up again and again.

- On page 42, in an article about FBI director Louis Freeh, it was written, "But Freeh's real problem is not purity. It's pride. In his three and a half years as FBI director, he, too, often seems compelled to declare his own righteousness. . . ."

- On page 47, in an article about collapsing peace talks between Israel and Palestine, it was written, "The king also accused Netanyahu of blocking the search for peace and seeking the 'deliberate humiliation of your so-called Palestinian partners.' . . . But his politics of humiliation may doom any effort to jump start the negotiations."
- On page 50, in an article about the record number of bankruptcy filings, it was written, "And bankruptcy lawyers say the sense of humiliation remains." One lawyer was quoted stating, "[Judges] don't see the shame."
- On page 9, in a letter to the editor by an aide to the Sultan of Brunei complaining about an article about bizarre and cruel treatment of a woman by the Sultan, he wrote that his boss "deserves a degree of recognition and respect which, regrettably, is so lacking in this article."[12]

The very day I read these articles, I heard a quote on TV from pioneering baseball great Jackie Robinson, the very model of dignity when he faced an onslaught of both scorn and praise when he broke the color barrier to professional baseball. He said, "I never cared about acceptance as much as I cared about respect."

The week earlier, on the CNN network's *Larry King Live* interview program, Larry King asked the Academy Award-winning actor Rod Steiger, "What makes you so good?" Steiger answered, "The fear of not being respected."[13]

This has become such a big theme in our lives that many even denigrate this "excuse" culture where we try to overlook the bad acts of young people since those acts are the results of "low self-esteem." This is as if to say that people don't have to be responsible for the consequences of their acts since we have to understand that it's not their fault, it's just their poor self-image.

Garry Trudeau in his comic strip Doonesbury parodied this sense of entitlement on April 2 and 3, 1997. A character goes up to his college professor with a copy of his grades in his hand and says, "This B+ is wrong, man! You're dissin' me here big time!" The next day, the character says to the professor, "It's not just me, man! When you give me a bogus grade, you're showing disrespect for my whole community!"[14]

But the reaction of people to their dignity being violated can be extreme and death is preferable to loss of this honor. In 1997, John E. Curtis Jr., the well-liked and successful C.E.O. of the biggest cafeteria chain in the country, Luby's, suddenly killed himself. As it was reported, "One possibility in Curtis's case: he could not bear the shame, or perhaps the cruelty, of laying off 1 percent of Luby's 13,000 person work force."[15]

SHAME: THE DEADLIEST OF ALL EMOTIONS

It's not just uneducated, neglected youths who react regrettably to the sting of shame. Even the highest-level corporate executives or leaders feel the same way. Two high-level Clinton administration figures may have reacted in a similar manner to Curtis. Admiral Jeremy Boorda killed himself after a very distinguished career just as it was about to be revealed that he was wearing a particular medal on his uniform which he might not have earned. Later he was vindicated. White House lawyer Vince Foster is said to have killed himself after facing the onslaught of accusations and criticism that would become almost a routine part of the job for major White House officials during that administration.

Still, though many people in our society react poorly to shame, most don't react in a way that they cause violence to others. But when violence does occur, it is almost exclusively the result of shame.

Another story told to me by prisoner Voy Cooks was about a younger prisoner he was trying to give advice to who wanted to fight him because Cooks may have logically trapped him in a point he couldn't defend. It was apparent the young man was embarrassed by having brought up a foolish point he couldn't defend. As Cooks tells it:

> I generally talk to a lot of young people about the whole concept of selling drugs. One particular fellow attempted to justify his drug selling by saying it was an economic necessity. You know, he had to pay rent and buy milk for the baby. When I refused to accept that rationale, he wanted to fight. What happened was, he and I had a discussion about selling in his community being a liability instead of an asset. And he was telling me about the lack of opportunity in his community for young black males, which I couldn't disagree with. So he was basically trying to tell me that he had no other options . . . that his economic survival depended on him selling drugs. So then I said to him, "Now that you're in prison, who's paying the rent? Who's feeding the

baby? Was it worth it?" Nobody likes to admit that they were a fool. So his emotions took over.

In other words, this young man found the revelation that he had made a foolish point impossible to live with. He sensed that only violence could wipe away his shame.

In a survey by the National Institute of Justice released in 1997, twice as many juvenile as adult arrestees agreed with the statement, "It is okay to shoot someone who disrespected you." Three out of 10 of all arrestees agreed with the statement, "Your crowd respects you if you have a gun."[16]

In another 1997 report by the National Institute of Justice entitled, "Violence Among Middle and High School Students," by Dr. Daniel Lockwood, it was concluded that:

> Aggravated assault and even homicide, which include young people as victims and offenders, often result from events similar to those triggering less serious offenses—transactions over seemingly trivial matters, occurring between people who know each other. . . . A "character contest" may develop in which neither party will back down. The disputants then create a "working agreement" that the situation calls for violence. . . . A key step in the transaction is often an event that the offender interprets as an offense requiring saving face.[17]

This is exactly what Eric Rodriguez, the now successful youth worker, was talking about when he described to me what occurred during his violent childhood:

> Fighting was something that was pretty common. In fact, it was a way I gained a lot of respect from people, or what I perceived as respect. Today, I look back in hindsight and see it was not respect, it's fear versus respect. But it definitely felt like respect at the time. People started looking up to me. I was fighting every single day. It didn't matter what it was about. Over trivial stuff. Someone steps on your sneakers and you're fighting. . . . We would get into fights with people just to fight. There would be a group of us who would walk down . . . we'd see another group of people, some guys, we'd get into a fight. Simple as that, for no particular reason, for the sake of fighting, for the adrenaline rush, to have your friends rave when you're done. It's that simple.

But why is it that while we all at some point experience shame, rejection, ridicule and embarrassment as the most painful emotions, we don't get so overwhelmed by them that we lash out and violently attack and kill others? There are some who do that very thing.

EARLY ABUSE AND THE FEAR OF
THE DEATH OF ONE'S SOUL

Dr. James Gilligan says that in his years of seeing the most violent men in maximum-security prisons on a daily basis he learned, often from independent sources, the history of victimization these men had experienced. They were rejected, physically abused, neglected and sexually abused in such excessive and often bizarre ways that it was easy to see how the extreme violence against them in their childhood developed into extreme violence against others. Dr. Gilligan writes:

> They have seen their closest relatives . . . murdered in front of their eyes, often by other family members. As children, these men were shot, axed, scalded, beaten, strangled, tortured, drugged, starved, suffocated, set on fire, thrown out of windows, raped or prostituted by mothers who were their "pimps"; their bones have been broken, they have been locked in closets or attics for extended periods, and one man I know was deliberately locked by his parents in an empty icebox until he suffered brain damage from oxygen deprivation before he was let out.[18]

Gilligan tells the story of the very first violent criminal he saw in therapy in prison—Randolph W., who told the story of how his father brutalized and terrorized all the members of his family. At first, Gilligan assumed he was being "conned" in order to gain his sympathy. Then Gilligan, to his surprise, learned that Randolph W.'s father was in that very same prison at that time for murdering his own daughter—Randolph W.'s sister.

For many the degradation during their childhood was so extreme that it leads to almost an absence of feeling—a death of the self. These once victims now turned violent individuals are so afraid of the loss of themselves that they'll lash out dangerously at anyone who they perceive dares to add to this shame. This is why a violent reaction might be so disproportionate to some petty, imagined slight that observers mistakenly presume it is a motiveless crime.

This is also, parenthetically, a towering argument against the ill-informed opinion of so many politicians that we're pampering young offenders in prisons and juvenile facilities and, if only we'd get tougher on them while they're there, they'd learn the error of their ways and straighten up. "Give 'em a cement slab to sleep on and no pampering and coddling!" is the attitude. A number of people have called into radio talk shows I've been on and advocated bringing back the concept of beating prisoners. What they don't understand is that these offenders have been beaten, brutalized, humiliated and abused throughout their lives and just continuing this in prison is not going to turn them into model citizens. It certainly won't act as a deterrent to crime. The offender's attitude would almost be, "So what else is new?"

THE MISGUIDED POPULARITY
OF SHAMING SENTENCES

Humiliating and brutalizing young prisoners further may satisfy and give pleasure to some observers and, on some level, may not even be unfair to an offender who viciously hurt or killed an innocent good citizen. But will it help reduce crime in this country and make us safer? Absolutely not. To embitter and shame a violent person will only make him more dangerous once he is released.

That is why when a politician like Sheriff Joe Arpaio of Maricopa County, Arizona, boasts that he plans to use chain gangs and tent cities for children who break the law and that "My philosophy is they will eat the same bologna, wear the same pink underwear [as the adult inmates],"[19] it is not a serious attempt to cut the crime rate and make the good members of the public safer. It is just a cynical attempt by a politician to get some votes even if it endangers the citizenry.

This is similar to the increasingly popular trend of "scarlet letter" sentencing — trying to emphasize humiliation in the punishments. In Maryland, juvenile offenders were ordered by a judge to apologize on their hands and knees. In California, a shoplifter was ordered by a judge to wear a T-shirt declaring, "I am a thief." In Texas, a thief was ordered to clean out stables for 600 hours. In another state, a man was ordered by the judge to allow his ex-wife to spit in his face. In Seattle, a judge ordered a woman to wear a sign, "I am a convicted child molester."

Occasionally, such shaming punishments might actually effectively degrade a generally good, nonviolent citizen in the mainstream who might have done something bad out of character. When such a citizen has his picture and name put in the newspaper for soliciting a prostitute or someone convicted of driving while intoxicated must put such a fluorescent sign admitting his crime on his car, they might regret their crime. It can't be said that in no situation would shaming ever work. But there are no empirical studies that this reduces recidivism. Politicians are acting on this purely from random anecdotal evidence. At any rate, it probably won't act as a deterrent since offenders, particularly youthful offenders, either (1) act on impulse and don't even think about whether they might get caught, or (2) even if they think about it, believe they won't get caught. Offenders don't generally commit crimes when they are fairly certain they'll get caught.

Still, University of Chicago law professor Dan Kahan thinks demeaning punishments have their place. He says the fact that they're often used as an alternative to jail is a positive.

> Some people tell outlandish horror stories—they say that shaming punishments will unleash this appetite to hound people. They'll be lynchings. We'll be launching ourselves into the Puritan age. That's possible. But what's the likelihood that that will happen versus the certainty that people will be imprisoned if you don't use shaming penalties? Nothing destroys your life nearly so completely as having spent time in jail.[20]

But the weakness in Kahan's argument is that if that is the great positive thing about shaming punishments—their use as an alternative to incarceration—it would be better to implement the alternatives to incarceration which have been proven to actually empower young people, such as making them get used to work, finish their education, get rid of their addictions, and make them into responsible family members. This will help them end their cycle of crime more effectively than just degrading them and making them angry and cynical. Empowerment versus embitterment.

THE POSITIVE ASPECTS OF PRIDE AND CONSCIENCE

The development of a moral sense of shame is itself not a bad emotion to have. In fact, it is necessary for children to acquire it. A child should feel pride when he or she achieves a good accomplishment such as helping others, and perhaps should feel ashamed when he or she has acted cruelly to someone.

"Shame is part of growing up and developing a conscience," says Harvard child psychiatrist Dr. Robert Coles. "If a child doesn't learn to be ashamed of that behavior, we're in real trouble by the age of 2 or 3."[21]

But holding a moral sense of shame within oneself is different from being degraded, demeaned and debased. Tom Myers, an official at the Erie County (Pennsylvania) Prison, also runs a program called the Shock Juvenile Awareness Program where he brings to the prison local students who are at risk of committing crimes which could land them in jail. He showed me some of the thank-you notes the youngsters sent him. The following one, which used the word "respect" again and again, was typical of many which seemed to exhibit a slight bit of that preoccupation with respect and yet, ultimately, a healthier view of it along with honor and pride:

> Going to the jail taught me a lot about respect. Sometimes all a person has is his or her self-respect. Most people demand respect. You owe everybody their respect. If you don't show people respect they will get very angry because they deserve your respect. Jail is a very harsh place. It is degrading and dehumanizing. They are treated like animals. I learned that everybody has something to teach. I learned that you should listen to and respect your elders.

But changing the attitudes of violent young lawbreakers to pull them away from their rigid reactions to being "dissed" or shamed won't be easy. Gang researcher W.B. Miller writes:

> It happens that great nations engage in national wars for almost identical reasons [that gangs do] . . . personal honor, prestige and defense against perceived threats to one's homeland. . . . When a solution to this problem [of fighting nations] has been found, we will at the same time have solved the problem of violent crimes in city gangs.[22]

In the case of violent young Americans, the solution is early intervention in their lives to rescue them from early childhood abuse, violence against them, poverty, racism and neglect—to build them up inside so that they won't fear their very destruction from a mere insult or slight. They will no longer have to lash out in a disproportionate, violent reaction, or kill because they have no interior defenses or feelings of self-worth to shore them up against the typical rejections and occasional demeaning treatment we all come up against from time to time. We should do this not only for them, but in our own self-interest, to protect the safety of we good citizens.

Chapter 6

The Solution

Intervention, Families, Role Models, the Media and Rehabilitation

Eric Rodriguez is the young man I described in the Introduction, who was essentially left to live on his own from the age of eight throughout the rest of his childhood after his father was jailed and his mother was frequently hospitalized from mental illness. Feeding and supporting himself, he turned to theft and violence. But when he was 14, he was approached by Molly Baldwin, the head of a youth services program called ROCA and a legendary figure in Chelsea, Massachusetts, who gets out of her office and walks the indifferent streets stopping kids, asking them about their lives and then coming back again and again.

> I was approached by Molly Baldwin, who said, "We are opening up a gym for folks who play basketball. If you want to come down, come down." She'd come back the next day and say, "Hello. Interesting. You're standing on the same corner. It's below zero out. Any particular reason?"
>
> And so, over a course of time, she would just strike conversations with me. That simple. It was enough. And she'd be consistent. And she would ask me how my day was and that was something nobody else was doing. Teachers would say, "You got detention because of this, you're not going to pass because of this." DSS says, "You've got to do this because your mother dah dah dah." And opposed to—here was this one place in the world that was saying, "Well, you know what . . . what do you like to do?" And then the next step to that was to really look at my attributes, what are the things that are working for me, and to say, "That's what I want to build in you. I don't care about all the

other stuff in you. Well, I care about it, but I want to focus in on the fact that you're a natural leader, you're pretty articulate, you're a sharp kid. These are skills." Nobody ever recognized that and when I first got involved in ROCA, it was literally drilled into my head that, "Hey, you have potential. You could do something with yourself."

And so I love basketball, so that was kind of the bait-and-switch and I really just came down once a week on Mondays to play basketball and she would say, "Why don't you bring your friends down?" and so I'd do that. We'd go down there just to play ball and really, over a course of time, she'd use that as a way to get to know me and to begin to develop a relationship with me. She'd start upping the ante in our conversations about my life and some decisions that I was making in my life or not making.

She gave me an opportunity to work. She asked, "Why are you doing what you're doing?" And I'd say, "Hey, I don't have money. I don't have food. I have to do something." She said, "Okay. How about if I offer you a job?" At that point on the first or 15th of every month, I could make a thousand dollars a night. She said, "I can't compete with what you're going to make out on the street. But I can give you something that's sustainable, that's going to be the entire summer and it's yours to do with what you'd like." That was pretty appealing. . . .

Why would I want that over $1,000 a night? I think it's a series of a few events. A friend of mine was murdered on the same corner that was the hot spot where most of my customers would come. My brother started using what we were selling, began to become the best customer. And I have to say a lot of my friends were being arrested, going to jail, and I knew it was a matter of time before I got caught. And I wasn't getting rich, despite making that type of money. It's a myth that drug dealers get rich out there. Nine out of 10 people who are out there selling, spend it faster than they make it and I was certainly one of them. . . .

I think that the opportunity afforded me was a pretty incredible one. I came into the job expecting it to be a typical youth employment project where I would come and they'd say, "Okay, you come in. From 9 to 10, you're going to sweep, from 10 to 11, you're going to file, from 11 to 12, you're going to blah, blah, blah. . . . And instead, she asked me, "What do you think this community is most in need of?" And I said, "Well, I see all these little kids who have nothing to do (at the time, I'm 14 years old). I know what they feel like. They're home. They're by themselves. Some of their parents aren't even around."

And Molly said, "Good. Come up with a plan for some type of program for kids from 8 to 11 years old." And I said, "I'm not sure I know how to do that." And she said, "You know, I bet you do. I bet you have tons of ideas. Why don't you take a crack at it." And little by little, I started realizing, hey, she's not going to do this for me. This is something I'm going to do for myself. And that became an incredible experience in my life, an opportunity to have somebody who hardly knew me to trust me enough to put in my hands a program and say, "Hey, it's for you to develop and tell me what it is."

If I were to say to you that was the changing point in my life, I'd be lying to you because it was really a roller coaster ride for about four years.

Eric Rodriguez's remarkable story is towering testimony that even if you don't have the best instrument for developing a good life—the family—which nothing else can truly replace, a young life can still be saved by having a responsible adult intervene and serve as a model and give you direction.

RESILIENT KIDS

It's just the way life is. It shouldn't have to be like that. Who'd want to live like that . . . shootin' and fightin and all that?

The above words were spoken by Ronny, a fifteen-year-old inner-city youth who was explaining to me the daily routine of his life. He had been sentenced to a rigorous Connecticut alternative to incarceration program because, "I got mad enough to beat the crap out of someone." Although he had, indeed, committed some reprehensibly bad behavior, the good news and saving grace was that Ronny actually had a clue that his way of life wasn't the best way of life. He put to rest the lie that violent youthful offenders genuinely enjoy their impulsive, unfulfilled existence. In the sentence, "It shouldn't have to be like that," Ronny exhibited an understanding of the possibilities out there beyond his limited world of urban violence. The sentence is towering proof that you can reach him—and others.

This brings up the larger issue of whether it would be possible to end much of youth crime by either rehabilitating young offenders or by intervening and changing their environment at a very young age before they get into trouble. Or should we just lock them up because "nothing works"? The age-old nature–nurture argument has become the touchstone of all political arguments on crime. In fact, Leon Kamin, a psychologist at Northeastern University, says that the simplest way to determine someone's political view is to ask them their thinking on genetics.

Fortunately, it is the view of the American people that the environment in which we raise young people is the key determining factor to whether they'll turn out to be good contributing citizens. In the April 21, 1997, issue of *U.S. News and World Report,* a comprehensive poll was released which asked whether "heredity and genes determine behavior or whether a person's environment and society determine how they behave?" Seventy-two percent of those polled answered that environment and society are most significant while only 18 percent stated a belief that heredity and genes are the most important.[1] If the public is right on this, then this is proof that if we make changes in the upbringing and environment of potential criminals, we can eliminate a large portion of crime in America.

And the American public is right. The bottom line is that virtually every poll shows that Americans believe that youth crime should be fought on two tracks simultaneously. They answer that very violent offenders should be treated harshly and incarcerated because we need to be protected from them. The public does not have much sympathy for and is in fact quite angry at violent criminals, even youths, who do not receive serious consequences for their actions. But, they say that at the same time, we need to either prevent the offenders from becoming criminals in the first place or to try to turn most of their lives around and back on the right track. Americans really do want most efforts put into prevention. But once a serious crime has been committed, they want a combination of harsh retribution and rehabilitation. For most, the attitude is, "Yes, lock him up, but while he's in there, do something with him. Don't just keep him in there sitting around with the older violent criminals so that once he gets released, he'll be as uneducated, unskilled as when he went in, only angrier and more violent."

Bob Kupec believes we are not powerless to change the lives of young people, and he's been on the front lines of working among offenders for years. Kupec was warden of five adult prisons in Connecticut, including the supermax. Now he spends his days running the day reporting center where young Ronny whom I spoke with and other youths on the beginning paths to crime leave their homes every day to attend regular classes, life skills classes, do rigorous community service and participate in programs. His view on this, after years on the front lines of working with lawbreakers, is that many politicians and so-called experts are hypocritical in their statements about the ability of young people to learn and transform themselves: "You can't say kids can't change, but then say, when they enter prison, they learn to be better criminals. You can't have it both ways."

The best solution to youth crime is to have everyone raised in an intact family where loving, committed parents devote a great deal of time to their children teaching them good values. Human personality is shaped early and this route is the best, bar none. Governments must not get in the way of the family and should shore it up at every turn.

But as this book illustrated earlier, this is not a realistic picture for absolutely everyone at the moment, as more and more children are being raised in single-parent homes and, even when there are two parents, they're often not around. What can we do then?

General Colin Powell, former chairman of the Joint Chiefs of Staff, addressed that question while visiting a Boys and Girls Club in a less than affluent area of Florida. He says he was sitting around talking with some kids and telling them about his own poverty-stricken childhood growing up in a tenement in the Bronx. Powell explained that he managed to thrive even in this environment because his parents provided him with a supportive, nurturing structure and encouraged him to believe in himself. Powell relates the rest of the story as follows:

> As I spoke, a nine-year-old boy raised his hand. "General," he asked, "Do you think if you didn't have two parents you would have made it?"
>
> That kid cut me to the quick. He was saying, "This isn't my world you're talking about. Can I still make it?" My answer was: "Yes, you can." That boy may not have had what I had growing up, but, I said, "There are people here who care for you, who will mentor you, who will watch over you and teach you right from wrong."[2]

Colin Powell is right in his belief that, as long as there are older people in a young person's life to give him direction and moral guidance, this can trump a bad neighborhood and the unfortunate absence of the best solution—good parents in our lives.

Powell's viewpoint supports what some psychologists have dubbed the "resiliency theory." Decades ago, child psychologist Emmy Werner began studying the progeny of abusive, poverty-stricken, substance-abusing and even mentally ill parents. Expecting to learn how deficiency trickles down from parent to child, Werner was astonished to learn that at least one-third of the children of these inadequate parents actually thrived and developed into stable, healthy, happy and successful grown-ups.[3]

Why do these "resilient kids" thrive and prosper while other kids raised in this kind of atmosphere are swallowed up and defeated by it? Originally, psychologists studying the resiliency theory focused on born traits such as a good I.Q. or a good temperament. But ultimately they learned you can mold a resilient kid by creating a resiliency route of mentors, teachers and volunteers rather than just leave it all up to the innate characteristics you were born with.

An article in the November 11, 1996, issue of *U.S. News and World Report* entitled "Invincible Kids," focused on one young person, Rudy Gonzalez, who grew up in Houston's East End barrio. His father had been killed in a barroom fight when Rudy was six. Rudy himself had a very violent streak. He had been in trouble with the police for banging another kid's head against the pavement until the blood flowed, and for punching a teacher. He slept through classes and robbed warehouses and stores. Ultimately, many of his friends joined gangs, dropped out of school, got girls pregnant and wound up in jail.

Somehow though, Rudy found his way into the urban branch of the Boy Scouts of America and under the wing of a city cop, John Trevino, who was the scoutmaster. Then a fortuitous thing happened. Rudy helped save the life of a kid stuck up to his neck in a muddy bayou. A newspaper picked up on the story and Rudy eventually went to the White House to be congratulated by President Bush. The upshot was that he saw the possibilities life had to offer. His open personality blossomed and he became particularly self-motivated. He set up a Scout project to serve his community and clean up a barrio cemetery. He made a goal to learn all he could about college scholarships and eventually entered Texas A&M to study accounting.

But the best action that Rudy Gonzalez took for himself was the thing that most resilient kids have in common: They manage to wind up with substitute parents sometimes by dumb luck, but more often by somehow seeking them out.

"We were just kids in the barrio without anything to do," says Rudy today. "We didn't have the YMCA or Little League, so we hung out, played sports, broke into warehouses and the school."[4]

We know that most kids can turn around their lives even after a bad start. What is sad is that with today's wholesale disinvestment in youth by the politicians, the opportunities are fewer and fewer. But when those opportunities are given out by the community in partnership with government in an organized, comprehensive way, the results have been nothing short of astonishing. As President Clinton said during the major national volunteerism summit on April 27, 1997, the important part of this partnership is not the government, but the community. He stated:

You and I both know that a lot of the problems facing our children are problems of the human heart, problems that can only be solved when there is a one-to-one connection, community by community, neighborhood by neighborhood, street by street, home by home, with every child in the country entitled to live out their God-given destiny.[5]

Such is the story of Boston in the 1990s and how its extraordinary partnership resulted in a phenomenon that broke all records in sending youth crime plummeting to the cellar.

HOW YOUTH CRIME DIVED IN ONE CITY

In 1990, the city of Boston made national news when citizens' groups requested the National Guard to patrol the streets because they had no confidence in the ability of the Boston police to control its violent youth gangs. That never happened. But the city did do something instead which resulted within half a dozen years in:

- The homicide rate in Boston dropped to a 30-year low
- Overall crime in Boston dropped to a 30-year low
- In 1997, the city received an award for having reduced crime overall more significantly than any other city in America.
- By late 1997, Boston had gone nearly two and a half years without a youth being killed by gunfire or stabbing. This was following years of record numbers of youth homicide victims.
- From 1993 to 1995, the juvenile arrest rate for aggravated assault and battery with a weapon dropped 65 percent.
- By 1998, the overall gun homicide rate for all age groups in Boston had dropped 80 percent.

Attorney General Janet Reno had the Justice Department circulate a pamphlet across the country called "One City's Success Story" which told the story of Boston.

President Bill Clinton remarked, "We know that if this can be done in Boston, it can be done in every community in every neighborhood of every size in the United States."

In fact, Boston Police Commissioner Paul Evans says that today his beeper goes off so rarely that he calls another number just to check to see if it's still in operating condition.

Boston's solution to youth crime consisted of this: Everyone who touched the lives of juveniles began talking to each other. It began in the wake of a gang-affiliated violent riot which took place inside the Morning Star Baptist Church in the neighborhood of Mattapan during a murdered young person's funeral. During the funeral a gang chased another kid into the church and stabbed him in front of those assembled. Considering this a "wake-up call," a partnership of hundreds of neighborhood groups, schools, youth workers, the courts, the district attorney's office, the police and the newly formed Ten Point Coalition which represented 54 churches, all put their heads together. This partnership blurred the once sharp lines between law enforcement and social service groups.

The partnership started with the premise that, as Commissioner Evans said, "The thing that's working is not just lock 'em up, lock 'em up." This is not to say that the police didn't take the law enforcement aspect seriously. In fact, through the use of academic research, police intelligence gathering and computers they targeted who they believed were the 300 or 400 most violent youthful offenders. But they went beyond this.

Boston police Lieutenant Gary French explains, "If you just whack the bad guys without doing other things for the neighborhood, you don't get as much bang for your buck. . . . We can come out and lock 'em up until the cows come home and it won't work unless there is intervention and prevention at an early age."

Boston's District Attorney Ralph Martin agrees and in a roundtable conference on juvenile crime with President Clinton held in Boston on February 19, 1997, he said, "That's a key phrase—restoring order—not only locking up the bad guys, which we're very good at, but helping to restore order so that people can fend for themselves after people have been taken off the streets."[6]

They learned that since there is not one core root of crime, there can't be a one-size-fits-all solution.

"Anyone who comes into a city like this and looks for one central cause just doesn't get it," says Commissioner Evans.

Among the myriad things being done are:

- Just as the police targeted the most violent youth, they also developed a list of 200 at-risk children not yet deeply involved but with a potential for joining gangs. Teams of ministers and police began visiting them at their homes and at their schools. That list expanded to 1,000 children. Besides just giving them moral advice, practical assistance was offered. During one potential flare-up of gang violence in May 1998, while meeting with nearly 30 middle school students, one minister, the Reverend Prince Woodberry, said, "You want a job? No problem. We can help. There's all kinds of summer programs, summer camps. I have a martial arts camp I'm doing this summer. You want to be down with that, I'll put you in there. You won't pay nothin'."[7] All but one of the middle school students that day signed lists for jobs or summer activities.

- Youth centers were set up such as the Bird Street Recreation Center which features tutoring, computers, sports, job preparation and peer leadership programs which focus on smoking prevention and sexuality issues.
- Nine hundred community crime watches have been set up. In a city of 47.3 square miles, this means 19 groups per square mile.
- The city has hired ex-offenders to work as go-betweens to settle disputes between gang members or nonviolent, but troubled, youths without gunfire.
- Operation Night Light was put into effect where probation officers got out of their desk-bound offices and into the community where they would go to the homes of their probationers at night to check up on them. As one probation officer, Bernie Fitzgerald, explained at the public roundtable discussion with President Bill Clinton on February 19, 1997, "What happened was we became sort of office-bound at one time. We didn't have a real sense of what was going on in the streets and the community. We were treating them between 8:30 and 4:30. . . . We had to find a different way to do our jobs. . . ."
- Prosecutors went out into the community, regularly attending crime watch meetings so people would get to know them and would not be shy about approaching them. Among other things, they speak to residents as how to give their input to judges and parole boards on items such as sentencing and parole dates. They also interact with the police long before arrests are made. This is a new approach for prosecutors, who have traditionally worked exclusively within the confines of the court building.

- An army of health outreach educators fans out into the neighborhoods giving advice on everything from AIDS to teen pregnancy, violence, infant mortality and smoking.
- There is an annual youth summit in which 1,500 youths participate, a youth line and a city youth council comprised of teenagers who regularly meet with the mayor.

One of the hallmarks of Boston's partnership is that so many agencies worked together so well and didn't have the turf wars that so many other locales experience among law enforcement entities. One of the best examples of this was the breakup of the notorious Intervale Posse, a longtime youth gang. The gang unit of the Boston Police Department worked in sync with the DEA; the district attorney's office; the National Guard; the Bureau of Alcohol, Tobacco and Firearms; the state attorney general's office; and a number of other agencies.

Then, once the arrests were made, other groups went into action to either realistically or even symbolically end the gang's dominance. That same morning workers from the Boston Housing Authority swarmed into the nearby projects and painted hallways, changed locks. They removed trash and hauled away abandoned cars. The famous "sneaker tree," from which the Intervale Posse had hung dozens of sneakers to show their dominance over the neighborhood, was cut down. The National Guard bulldozed a lot where the gang would hang out and watch an outdoor television powered by a long extension cord. Next, the city's Inspectional Services Department leveled abandoned buildings, boarded up others which were used to stash or sell drugs, erased graffiti and fenced in certain lots. They put pressure on absentee landlords who rented out apartments to active drug dealers. They appointed more than 70 building "captains" to act as liaisons between tenants and managers. Parole officers moved quickly to violate offenders. Members of the Street Workers program and the Youth Violence Strike Force swarmed in to the area offering jobs and afterschool programs and warned everyone of continued enforcement. A local food pantry began donating thousands of pounds of food to the neighborhood each week. The Red Cross and other groups began to conduct nutrition classes, CPR classes and health workshops. Volunteers constructed a playground and began a graffiti removal program. They were smart enough to know that merely "being tough" and making arrests followed by jail would not be enough. Within a year, assaults, robberies, drug charges and other serious crimes dropped by more than 50 percent, and emergency 911 calls from the neighborhood dropped by 40 percent.[8]

COMMUNITY POLICING AND FAITH-BASED PROGRAMS

The two main components of Boston's remarkable partnership are community policing and the involvement of the churches.

Boston was one of the first cities to put into practice community policing to try to undo the unfortunate trend which had begun across the country in the 1960s of taking cops off the beat and out of the neighborhoods. Instead, from the '60s to the early '90s, police would come into neighborhoods only after a 911 call had been made. They knew no one in the community and would swoop in like visiting aliens. You only saw one of these crisis-oriented policemen when there was trouble or, more specifically, when you were in trouble. The police were often perceived as the bad guys. This was mostly because you didn't know them and they weren't a daily friendly presence in your life. They could go after you, but would they ever be there to help? Also, when community people did contact the police, many people would only call them when it was the most dire emergency and there was no way of getting around it.

"Nine out of 10 times the only time a youth will call a police officer is when a friend has been shot, or in a domestic relationship where dads hit moms," says William Morales, a former convict who now works with Urban Edge, a housing and antiviolence group in Boston.[9]

Never really getting to know a police officer and only getting to see them during an emergency response, children and, in fact, the rest of the community, never got a chance to build up a relationship with them. The neighbors and the police both lost because of this since, if they couldn't build up trust, no one would confide in the police or even inform them where, specifically, the crime is going on. Even neighborhoods that were regularly patrolled were patrolled by police officers in squad cars. It was believed that police officers could cover more ground this way and you'd need fewer officers through being linked merely by phone and radio.

Donald Stern, the U.S. Attorney to Massachusetts who has worked closely with the partnership to end crime in the city of Boston, says:

> In the old days, there was a lot of mistrust and distrust. Probation offi-
> cers wouldn't go out of their offices, the police were mostly respond-
> ing to 911 calls, prosecutors just looked at what came in the door to
> decide what to act on, the feds had their heads in the clouds and didn't
> know what was happening on the streets. And the community may
> have viewed the police as an invasion force. . . . There has been a sea
> change.[10]

Today in Boston that trust is being built up. If you see the same cop on
the street every day, chat with him and go to neighborhood meetings
where he shows up to participate, you have no hesitation in letting him
know what's going on in the community.

"If someone comes to a meeting and says, 'Someone has moved
across the street from me and I think something's going on,' the cops will
check it out," says Louise Carcione, who heads a neighborhood council in
the city.[11] In one neighborhood where the residents were concerned about
too much prostitution, they organized themselves to videotape the license
plates of the customers' cars coming into the area so they could identify
the chief offenders. They always let the police know when they would be
doing this and worked in tandem with them.

Cooperation also helps clear up misunderstandings between the police and the community. At one particular meeting between area residents
and the police in the basement of a neighborhood police station, the residents wanted to know the reason for the delay in shutting down one
house out of which everyone knew drugs were being sold. The police
captain at the meeting had to explain that the dealers in that house were
part of a much bigger drug operation and, unfortunately at that time, the
police had been unable to get the dealers to sell to one of their undercover
officers which would therefore give them the right to search the house.
The officer further explained that if the police visibility were built up in
front of that drug house, it could reveal their plans to ultimately make the
arrests.

"We don't have the evidence we need," said Captain Bob Dunford. "If
you want a Band-Aid, I'll give you a Band-Aid. But we're trying to eradicate the problem."

The neighborhood residents, having spoken to the police and gotten
an explanation, now at least understood the police a little better. They
know what police can and cannot do. Police have had to explain that they
just can't just search a young person's pockets or take him to the police station without some kind of evidence.

In the past, each area may have had one designated community outreach officer. But the difference is that now, it's not just one designee; community policing is integrated throughout the force.

As Dunford said to President Clinton at the 1997 roundtable discussion on Boston's youth crime successes, "It's communication. We do a lot of talking with each other. But, more importantly, we listen to each other. [The neighbors] have a real voice in how we police. . . ."[12]

Kids know them, also. In fact, some police officers in Boston started visiting schools and passing out collectable "cop cards" with their photographs on them. If the kids then visited them at the police station on Wednesday nights, they would autograph the cards.

While community policing has been the centerpiece of President Clinton's crime strategy, there is a great deal of consensus on it. Community policing is "a policy area where liberal and conservative thinking has converged in recent years," wrote political columnist David Broder in his February 26, 1997, column. Bill Bratton, the celebrated former police commissioner of both Boston and New York City, who has received much of the credit for introducing community policing to those cities, says, "American police chiefs—unlike the Congress of the United States that is so far away from reality—know that you can't just be tough on crime. You can't just lock them up."

Another unlikely alliance between conservatives and liberals is based on the belief that only a more powerful set of values can fight the criminal influences on young people today. Without two parents in the home or a caring cohesive community around them, the one institution that is often the only constant in their neighborhood is the church. In depressed and deteriorating neighborhoods, the black church has been a bulwark and the one constant that has not abandoned its people. The wry comment used to be that as businesses, the middle class and all other standard establishments would flee a declining area, the last two institutions left in a slum would always be liquor stores and churches, and there is truth to that. So now, with the government's commitment to young people declining, "faith-based" social programs are on the upswing. For years, churches have run everything from soup kitchens to drug programs to basketball leagues but weren't always noticed below the radar screen. Today everyone is turning to them because they realize that, when it comes to trying to save young people, they may be about the only game in town.

As the Reverend Jeffrey Brown of Boston's Ten Point Coalition of religious leaders told President Clinton at the roundtable conference on youth violence in February 1997, "We provide hope and develop within our young people a spiritual discipline against the resentment that they fear."[13]

Boston's Ten Point Coalition was formed in the early 1990s in the wake of an almost out-of-control wave of youth violence. Today their presence is ubiquitous, almost everywhere in the minority community. As stated previously, at the hint of renewed gang violence or any sort of trouble, the ministers enter the public schools or make late-night visits to the homes of at-risk youth. They run programs such as one church's Ella J. Baker House, which works with 1,300 youths in a dizzying array of programs such as recreational, tutoring, job providing and violence prevention. They're the main clearinghouse and troubleshooting institution doing everything from taking children to the movies, finding money for baseball uniforms, locating a place to live for a teenager just thrown out of home and settling individual disputes among children before they escalate. They are even a presence at the local court, using one of their youth workers as an advocate looking for alternatives to incarceration for some youthful offenders.

In the Ten Point Coalition's remarkable alliance with the police, they prefer to save a young person if he's winnable, but won't hesitate to help the police identify the toughest ones from whom others need to be protected. Police Commissioner Paul Evans says, "We can put our heads together and say this kid has gotten into trouble, but he's a good kid—let's try extra hard to get him the services he needs. This one, we can't save—and if we don't get him off the streets and into prison, he's not going to make it."

The results have been nothing less than miraculous. Criminologist John J. DiIulio, Jr. testified before the U.S. Senate's Subcommittee on Youth Violence in February 1996 that, in his opinion, the question of whether there will be a coming youth crime wave:

> . . . will depend greatly on how much local, community-level and faith-based institutions do to save their children—and the rest of us—before it's too late. With respect to inner city youth crime, our guiding principle should be, "Fill churches, not jails."[14]

DiIulio went on to cite studies that showed that even when youths don't attend church, but the neighbors around them do, the young person is less likely to commit crimes and more likely to stay in school and have a job. It may sound fantastic, but it's true that merely having good external influences around you are enough to turn your life around.

President Clinton, in a 1995 speech to high school students, said much the same thing:

> Don't you believe that if every kid in every difficult neighborhood in America were in a religious institution on weekends—a synagogue on Saturday, a church on Sunday, a mosque on Friday—don't you really believe that the drug rate, the crime rate, the violence rate, the sense of self-destruction would go way down and the quality and character of this country would go way up?

Washington's frustration, after years of trying to fight crime and poverty with the failed policies of either trying to spend our way or arrest our way out of the problem, is now turning it to these faith-based organizations. A 1996 Congressional bill referred to as "charitable choice" gives states the power to contract with church-based organizations. These organizations will run social service programs and provide moral leadership. They are not permitted to proselytize but can maintain their religious character. There is also an initiative for a tax credit for those who contribute to these programs.

Much of the success of this growing trend of faith-based social programs is anecdotal, but in Boston it seems to be working. It appears logical that, with the absence of so many parents from the lives of children and the government's disinvestment in children, any attempt to fight moral poverty would be welcome and effective. I asked 15-year-old Tyrell how he had come to abandon his life of violence and actually become part of an organization where he serves as an antiviolence counselor to his peers. He answered simply, "Somebody changed my way of thinking—God."

The Reverend Eugene Rivers, a Pentecostal minister and one of the dynamic leaders of Boston's Ten Point Coalition, said: "We were poor before, but we were never as crazy as this. What's happened is that hope has died, and secular liberals can't speak to the death of hope. They don't have the grammar or the vocabulary for it. We do."

Or as one priest working at a drug abuse program said, "These are God's creations. They were put here for a greater reason than to buy sneakers."[15]

OTHER FORMS OF INTERVENTION

Scores of municipalities across the country come and visit Boston to see what they can imitate for their own cities' youth programs. It is only logical. As President Clinton said after a visit to Boston in June 1997, "When you know what works and you do it and you see children's lives reclaimed, it becomes unconscionable not to do more."

Minneapolis was one such municipality. After two years of unprecedented violence in that city, they decided to model their crime prevention program specifically after Boston. Minneapolis was introduced to probation officers riding alongside cops at night just like Boston's Operation Night Light; meetings among federal, state and local agencies; warrant sweeps; violence prevention programs; and regular meetings between law enforcement authorities and neighborhood groups. And, although, they had 28 homicides in the first five months of 1997, during the first two months in which they implemented their Boston-style program there were none.

"We're stealing every idea that Boston hasn't nailed down," says Minneapolis probation supervisor and former police lieutenant Jim Robertson. "Look what's happened to your body count, and look what's happened to ours. You're doing something right."[16] Yet Boston is only one example of a strategy which has sent the crime rate into a nose-dive compared to merely relying on arrest and incarceration.

The earlier the intervention, the better. As one veteran public school teacher told me, "If you wait till middle school or high school and hope some magic person will suddenly enter and turn some kid's life around . . . I'd like to see it happen. Well, it does happen sometimes, but it doesn't happen much."

For example, according to a 1997 report of the Justice Department entitled "Mentoring—A Proven Delinquency Prevention Strategy," children who participated in a Big Brother/Big Sister program were 46 percent less likely to start using drugs, 27 percent less likely to start using alcohol, 32 percent less likely to strike someone and 50 percent less likely to skip school. It reported that a similar program, Project Jump, matching troubled youths one to one with an adult, showed similar results.[17]

Connecticut's nationally famous Alternatives to Incarceration program brought crime down so dramatically throughout the 1990s at a fraction of the cost of incarceration that the governor requested they set up a similar program for youth. In a typical use, a young person who is relatively nonviolent but still headed for incarceration will, instead, be admitted into a day reporting program. That means he or she will get to live at home, but report to the day reporting center seven days a week from 8:00 in the morning until well into the evening. Here it will be a full day of classes, community service, recreation, counseling and group meetings on things like anger management, nutrition and HIV awareness. At one juvenile reporting center I visited in Hartford, called ADAPT, students were getting such individualized teaching that within a matter of weeks, test results were showing that even the toughest street kids were jumping on average about five grade levels. I spoke to one 15-year-old, Ronny, who had just returned from a field trip to the Beardsley Zoo and, as I was walking past him, was now using a computer to research information on the eagles which had fascinated him. He gave me an enthusiastic update on them along with statistics and opinions on endangered species. Ronny told me, "People be trying to kill animals for fun and stuff like that, and sometimes by accidents like oil spills. They could take some of these animals and keep them some place for a while where they could have more animal babies." Daily community service included cleaning up hiking trails and churches and even carrying the luggage and escorting visiting athletes in the Special Olympics to their rooms. One example of bringing these youths out of their worlds and into a more compassionate life is that at the end of each race in the Special Olympics, there is a designated "hugger" at the end of the line to give the athlete a hug. Many of these tough street kids in the alternatives to incarceration program worked as "huggers." This Connecticut program is so much cheaper than warehousing young people in cells, but more importantly their rearrest rate went way down. One boy in the ADAPT program told me, "It'd be easier in jail. I'd rather be here because it's harder. Without struggle there can be no success. What you gonna achieve?"

Republican Governor Christine Todd Whitman of New Jersey had this sort of program in mind when she declared at a July 19, 1995, luncheon before the National Council on Crime and Delinquency in Washington, D.C.:

> A judge in one county has many options to craft appropriate orders for young offenders. In the next county over, especially if it is urban, a judge may have very few options between probation and incarceration. That's like having to choose between an aspirin and a lobotomy for a migraine.[18]

Not every youth crime prevention program is effective and the list of them must be culled. For example, the politically popular boot camps for juveniles were effective in keeping down the recidivism rates for juveniles only if there was a good follow-through aftercare program once released.

Analysts at the RAND Corporation studied the benefits in crime reduction of incarcerating more people as opposed to four different early-childhood intervention programs. They looked at programs such as (1) home visits by professionals beginning before birth through the first two years of childhood followed by day care; (2) training for parents and therapy for young children who have exhibited aggressive behavior; (3) incentives to induce disadvantaged high school students to graduate; and (4) monitoring and supervising high school-age kids who have already exhibited delinquent behavior.

The results, presented in a 1996 report entitled *Diverting Children from a Life of Crime,* were that:

- California's three-strikes-and-you're-out program of more and lengthier incarceration did result in a 21 percent reduction in crime for a cost of $5.5 billion a year.
- For less than another $1 billion spent on parent training and graduation incentives, that crime reduction could be roughly doubled.[19]

If you want to see the ineffectiveness of concentrating almost all anti-youth-crime efforts on incarceration, just take a look at California and compare it to Boston or New York. While Boston and New York hit record lows for violent crime after introducing the strategies discussed above such as community policing and early intervention, California jailed its juveniles at a rate higher than any other state, more than twice the national average. It also had the highest youth unemployment rate. Subsequently, the number of California teens who were murdered more than doubled.

California should heed the point made by President Clinton at a speech on June 11, 1997, at the Justice Department Symposium on Youth Violence which he specifically chose to hold in Boston. There he cited Boston as the model for other places to follow, declaring that:

> This is not rocket science. It's replication. We know what works. There is no excuse for not doing what works. . . . I understand that you can pass a bill and make it very popular if all it does is seem to penalize people. And I am not against tougher penalties.[20]

It is far preferable and simpler to build positive children than to rebuild adults gone bad. Unfortunately, the opposite is happening. There is a growing disinvestment in children. For example, out of almost 3 million children eligible for the early Head Start program, there are currently spaces for only 32,000. In my state, there are more than 12,000 children on waiting lists for day care.

This neglect and failure to intervene on behalf of youngsters is regrettable not just for them, but for ourselves. A Justice Department study highlighted in a 1996 report entitled "The Cycle of Violence Revisited" reported examining the lives of more than 1,500 child victims identified in court cases from 1967 to 1971 as being the victims of abuse or neglect. By 1994, almost half had been arrested for a serious offense, 18 percent for a violent offense.[21]

There could not be a better example than that of Kipland Kinkel who killed his parents and then shot 24 of his classmates, two of them fatally in Springfield, Oregon, in May 1998. Despite the fact that he spoke openly about building bombs, had been suspended for bringing a gun to school, bragged about torturing animals and commented that he'd like to kill someone, he was never referred for counseling. Due to budget cuts, his school did not have the requisite number of counselors. This catastrophe underscores the dangers when such services are either cut or made difficult to access. Across the country, counseling has also been more difficult to obtain with the rise of managed care. Dr. Howard Spivak, a pediatrician and vice president of community health programs for the New England Medical Center, tells the story of having to make 14 phone calls in order to find counseling services that were covered by insurance for a suicidal boy.

"It was a nightmare," said Spivak, who is also chairman of the American Academy of Pediatrics Committee on Violence. "If it's hard for me, what is it like for a family trying to find services?"[22]

All too often when we neglect a young person, it is we good citizens who endanger ourselves.

Chapter 7

Conclusion

A 15-Point Plan

Charles Barkley, a forward for the Phoenix Suns basketball team, created quite a stir during the 1993 NBA playoffs when, in a Nike shoes commercial, he stated: "I am not a role model. I am not paid to be a role model. I am paid to wreak havoc on the basketball court. Parents should be role models. Just because I dunk a basketball doesn't mean I should raise your kids."

Barkley was both right and wrong. Yes, parents should be the primary mentors and models in the lives of their children. But, in the all-too-common absence of that, young people will seek out their own models. They may pick basketball players or rock musicians or actors. But even more unfortunate is when they select gang members, violent film and television characters or older youths in crisis as their role models. In the absence of positive role models—older responsible neighbors, teachers, clergy or relatives—children will still always select someone, anyone, on whom to model themselves. This because, as author Barry Lopez sadly noted, "A growing hallmark of Western culture is actual and psychological detachment of individuals from each other."[1] That void will be filled one way or the other.

If young people at an early age aren't surrounded with interested parents, cohesive communities or other positive role models who just fortunately are around, then we have to make proactive responses to intervene with programs of mentors and people to look up to.

To ignore this, and simply wait for youths to get into serious trouble before stepping in, is a prescription for disaster. To then step in and spend millions for harsh punishments and lengthy prison terms in adult prisons after a tragedy occurs, will provide little solace to the victims and their families. It will make us safer and be much cheaper to prevent deaths and crimes before they occur, than to spend millions after the fact.

A politician may cynically con the public by proposing prisons as the sole weapon in our arsenal against crime, but no society can hold itself together with prisons. If this were true, America would be the safest country on earth. Our prison population has risen sixfold in the last quarter century and is rapidly approaching the 2 million inmate mark. Do you feel safer? Our nation's prisons cost about $50 billion a year to run, but when you add in the price of police, medical bills, lost property, courts, insurance, etc., the price of crime in the United States is about half a trillion dollars a year—twice the size of the Pentagon's annual budget.[2] Wouldn't it make sense to take a small portion from the corrections budget and put it toward crime prevention instead? One older prisoner I spoke with, a veteran of many prison sentences, concludes that:

> When you say that these kids are beyond redemption, you don't have to do anything. See, you're just free to levy criticism all over the place, which is an easy thing to do. What's not so easy is finding a way to communicate with these youths and tapping into their potential.

This is particularly true in light of the research that shows us that prisons do not deter criminals from committing crimes. Most offenders, but particularly youthful offenders, commit crimes on impulse. They rarely think about the consequences but when they do, they assume they won't get caught. Where prisons are effective is in incapacitating criminals from committing crimes while they are actually in custody. This is why very violent young people should be held in custody. But so many facilities are crime schools, particularly the adult prisons where the rearrest rates for young people shortly after their release can be as high as 85 percent. This is why children should be kept out of adult prisons. But wherever children are held, more must be done with them to turn their lives around rather than just holding them, marking time, in these violent warehouses.

The thing that is so frustrating is that a great deal of research has been done and we really do know how to greatly cut youth crime. The causes of youth crime are complex and varied and don't lend themselves to just one cookie-cutter solution.

Surprisingly, the American public is way ahead of the politicians on the solution to crime. A number of surveys and polls conducted in the 1990s show that, contrary to what was thought, Americans don't fall for overly simplified solutions and are remarkably sophisticated in their opinions. They want an eclectic combination of tough penalties and, at the same time, prevention and rehabilitation. A poll released in March 1998 by the Justice Policy Institute and the Youth Law Center revealed that 74 percent of the public believes specific funding should be set aside for prevention programs.

Jean Johnson, in an article titled, "Americans' Views on Crime and Law Enforcement," which summarized a number of surveys in the September 1997 issue of the *National Institute of Justice Journal,* concluded:

> For youngsters in particular, people want the preventive approach— "stop them before they start, if you can." But for most Americans, the worst possible lesson for young offenders would be to not get caught or to receive the "slap on the wrist" of probation. . . . Most Americans are convinced that the young person who "gets away with it" is all the more likely to continue a life of crime.[3]

In other words, do everything you can do to prevent the child from getting into trouble, but if he or she does, then crack down on them with consequences. However, for those who do get incarcerated, they had better not be left there just warehoused, sitting around doing nothing. The American public believes in rehabilitation for most young people and wants to see young people on the wrong track turned around through education, counseling, substance abuse therapy and skills training.

In a survey published in May 1997 by Mass INC entitled "The Public's View," voters selected what they believed were the best crime control measures. The top-ranking choice was more community policing, followed by putting more emphasis and money on handling abused, neglected and problem children prior to the time they get into trouble. Third was drug testing for probationers and parolees and cracking down on those who flunk. Very low on the survey was the concept of incarcerating all violent juvenile offenders or mandatory prison sentences with no parole for juveniles. The survey reported:

> These results do not allow for an easy categorization of the public's view. In fact, they appear to represent a genuine receptivity to a blend of what are often too simplistically called "tough" crime control measures (e.g., measures focused on punishment, restitution and tighter checking on and control over probationers and parolees) with a number of measures that are often too simplistically labeled "soft" (e.g., measures focused on rehabilitation and prevention). "Blend" means just that—not "soft" as a *substitute* for "tough," or vice versa.[4]

The public's view is shared by those on the front lines of crime fight-ing—the police. That's what Salt Lake City Police Chief Ruben Ortega said as he argued for more after-school programs in an article appearing in the April 27, 1998 issue of *Newsweek* entitled, "It's 4:00 p.m. Do You Know Where Your Children Are?" Ortega stated: "We've come to the realization that we're not going to arrest our way out of this problem. If we don't change our strategy, we'll be complaining in five or 10 years about how bad crime has gotten again."

That's exactly what Denver Police Chief Donald L. Michaud said:

> Law enforcement professionals know that we cannot just arrest and incarcerate our way out of delinquency and crime. There must be a blend between enforcement and prevention. It is clear that meaningful prevention measures must start with early child care, and that must be followed up with well-crafted after-school programs designed to give kids the opportunity to succeed and make appropriate choices. Ade-quate funding for meaningful programs is key.

Art Reddy, vice president of the 8,000-member International Union of Police Associations, agrees, stating, "It's far cheaper to prevent children from getting in trouble than to arrest, prosecute and incarcerate them after the fact."[5]

His thoughts are echoed by former Buffalo Police Commissioner Gil Kerlikowske, who asserts, "We've got to tell the American people that we'll win the war on crime when we're ready to invest our time, energy and our tax dollars in America's most vulnerable before they become America's most wanted."[6]

In fact, in 1996, a national survey of police chiefs determined that 90 percent of them agreed with the following statement:

> America could sharply reduce crime if government invested more in programs to help children and youth get a good start by fully funding Head Start for infants and toddlers, preventing child abuse, providing parenting training for high-risk families, improving schools and pro-viding after school programs and mentoring. . . . [I]f America does not pay for greater investments in programs to help children and youth now, we will all pay far more later in crime, welfare and other costs.

When the results of this poll of police chiefs, commissioned by the Washington, D.C.,-based organization of police, prosecutors and crime victims called Fight Crime: Invest in Kids was announced on July 26, 1996, Patrick Murphy, the former police chief of New York City, Detroit, Wash-ington, D.C., and Syracuse, said, "When I hear someone say we can't afford investments in programs that help kids get the right start, I see more bright yellow crime scene tape, more prisons, hundreds of police officers and thousands of good men and women and boys and girls lying in pools of blood, more families crying. I've seen too much of that."

The bottom line for the solution to youth crime in America couldn't have been summed up more succinctly than the way Attorney General Janet Reno put it at the National Forum on Youth Violence in Chantilly, Virginia, on May 31, 1995. She said:

> I try to talk to a child when I go to a community, a child who has been in trouble, who is in trouble, who is in detention, and I ask, "What could we do to prevent the trouble in the first place?" The reply generally is, "Somebody to talk to, something to do in the afternoon, something to make me feel like I am making a difference." It's simple.[7]

It's essentially what one 16-year-old, whom I'll call Sam, who lives in a very tough urban neighborhood, told me. He goes to school, works, plays sports and works for a community youth organization. He says, "I'm involved in a lot of stuff. I don't have a chance to do bad things. Or maybe I see bad stuff and don't want to do it. Kids should just get involved and keep really busy. Just keep us busy. A lot of kids don't have stuff to do."

To elaborate and flesh out both Janet Reno's and Sam's concise advice, I propose the following 15 solutions to eradicate youth crime:

1. Anything at all that can shore up and strengthen the American family. This includes more jobs with a living wage for the working poor, housing and access to services such as counseling for families in trouble, parent support groups, family crisis intervention, parenting and family skills training and permanent planning for foster children.

2. Intervention in the lives of young people at a very young age, even as early as prior to birth through such things as parenting classes to their mothers and fathers along with adequate prenatal care to the mother.

   At the same time, the media, particularly television, should fulfill its remarkable promise and use its power to reach both children and teens with programs and messages designed to help them cope with life. This is in no way a call for censorship of all the meaningless and violent programs currently on today.

But it is preferable that the sheer volume of these be balanced with positive programs that would be helpful and empowering to kids out in the world.

3. No automatic transfer of juvenile offenders to adult courts and adult prisons no matter how monstrous the crime. A hearing should be held where the prosecution must prove to the judge that there is almost no reasonable likelihood that the child can be rehabilitated.

4. No minor should ever be held in an adult lockup, jail or prison in sight or sound, let alone physical contact with adult prisoners. Aside from the brutality that is frequently inflicted upon the children, spending time with older, more violent criminals is akin to a violence training school. We will all be more endangered upon their release.

5. The remaining large juvenile reform or training schools should be abandoned for smaller, community-based rehabilitation centers where youthful offenders can receive education, job training and counseling. These have proven much more effective in cutting down the rearrest rate upon release.

6. Whenever possible there should be alternative to incarceration programs for nonviolent youthful offenders where the youngsters can go to school, perform rigorous community service, participate in groups and receive either substance abuse or psychological counseling if necessary. These are dramatically cheaper, but more importantly they also cut down the recidivism rate and make us safer. Additionally, children should not be jailed for age status offenses such as being a truant or a runaway. Services, rather than jail, will be more effective.

7. Keep schools open all afternoon until early evening with programs for which there is no charge. These include recreation, tutoring, mentoring and cultural activities. Since this is the peak crime-committing period of the day for juveniles—after school, but before parents come home from work—this will keep youngsters motivated and busy. It will help the public remain safe.

8. Prohibit the death penalty for children.

9. Provide adequate day care for children. Ideally, very young children should be with a parent. But, if, realistically, that is not possible, then this is preferable to either having them remain alone or spending too many hours of one's most formative years

merely being warehoused in a poor, unstimulating arrangement.

10. Although adults have the right to own a gun, there should be childproof locks on all of them; mandatory gun storage laws so adults will be liable if children get possession of their guns; no semiautomatic or automatic weapons since an offender is able to kill too many people before he can be stopped, and tougher gun registration laws which still permit people to own them. There should be more programs like the renowned Boston Gun Project which shattered all stereotypes that with 200 million guns out there in the public, any kid could steal a gun or get one by way of another state with less stringent gun controls. Through a variety of innovative methods, they found they could much more easily track down dealers and purchasers. But more importantly, they attacked things on the demand side. They found that since most youths carry guns for protection out of fear, if they cracked down on violent individuals and lessened the climate of fear, the number of guns went way down. This program helped to virtually end gun violence in what had only shortly before reached nearly epidemic proportions.

11. Faith-based programs giving children some kind of direction, spiritual purpose and guidance have also proven to lower the rate of youth crime.

12. When students bring weapons to school or engage in particularly assaultive behavior, the dilemma is this—yes, they should be removed from the school in order to protect the safety of students and teachers. But how does it help us take a troubled, potentially dangerous kid and just suspend or expel him—in other words, reward him by telling him he now doesn't have to go to school? Now he'll be free all day (typically without parents around), without direction, without any efforts being made to change help him turn his life around, and become an increasing danger to all of us. It is the worst solution for public safety. There is an alternative to either one of these two untenable actions—expulsion or letting him stay. Instead, the student should be removed from the school, but not just sent out on his own. He or she should go into an intensive treatment program specifically designed for weapons-toting juveniles. This is not some liberal idea. Police overwhelmingly back it because where it's been used so far, it has been so effective and the recidivism rates of

these troubled, dangerous students went into a freefall. In Boston, the Counseling and Intervention Center has only a 9 percent recidivism rate while the Safe Alternative and Violence Education program in San Jose, California, has a similar drop in these kids ever again being caught with a weapon.

13. Comunity policing, where individual police officers become known fixtures in the neighborhood and work together with the community, has been responsible for astonishing drops in crime. Ironically, this crime reduction occurs without more arrests or incarcerations. Community policing is cheaper and makes us safer because it results in crime prevention—not merely after-the-fact punishments.

14. Strategies must be developed to anticipate and intercept those youths who may not be suspected as potentially violent, yet commit horrifically brutal acts such as the infamous series of mass murders at schools in 1997 and 1998. Despite the tremendous coverage of these savage acts, they are extremely rare. Still, after each of these incidents, it is almost always acknowledged that these youthful killers actually left numerous clues, whether on their bedroom walls or in the threats they made in the schoolyard. Parents must be educated to recognize these clues, and schools must do the same and move quickly.

15. Mentoring programs, both public and private, should be the cornerstone of youth crime prevention since, although the family is best, if that is not possible, other supportive adults must be present in the lives of the young.

It is the fact that we actually do know what causes youth crime which gives us such room for hope. "What this whole superpredator argument misses is that [increasing teen violence] is not some inexorable natural progression," argues David Kennedy, a senior researcher at Harvard's Kennedy School of Government. "It's a product of very specific dynamics."[8]

We know what to do.

The previously cited 1997 Chicago study on the causes of crime and violence which found the very lowest violence in "cohesive communities" where neighbors stuck their heads out their windows and minded each others' business gave its chief author, Dr. Felton Earls, such room for hope. "Our study strikes kind of an optimistic note," says Earls. "There's something to work with here."[9]

No less a cause for optimism is the electrifying success of community policing—the cop walking the beat. For example, New York City's murder rate dropped an astounding 70 percent during a five-year period during the 1990s while, at the same time the rise in their incarceration rate was the lowest in the Northeast and the fifth lowest in the country—one tenth the national average.[10] This is absolute proof that only locking up more people as the sole strategy for crime fighting doesn't work. Prevention does.

"Every place that I have examined where community policing has occurred, there has been a dramatic drop in crime, particularly violent crime," said University of Pennsylvania criminologist Marvin Wolfgang.[11]

We know what to do. Barry Krisberg of the National Council on Crime and Delinquency resounds with optimism when he notes that violence prone youths of the future "are now three to five years old. We could change the crime projections if we wanted."[12]

We must fiercely champion those weakest among us—our littlest Americans—from those who would wreck them. And do it neighborhood by neighborhood, block by block.

Intervening in the lives of young people before they get into trouble, rather than ignoring them and then spending money to lock them up, is the best route to making us safer. It is the very best our culture can do. We should not beat up on and continue to make war on children because, even from a pragmatic and totally selfish point of view, it will, in the final analysis, only endanger us.

We know exactly what works to eliminate most crime . . . to get in touch with what President Lincoln once referred to as the better angels of our nature. Not to do it would be shameful.

Notes

Preface

1. Speech at the American Enterprise Institute's Francis Boyer Annual Dinner, December 4, 1997, as televised on C-SPAN.
2. Speech at National Conference on Violence, Boston, March 27, 1998.
3. Robert Coles, *The Moral Intelligence of Children* (New York: Random House, 1997).

Chapter 1
Introduction and Overview: Children as the Enemy

1. Ted Gest with Victoria Pope, "Crime Time Bomb," *U.S. News and World Report* (March 25, 1996), p. 30.
2. Howard Spivak and Deborah Prothrow-Stith, "Stop Demonizing Our Youth," *Boston Globe* (July 27, 1997), p. 14; Richard Lacayo, "Teen Crime," *Time* (July 21, 1997), p. 26, 29); Ted Gest with Victoria Pope, "Crime Time Bomb," *U.S. News and World Report* (March 25, 1996), p. 30; James Alan Fox, *Trends in Juvenile Justice: A Report to the United States Attorney General on Current and Future Rates of Juvenile Offending* (Washington, D.C.: Bureau of Justice Statistics, March 1996), p. 2; Laura Meckler, "Drug Use Up Among Young Adults, US Report Finds," Associated Press (August 7, 1997); Darlene Superville, "Youth Cite Rise in Drugs," Associated Press (August 14, 1997).
3. James Traub, "The Criminals of Tomorrow," *New Yorker* (November 4, 1996), p. 52.
4. Most Adults Believe Children Lack Values, Poll Suggests," Associated Press (June 27, 1997).
5. Walter Kirn, "Crybaby Boomers," *New York Times* (July 2, 1997).

6. Anna J. Bray, "Who Are the Victims of Crime?," *Investor's Business Daily* (December 12, 1994), p. A-1.
7. Lisa Stansky, "Age of Innocence," *ABA Journal* (November, 1996), p. 66.
8. *Ibid.*, p. 61.
9. John Siegenthaler, "Interview with Joseph McNamara," MSNBC News (June 11, 1997).
10. Michael J. Sniffen, "Arrest Rate for Juveniles Dropped in '95," Associated Press (August 9, 1996); Gary Fields, "Youth Violent Crime Falls 9.2%, *USA Today* (October 3, 1997); Michael J. Sniffen, "Youth Crime Fell in '97, Reno Says," Associated Press (November 20, 1998).
11. "Despite String of Shootings, U.S. Says School Crime is Down." Associated Press (October 15, 1998); Elizabeth Donohue, Vincent Schiraldi, and Jason Ziedenberg, "School House Hype: School Shootings and the Real Risks Kids Face in America," *Justice Policy Institute Policy Report* (Washington, D.C.: Justice Policy Institute, July, 1998), pp. 4–5.
12. Gary Fields, "Youth Violent Crime Falls 9.2%," *USA Today* (October 3, 1997), p. 1A; Vincent Schiraldi and Mark Kappelhoff, "As Crime Drops Experts Backpedal—Where Have the 'Super Predators' Gone?" *JINN* (May 2, 1997); Steven A. Holmes, "It's Awful! It's Terrible! It's . . . Never Mind," *New York Times* (July 6, 1997), p. 3; Eric Lotke and Vincent Schiraldi, *An Analysis of Juvenile Homicides: Where They Occur and the Effectiveness of Adult Court Intervention* (Washington, D.C.: National Center on Institutions and Alternatives and Center on Criminal and Juvenile Justice, 1996).
13. Beth Carter, "Federal Juvenile Proposals in Perspective," *Crime & Politics in the 1990's* (Washington, D.C.: Campaign for an Effective Crime Policy, May, 1997), p. 3; Lori Montgomery, "A Divide on What's Fueling Youth Crime: Teens Raised for Violence or Just Well Armed," *Philadelphia Inquirer* (July 28, 1996), p. 1.
14. Vincent Schiraldi and Mark Kappelhoff, "As Crime Drops Experts Backpedal—Where Have the 'Super Predators' Gone?" *JINN* (May 2, 1997), p. 3.
15. Fox Butterfield, " States Revamping Youth Crime Laws," *New York Times* (May 12, 1996), p. 1.
16. Howard N. Snyder, Melissa Sickmund and Eileen Poe-Yamagata, *Juvenile Offenders and Victims: 1996 Update on Violence* (Washington, D. C.: Office of Juvenile Justice and Delinquency Prevention, June 1997).
17. Meg Greenfield, "Sexual Harasser?" *Newsweek* (October 7, 1998), p. 90.

18. David Broder, "Funding Prevention Still Fights Crime Best," syndicated column (July 28, 1996).
19. *Ibid.*
20. Lisa Stansky, "Age of Innocence," *ABA Journal* (November, 1996) p. 62.
21. *Ibid.,* p. 63.
22. *Ibid.,* p. 62.
23. "New Poll of Police Chiefs Shows Overwhelming Agreement," press release (Washington, D.C.: Fight Crime: Invest in Kids, July 26, 1996).
24. Jonathan Alter, "Taking the Short View," *Newsweek* (May 5, 1997), p. 32.
25. President Clinton speaking at the U.S. Justice Department Symposium on Youth Violence held in Boston, June 11, 1997.
26. Robert Coles, *The Moral Intelligence of Children* (New York: Random House, 1997), p. 58.
27. Jack Levin and Heather Beth Johnson, "Preventing Student Violence," *Boston Globe* (September 23, 1997), p. A 13.
28. Gil Garcetti, "In Their Own Words," *NBC Nightly News* (May 9, 1997).
29. Editorial Board, "A System Sentencing Itself to Despair," *Los Angeles Times* (April 25, 1993), p. M4.
30. "New Poll of Police Chiefs Shows Overwhelming Agreement," press release (Washington, D.C.: Fight Crime: Invest in Kids, July 26, 1996).

Chapter 2
A Coming Youth Crime Wave by a Nation of Sociopaths

1. "Most Adults Believe Children Lack Values, One Poll Suggests," Associated Press (June 27, 1997).
2. Logan Pearsall Smith, *All Trivia: Trivia, More Trivia, Afterthoughts, Last Words* (New York: Harcourt Brace, 1945).
3. Maria Eftimiades, Susan Christian Goulding, Anthony Duignan-Cabrera, Don Campbell and Jane Sims Podesta, "Why Are Kids Killing?" *People* (June 23, 1997), p. 46.
4. John Ellement, "Teenager Convicted in Dorchester Slaying, but a Mother's Pain Lingers," *Boston Globe* (November 27, 1997), p. B 3.
5. Howard Spivak and Deborah Prothrow-Stith, "Stop Demonizing Our Youth," *Boston Globe* (July 27, 1997), p. 14; Richard Lacayo, "Teen

Crime," *Time* (July 21, 1997), pp. 26, 29; Ted Gest with Victoria Pope, "Crime Time Bomb," *U.S. News and World Report* (March 25, 1996), p. 30; James Alan Fox, *Trends in Juvenile Justice: A Report to the United States Attorney General on Current and Future Rates of Juvenile Offending* (Washington, D.C.: Bureau of Justice Statistics, March, 1996), p. 2; Michael Grunwald, "Stopping the Cycle: Gains Found in Therapy for Young Sex Offenders," *Boston Globe* (January 19, 1998).

6. "U.S. Children Face High Risk of Violent Death," CNN Interactive web site (February 7, 1997).

7. Joyce Purnick, "Youth Crime: Should Laws Be Tougher," *New York Times* (May 9, 1997), p. B1; Howard N. Snyder, Melissa Sickmund and Eileen Poe-Yamagata, *Juvenile Offenders and Victims: 1996 Update on Violence* (Washington, D. C.: Office of Juvenile Justice and Delinquency Prevention, June, 1997), p. 15.

8. Howard N. Snyder, Melissa Sickmund and Eileen Poe-Yamagata, *Juvenile Offenders and Victims: 1996 Update on Violence* (Washington, D. C.: Office of Juvenile Justice and Delinquency Prevention, June, 1997), p. 15.

9. Melissa Rossi, "They Kill," *George* (June/July, 1996).

10. Bret Easton Ellis, "Why Kids Are Ruining America," *George* (June/July, 1996).

11. President Clinton speaking at the Justice Department Symposium on Violent Youth Crime, Boston, June 11, 1997.

12. Michael J. Sniffen, "Arrest Rate for Juveniles Dropped in '95," Associated Press (August 9, 1996); Gary Fields, "Youth Violent Crime Falls 9.2%," *USA Today* (October 3, 1997), p. 1A; Michael J. Sniffen, "Youth Crime Fell in '97, Reno Says," Associated Press (November 20, 1997). Howard N. Snyder, *Juvenile Arrests 1995* (Washington, D.C.: Office of Juvenile Justice and Delinquency Prevention, February, 1997), p. 2; Patricia King and Andrew Murr, "A Son Who Spun Out of Control," *Newsweek* (June 1, 1998), p. 33.

13. Gary Fields, "Youth Violent Crime Falls 9.2 %," *USA Today* (October 3, 1997), p. 1A; Vincent Schiraldi and Mark Kappelhoff, "As Crime Drops Experts Backpedal—Where Have the 'Superpredators' Gone?" *JINN* (May 2, 1997); Steven A. Holmes, "It's Awful! It's Terrible! It's . . . Never Mind," *New York Times* (July 6, 1997), p. 3; Eric Lotke and Vincent Schiraldi, *An Analysis of Juvenile Homicides: Where They Occur and the Effectiveness of Adult Court Intervention* (Washington, D.C.: National Center on Institutions and Alternatives and Center on Criminal and Juvenile Justice, 1996).

14. Fox Butterfield, "After 10 Years, Juvenile Crime Begins to Drop," *New York Times* (August 9, 1996), p. A 25.

15. Darrell K. Gilliard and Allen J. Beck, *Prisoners in 1997* (Washington, D.C.: Bureau of Justice Statistics, August, 1998), p. 3; Michael J. Sniffen, "U.S. Prison Population Up, Report Finds," Associated Press (August 3, 1998); Dolores Kong, "Few Reliable Signs to Predict Youth Violence," *Boston Globe* (October 3, 1997), p. B6.

16. Debra Rosenberg and Evan Thomas, " 'I Didn't Do Anything,' " *Newsweek* (November 10, 1997), p. 60.

17. Daniel Pedersen and Sarah Van Boven, "Tragedy in a Small Place," *Newsweek* (December 15, 1997), p. 30; Ted Bridis, "A Day Later, Teary Kentucky Students Return to Class," Associated Press (December 3, 1997).

18. Ted Robert Gurr, *Violence in America, Vol. 1: The History of Crime* (Newbury Park, CA: Sage Publishing, 1989), pp. 1–79; Edward L. Ayers, *Vengeance and Justice: Crime and Punishment in the Nineteenth Century American South* (New York: Oxford University Press, 1984).

19. Iver Peterson, "In Spate of Killings, County Asks, 'Why?,' " *New York Times* (July 20, 1998), p. A17.

20. Ellen O'Brien, "Arkansas Cases Reopens Child Justice Debate," *Boston Globe* (March 27, 1998), p. A24.

21. Maria Eftimiades, Susan Christian Goulding, Anthony Duignan-Cabrera, Don Campbell and Jane Sims Podesta, "Why Are Kids Killing?" *People* (June 23, 1997), p. 53

22. "A Chilling Shift in Profiles of Those Who Kill Newborns," Knight-Ridder Service (November 27, 1997).

23. "Feuding Girls Get a Courthouse Warning," Associated Press (December 2, 1997).

24. Richard Louv, "Blaming Kids for Crime," Kids Campaign web site (November 30, 1997).

25. "Juveniles Could Face Chain Gangs," Associated Press (August 31, 1997).

26. Fagan, Schiff and Orden, *The Comparative Impacts of Juvenile and Criminal Court Sanctions on Adolescent Felony Offenders* (Washington, D.C.: National Institute of Justice, 1991); Rudman, Hartstone, Fagan and Moore, "Violent Youth in Adult Court: Process and Punishment," p. 32, *Crime and Delinquency* (1986), p. 75.

27. Richard Louv, "Blaming Kids for Crime," Kids Campaign web site (November 30, 1997).

28. Beth Carter, "Federal Juvenile Proposals in Perspective," *Crime and Politics in the 1990's* (Washington, D.C.: Campaign for an Effective Crime Policy, May 1997), p. 3; Lori Montgomery, "A Divide on What's Fueling Youth Crime: Teens Raised for Violence or Just Well Armed," *Philadelphia Inquirer* (July 28, 1996), p. 1.

29. Heather Knight, "Report on Youth Says Education, Health and Crime Up," *Los Angeles Times* Syndicate (July 3, 1997); Richard Chacon, "College Freshmen Called More Detached," *Boston Globe* (January 12, 1998), p. A4; *Facts at a Glance* (Washington, D.C.: Child Trends, Inc., October 1996); Laura Meckler, "Teenage Birth Rates Drop Nationwide," Associated Press (May 1, 1998); Beth Gardiner, "Study Cites Sharp Drop in Teen Pregnancy Rate," Associated Press (October 16, 1998)

30. N. Zill, K.A. Moore, C.W. Nord and T. Stiff, *Welfare Mothers as Potential Employees: A Statistical Profile Based on National Survey Date* (Washington, D.C.: Child Trends, Inc., 1991), p. 6; *Facts at a Glance* (Washington, D.C.: Child Trends, Inc., October, 1996). *KIDS COUNT Date Book: 1993, State Profiles of Child Well-Being* (Baltimore: Annie E. Casey Foundation, 1993), p.13.

31. Laura Meckler, "Poverty in U.S. a 'Revolving Door,' Census Study Finds," Associated Press (August 10, 1998).

32. *Survey of State Prison Inmates, 1991* (Washington, D.C.: U.S. Department of Justice, March, 1993); Anna Bray, "Who Are the Victims of Crime," *Investor's Business Daily* (December 12, 1994), p. A1; Patrick F. Fagan, "The Breakdown of Families Causes Violence," *Violence: Opposing Viewpoints* (San Diego: Greenhaven Press, 1996), p. 86; Grogger, "Crime: The Influence of Early Childbearing on the Cost of Incarceration," *Kids Having Kids: Economic Costs and Social Consequences of Teen Pregnancy*, ed. Rebecca Maynard (Washington, D.C.: Urban Institute Press, 1997), "Murder Risk High in Babies Born to Teens," Associated Press (October 22, 1998).

33. Robert M. Goerge and Boong Joo Lee, "Abuse and Neglect: Effects of Early Childbearing on Abuse and Neglect of Children," *Kids Having Kids: Economic Costs and Social Consequences of Teen Pregnancy*, ed. Rebecca Maynard (Washington D.C.: Urban Institute Press, 1997).

34. Patrick F. Fagan, "The Breakdown of Families Causes Violence," *Violence: Opposing Viewpoints* (San Diego: Greenhaven Press, 1996), p. 91.

35. *Ibid.*

36. Jonathan Alter, "It's 4:00 p.m. Do You Know Where Your Children Are?," *Newsweek* (April 27, 1998), pp. 28–33.

37. Sandy Coleman, "Q & A with Jack Levin, Director, Program for the Study of Violence," *Boston Globe* (October 5, 1997), p. 2—City.

38. "Major Cities Police Chiefs Organization Calls for Child Care, After School Programs," press release (Washington, D.C.: Fight Crime: Invest in Kids, February 19, 1998).

39. Barbara Kantrowitz, "Off to a Good Start," *Newsweek* (Special Issue, Spring/Summer, 1997), p. 9; LynNell Hancock and Pat Wingert, "The New Preschool," *Newsweek* (Special Issue, Spring/Summer, 1997), p. 36.

40. Roberta Bergman, "Letters: Putting Kids First," *Newsweek* (November 24, 1998), p. 18.

41. LynNell Hancock and Pat Wingert, "The New Preschool," *Newsweek* (Special Issue, Spring/Summer, 1997), p. 37.

42. Albert R. Hunt, "John Kerry and a Children's Crusade," *Wall Street Journal* (April 16, 1998), p. A 23; Marie T. Oates and Rosemary Jordano, "Silent Crisis of Child Care," *Boston Globe* (November 2, 1998), p. A19.

43. Ellen Goodman, "Rethinking Child Care: 'There's Gotta Be a Better Way,' " *Boston Globe* (January 15, 1998), p. A23.

44. Mimi Hall, "Conservatives: Clinton Broke Vow on Spending," *USA Today* (January 8, 1998), p. 6A.

45. George Will, "The EOBG Marches On," *Newsweek* (January 19, 1998), p. 72.

46. *The Economic Report of the President Transmitted to the Congress* (1995), pp. 178–179; "Welfare Reform Seen from a Children's Perspective," *Child Poverty News & Issues* Vol. 5, No. 2, 1995), p. 2; "Washington to the States: Ready or Not, Here It Comes," *The National Association of Child Advocates Multi-State Children's Budget Watch Report—1996* (Washington, D.C.: NACA, November 20, 1996), p. 3; Timothy Smeeding, "U.S. Poverty and Income Security Policy in a Cross National Perspective," Luxembourg Income Study, working paper 70 (October 1991); Deborah Mathis, "Children in Poverty," *USA Today* (July 10, 1998), p. 3A.

47. Barbara Vobejda, "Census: Income Up, Poverty Declines," *Washington Post* Syndicate (September 25, 1998).

48. James Wilson, Speaking at the Francis Boyer Award Dinner of the American Enterprise Institute, UCLA, Los Angeles (December 4, 1997).

49. Randolph T. Holhut, "Teen Violence: The Myths and the Realities," The Written Word On-Line Journal (1996).

50. Scott Stossel, "The Man Who Counts the Killings," *Atlantic Monthly* (May, 1997), pp. 90, 96.
51. Theodore Fenn, "A Nation Gone Delinquent," *Washington Ripple* Vol. VIII, No. III (May 1994).
52. John Stamper, "TV Violence Without Consequences Has Researchers Upset," *Saint Paul Pioneer Press* (April 17, 1998), p. 3A.
53. Howard Kurtz, "Murder Rates Drop, But Coverage Soars," *Washington Post* Syndicate (August 13, 1997).
54. Scott Stossel, "The Man Who Counts the Killings," *Atlantic Monthly* (May 1997), p. 94.
55. Howard Kurtz, "Murder Rates Drop, But Coverage Soars," *Washington Post* Syndicate (August 13, 1997); Derrick Z. Jackson, "No Wonder We're Afraid of Youth," *Boston Globe* (September 10, 1997), p. A15.
56. *Ibid.*
57. John Leland, "Violence Reel to Real," *Newsweek* (December 11, 1995), p. 11.
58. "Violence: Call It Lethal Delivery," *Newsweek* (September 22, 1997), p. 10.
59. Sharon Begley, "How to Build a Baby's Brain," *Newsweek* (Special Issue, Spring/Summer, 1997), p. 31.
60. Fran Lebowitz, "Fran Lebowitz on Age," *Vanity Fair* (January, 1998), p. 95.
61. Colin Powell, "I Wasn't Left to Myself," *Newsweek* (April 27, 1998), p. 32.
62. Dolores Kong, "Study Shows Cohesiveness Curbs Neighborhood Violence," *Boston Globe* (August 15, 1997), p. A9.
63. Richard Rodriguez, "The Coming Mayhem," *Los Angeles Times* (January 21, 1996), p. M1.
64. Jonathan Alter, "It's 4:00 P.M. Do You Know Where Your Children Are?," *Newsweek* (April 27, 1998), pp. 28–33.
65. Hillary Rodham Clinton, *It Takes a Village* (New York: Simon and Schuster, 1996), p. 12.
66. "Quotes from Bob Dole," Republican National Committee web site (August 1996).
67. Kerby Anderson and Penna Dexter, "Special Report: Hillary Clinton's Book Exposed as a Smokescreen," International Christian media web site, (December 16, 1997).

68. James Wilson, Speaking at the Francis Boyer Award Dinner of the American Enterprise Institute, UCLA, Los Angeles (December 4, 1997).

69. Margaret Baird, "Letters: Putting Kids First," *Newsweek* (November 24, 1998), p. 18.

70. James Carroll, "When Families Shatter," *Boston Globe* (June 3, 1997), p. A 17.

71. Jennifer Wynn, "Letters: Lobbying for Love," *New York* (June 16, 1997), p. 8.

72. Jennifer Vogel, "Violent Juveniles Should Not Be Tried as Adults," *Violence: Opposing Viewpoints* (San Diego: Greenhaven Press, 1996), p. 190.

73. *National Summary of Injury Mortality Data, 1987–1994* (Atlanta, GA: Centers for Disease Control and Prevention, National Center for Injury Prevention and Control, 1996); John Gibeaut, "Nobody's Child," *ABA Journal* (December 1997), p. 45; A.J. Sedlak and D.D. Broadhurst, *Third National Incidence Study of Child Abuse and Neglect* (Washington, D.C.: U.S. Department of Health and Human Services, National Center on Child Abuse and Neglect, September 1996); Terence Thornberry, "Violent Families and Youth Violence," *Fact Sheet* (Washington. D.C.: U.S. Department of Justice, December 1994); Craig A. Perkins, "Age Patterns of Victims of Serious Violent Crime," *Special Report* (Washington, D.C.: U.S. Bureau of Justice Statistics, September 1997), p. 1; Howard N. Snyder, Melissa Sickmund and Eileen Poe-Yamagata, *Juvenile Offenders and Victims: 1996 Update on Violence* (Washington, D. C.: Office of Juvenile Justice and Delinquency Prevention, June 1997), p. 14; "Rate of Suicide Doubles Since '80 for Black Youth," Associated Press (March 20, 1998); "Study Details Teens' Troubles," Reuters (November 13, 1998)

74. John McCormick, "Chicago Hope," *Newsweek* (March 24, 1997), p. 68.

75. John Gibeaut, "Lucas Deserved Better," *ABA Journal* (December 1997), p. 52.

76. Sharon Begley, "How to Build a Baby's Brain," *Newsweek* (Special Issue, Spring/Summer, 1997), pp. 31–32; Debra Rosenberg, "Raising a Moral Child," *Newsweek* (Special Issue, Spring/Summer, 1997), p. 93.

77. Dr. James Gilligan, "Why Young People Are the Main Victims and the Main Perpetrators of Violence Toward Each Other," *Speech* (Boston:

Third Annual National Conference on Young People, November 6, 1997).

78. *Uniform Crime Reports—1994* (Washington, D.C.: FBI, 1995).

79. John J. DiIulio Jr., "A Lack of Moral Guidance Causes Juvenile Crime and Violence," *Juvenile Crime: Opposing Viewpoints* (San Diego: Greenhaven Press, 1997), p. 112.

80. Vincent Schiraldi and Mark Kappelhoff, "As Crime Drops Experts Backpedal—Where Have the 'Super Predators' Gone?" *JINN* (May 2, 1997).

81. Robert E. Shepherd Jr., "How the Media Misrepresents Juvenile Policies," *ABA Criminal Justice* (Winter 1998), p. 37.

82. Steven A. Holmes, "It's Awful! It's Terrible! It's . . . Never Mind," *New York Times* (July 6, 1997), p. 3; Eric Lotke and Vincent Schiraldi, *An Analysis of Juvenile Homicides: Where They Occur and the Effectiveness of Adult Court Intervention* (Washington, D.C.: National Center on Institutions and Alternatives and Center on Criminal and Juvenile Justice, 1996).

83. Thomas V. Brady, *Measuring What Matters Most: Part One: Measures of Crime, Fear and Disorder* (Washington, D.C.: National Institute of Justice, December 1996), p. 3.

84. Debra Rosenberg, "Raising a Moral Child," *Newsweek* (Special Issue, Spring/Summer, 1997), p. 92.

Chapter 3
The Everydayness of Firearms

1. Ted Bridis, "Fourteen Year Old Opens Fire; Three Girls Dead," Associated Press (December 2, 1997).

2. Philip J. Cook and Jens Ludwig, "Guns in America: National Survey on Private Ownership and Use of Firearms," *Research in Brief* (Washington, D.C.: National Institute of Justice, May 1997), p. 1.

3. Vincent Schiraldi, "Making Sense of Juvenile Homicides in America," *ABA Criminal Justice* (Summer 1998), p. 63.

4. "U.S. Tops in Gun Deaths, CDC Says," Associated Press (April 17, 1998).

5. "Overview: School Shootings," *New York Times* (March 27, 1998), p. A14.

6. "Public Schools Expelled 6,000 Caught with Guns, Report Says," Associated Press (May 9, 1998).

7. Stuart Greenbaum, "Kids and Guns: From Playgrounds to Battle-grounds," *Juvenile Justice* (Washington, D.C.: Office of Juvenile Justice and Delinquency Prevention, September 1997), p. 3; Howard N. Snyder, Melissa Sickmund and Eileen Poe-Yamagata, "Juvenile Offenders and Victims: 1996 Update on Violence," *Statistics Summary* (Washington, D.C.: Office of Juvenile Justice and Delinquency Prevention, February 1996), pp. 2, 24.

8. R. McEnery, *Today's Schoolyard Bully Just Might Be Armed* (Asbury Park, NJ: Asbury Park Press, February 28, 1996); "Teen Violent Death Rate," *1996 KIDS COUNT Summary and Findings* (Baltimore: Annie E. Casey Foundation, 1996); James Alan Fox, *Supplementary Homicide Reports 1976–1994* (Washington, D.C.: FBI machine readable data file, 1996); Glen Johnson, "Safety Efforts Tied to Drop in Child Deaths," Associated Press (May 5, 1998); Doug Levy, "Injury Deaths Down, Gun Homicides Up Among Kids," *USA Today* (February 29, 1996), p. 10D; "Homicide Rate in Young Men Studied," Associated Press (October 14, 1994); Howard N. Snyder, Melissa Sickmund and Eileen Poe-Yamagata, "Juvenile Offenders and Victims: 1996 Update on Violence," *Statistics Summary* (Washington, D.C.: Office of Juvenile Justice and Delinquency Prevention, February 1996), pp. 21.

9. "Homicide Rate in Young Men Studied," Associated Press (October 14, 1994).

10. "Gunshot Wounds Called Epidemic," Associated Press (February 3, 1998).

11. James C. Howell, "Youth Gang Drug Trafficking and Homicide: Policy and Program Implications," *Juvenile Justice* (Washington, D.C.: Office of Juvenile Justice and Delinquency Prevention, December 1997), p. 12.

12. S. H. Decker and B. Van Winkle, *Life in the Gang: Family, Friends and Violence* (New York: Cambridge University Press, 1996), pp. 185–186.

13. James C. Howell, "Gangs," *Fact Sheet #12* (Washington, D.C.: Office of Juvenile Justice and Delinquency Prevention, April 1994).

14. Lori Montgomery, "A Divide on What's Fueling Youth Crime: Teens Raised for Violence or Just Well Armed," *Philadelphia Inquirer* (July 28, 1996), p. 1

15. Wendy Kaminer, "Crime and Community," *Atlantic Monthly* (May 1994), p. 120.

16. "Weapon-Carrying Among High School Students—United States, 1990," *Morbidity and Mortality Weekly Report* Vol. 40, No. 40 (October

11, 1991) pp. 681–684; "Behaviors Related to Unintentional and Intentional Injuries Among High School Students—United States, 1991," *Morbidity and Mortality Weekly Report* Vol. 41, No. 41 (October 16, 1992), pp. 760–767; "41 Percent of Large U.S. Cities in Poll Report Serious School Violence," Associated Press (November 2, 1994); Melissa Sickmund, Howard N. Snyder and Eileen Poe-Yamagata, *Juvenile Offenders and Victims: 1997 Update on Violence* (Washington, D.C.: National Center for Juvenile Justice, August 1997), p. 14.

17. Brian MacQuarrie, "Saugus Mourns Boy Killed by Gunshot," *Boston Globe* (December 30, 1998), p. B10.

18. Tom Farmer, "Teen Who Shot Twin Makes Plea for Safety," *Boston Herald* (January 12, 1998), p. 18; Thomas Grillo, "Wareham Gun Tragedy Called an Accident," *Boston Globe* (January 12, 1998), p. B2; Paul E. Kandarian, "In a Flash, Wareham Twin Loses His Life," *Boston Globe* (January 12, 1998), p. B2

19. Philip J. Cook and Jens Ludwig, "Guns in America: National Survey on Private Ownership and Use of Firearms," *Research in Brief* (Washington, D.C.: National Institute of Justice, May 1997), p. 7.

20. Melissa Sickmund, Howard N. Snyder and Eileen Poe-Yamagata, *Juvenile Offenders and Victims: 1997 Update on Violence* (Washington, D.C.: National Center for Juvenile Justice, August 1997), p. 3.

21. *Ibid.*

22. Stuart Greenbaum, "Kids and Guns: From Playgrounds to Battlegrounds," *Juvenile Justice* (Washington, D.C.: Office of Juvenile Justice and Delinquency Prevention, September 1997), p. 4.

23. A. L. Kellermann, F.P. Rivara, G. Soames, D.T. Reay, J. Francisco, G. Banton, J. Prodzinski, C. Fligner and B. B. Hackman, "Suicide in the Home in Relationship to Gun Ownership," *New England Journal of Medicine* (1992), pp. 467–472.

24. Doug Levy, "Injury Deaths Down, Gun Homicides Up Among Kids," *USA Today* (February 29, 1996), p. 10D.

25. "Fatal and Non-Fatal Suicide Attempts Among Adolescents—Oregon 1988–1993," *Morbidity and Mortality Weekly Report* Vol. 44, No. 16 (April 28, 1994).

26. "Verbatim: Crime in America With Steve Roberts," U.S. News Online on CompuServe (March 15, 1994).

27. Michael Males, *Scapegoat Generation: America's War on Adolescents* (Monroe, ME: Common Courage Press, 1996).

28. Howard N. Snyder, Melissa Sickmund and Eileen Poe-Yamagata, *Juvenile Offenders and Victims: 1996 Update on Violence* (Washington, D.C.: National Center for Juvenile Justice, February, 1997), p. 2; Lawrence A. Greenfeld *et al.*, *Violence By Intimates: Bureau of Justice Statistics Factbook* (Washington, D.C.: U.S. Department of Justice, March 1998), p. 19.

29. *A Survey of Experiences, Perceptions and Apprehensions About Guns Among Young People in America* (New York: Louis Harris and Associates, 1993).

30. John Gibeaut, "Gang Busters," *ABA Journal* (January 1998), p. 66; G. David Curry, Richard A. Ball and Scott H. Decker, "Estimating the National Scope of Gang Crime from Law Enforcement Data," *Research in Brief* (Washington, D.C.: National Institute of Justice, August 1996), p. 2; Michael J. Sniffen, "Study Finds Increased Violence, Gang Involvement at Schools," Associated Press (April 13, 1998).

31. John Gibeaut, "Gang Busters," *ABA Journal* (January 1998), p. 65.

32. R. Block and C. R. Block, "Street Gang Crime in Chicago," *Research in Brief* (Washington, D.C.: National Institute of Justice, 1993), p. 7.

33. James C. Howell, "Gangs," *Fact Sheet #12* (Washington, D.C.: Office of Juvenile Justice and Delinquency Prevention, April 1994).

34. John Gibeaut, "Gang Busters," *ABA Journal* (January 1998), pp. 64–65.

35. *Ibid.*

36. James C. Howell, "Gangs," *Fact Sheet #12* (Washington, D.C.: Office of Juvenile Justice and Delinquency Prevention, April 1994).

37. Claire Johnson, Barbara Webster and Edward Connors, "Prosecuting Gangs: A National Assessment," *Research in Brief* (Washington, D.C.: National Institute of Justice, February 1995), p. 1.

38. James D. Wright, Joseph F. Sheley and M. Dwayne Smith, "Kids, Guns and Killing Fields," *Society* Vol. 30, No. 1 (1992), pp. 88–89.

39. Dolores Kong, "States Loses Funds to Track Gun Injuries," *Boston Globe* (September 25, 1997), p. B2; *Crime and Justice Trends in the District of Columbia* (Washington, D.C.: National Council on Crime and Delinquency and the District of Columbia Office of Grants Management and Development, Fall 1997); Douglas S. Weil and Rebecca Knox, *Evaluating the Impact of Virginia's "One-Gun-a-Month Law"* (Washington, D.C.: Center to Prevent Handgun Violence, 1995), p. 1; Blaine Harden, "Boston's Approach to Juvenile Crime Encircles Youth, Reduces Slayings," *Washington Post* (October 23, 1997), p. A3; "Gun Laws Are Linked to a Decline in

Deaths," Associated Press (October 2, 1998); "Fewer Youth Die by Gun, Data Show," Associated Press (September 24, 1997); Howard N. Snyder, "Juvenile Arrests 1995," *Juvenile Justice Bulletin* (February 1997), p. 8; "Checks Blocked 70,000 from Guns, US Says," Associated Press (September 5, 1997); Michael J. Sniffen, "Brady Law Checks Halted 69,00 Gun Sales in 1997," Associated Press (June 22, 1998); Russ Buettner, "City Gun Permits Are Falling Like Lead," *New York Daily News* (October 2, 1997), p. 5; "Brady Law Will Cover Rifles in November," Knight Ridder Service (August 9, 1998).

40. Paul Kandarian, "Gun Safety Is Father's Crusade," *Boston Globe* (February 1, 1998), p. B7.

41. E. Choi *et al.* "Deaths Due to Firearm Injuries in Children," *Journal of Forensic Sciences* (1994); *Child's Play: A Study of 266 Unintentional Handgun Shootings of Children,* (Washington, D.C.: Center to Prevent Handgun Violence, July 2, 1988); *Morbidity and Mortality Weekly Report* (February 7, 1997), p. 101.

42. Abbe Smith and Lael E.H. Chester, "Cruel Punishment for Juveniles," *Boston Globe* (July 17, 1996), p. A15.

43. James D. Wright and Joseph Sheley, "Teenage Violence and the Underclass," *Peace Review* (Fall, 1992), p. 35.

44. "Reno Promotes Youth Crime Prevention," Associated Press (September 11, 1997).

Chapter 4
Adult Trials and Prisons for Juveniles

1. Barry Krisberg, David Onek, Michael Jones and Ira Schwartz, "Juveniles in State Custody: Prospects for Community-Based Care of Troubled Adolescents," NCCD Focus (May, 1993), p. 6.

2. *Unlocking Juvenile Corrections: Evaluating the Massachusetts Department of Youth Services* (Washington, D.C.: National Council on Crime and Delinquency, 1991), p. 9.

3. *Ibid.,* p. 25.

4. Eileen McNamara, "Political Capital from a Tragedy," *Boston Globe* (October 11, 1997).

5. Gerald B. Lefcourt, "Congress Confronts the Baby Boomerang: Bad Ideas from People Old Enough to Know Better," *The Champion* (January/February 1998), p. 52; Melissa Sickmund, Howard N. Snyder

and Eileen Poe-Yamagata, *Juvenile Offenders and Victims: 1997 Update on Violence* (Washington, D.C.: National Center for Juvenile Justice, August 1997), p. 31.

6. Melissa Sickmund, Howard N. Snyder and Eileen Poe-Yamagata, *Juvenile Offenders and Victims: 1997 Update on Violence* (Washington, D.C.: National Center for Juvenile Justice, August 1997), p. 30, 39. Patricia Torbet, Richard Gable, Hunter Hurst IV, Imogene Montgomery, Linda Szymanski and Douglas Thomas, *State Responses to Serious and Violent Juvenile Crime* (Washington, D.C.: Office of Juvenile Justice and Delinquency Prevention, July 1996), p. 59; *Comprehensive Strategy for Serious, Violent and Chronic Juvenile Offenders* (Washington, D.C.: Office of Juvenile Justice and Delinquency Prevention, 1994), p. 5; Melissa Sickmund, Howard N. Snyder and Eileen Poe-Yamagata, *Juvenile Offenders and Victims: 1997 Update on Violence* (Washington, D.C.: National Center for Juvenile Justice, August 1997), p. 39; James Austin *et al. Juveniles Taken into Custody: Fiscal Year 1993—Statistics Report* (Washington, D.C.: Office of Juvenile Justice and Delinquency Prevention, September 1995); Bradette Jepsen, "Supervising Youthful Offenders," *Corrections Today* (June 1997), p. 68; Dale Parent, Terence Dunworth, Douglas McDonald and William Rhodes, *Transferring Serious Juvenile Offenders to Adult Courts* (Washington, D.C.: U.S. Department of Justice, January 1997), p. 1. Stanley Meisler, "Youths' Prison Plight Faulted," *Los Angeles Times* Syndicate (November 18, 1998).

7. Sean Hannity, *Hannity and Colmes*, Fox News (November 21, 1997).

8. Carolyn Skorneck, "Tougher Test for Young Defendants," Associated Press (May 9, 1997).

9. *Ibid.*

10. Ellen O'Brien, "Arkansas Case Reopens Child Justice Debate," *Boston Globe* (March 27, 1998), p. A24.

11. Melissa Sickmund, Howard N. Snyder and Eileen Poe-Yamagata, *Juvenile Offenders and Victims: 1997 Update on Violence* (Washington, D.C.: National Center for Juvenile Justice, August 1997), p. 31; John A. Butts and Howard N. Snyder, "The Youngest Delinquents: Offenders Under Age 15," *Juvenile Justice Bulletin* (September 1997) pp. 5, 7.

12. John A. Butts and Howard N. Snyder, "The Youngest Delinquents: Offenders Under Age 15," *Juvenile Justice Bulletin* (September 1997), pp. 5, 7. Melissa Sickmund, Howard N. Snyder and Eileen Poe-Yamagata, *Juvenile Offenders and Victims: 1997 Update on Violence* (Wash-

ington, D.C.: National Center for Juvenile Justice, August 1997), pp. 31, 42.

13. Marc Mauer and Tracy Huling, *Young Black Americans and the Criminal Justice System: Five Years Later* (Washington, D.C.: Sentencing Project, 1995).

14. "Hobbling a Generation II," *Report of National Center on Institutions and Alternatives* (Alexandria,VA: NCIA, 1992), p. 3; D. Altschuler, *The State of the Region: Youth Crime and Juvenile Justice in Maryland and Baltimore* (Baltimore: Johns Hopkins Institute for Police Study, Fall 1992), p. vi.

15. Jerome G. Miller, *Search and Destroy: African American Males in the Criminal Justice System* (London: Cambridge University Press, 1996)

16. Joe Clark, "Beyond the News," Fox News (July 11, 1998).

17. Jack Levin and Jack McDevitt,"Yes, We Need Hate Crime Laws," *Boston Globe* (July 28, 1998), p. A15; Jack Levin and Jack McDevitt, *Hate Crimes* (New York: Plenum Press, 1993).

18. Barbara Tatem Kelley, David Huizinga, Terence P. Thornberry, and Rolf Loeber, "Epidemology of Serious Violence," *Juvenile Justice Bulletin* (June 1997), p. 9; Teresa Howard, "Settin' It Off: Female Offenders Just May Be Juvenile Crime's Best Kept Secret," *The Source* (August 1997), p. 130; Sheila R. Peters and Sharon D. Peters, "Violent Adolescent Females," *Corrections Today* (June 1998), p. 28.

19. Ruth H. Wells, "America's Delinquent Daughters Have Nowhere to Turn," *Corrections Compendium* (1994).

20. Ric Kahn, "Among Young Women, Crime Is On the Rise," *Boston Globe* (December 11, 1996), p. B7.

21. Eileen Poe-Yamagata and Jeffrey A. Butts, "Female Offenders in the Juvenile Justice System," *Statistics Summary* (Washington, D.C.: Office of Juvenile Justice and Delinquency Prevention, June 1996), pp. 10–13.

22. Melissa Sickmund, Howard N. Snyder and Eileen Poe-Yamagata, *Juvenile Offenders and Victims: 1997 Update on Violence* (Washington, D.C.: National Center for Juvenile Justice, August 1997), pp. 31, 42.

23. Testimony of Mark I. Soler before the Youth Violence Subcommittee of the Judiciary Committee of the United States Senate on the Core Requirements of the Juvenile Justice Act and the Violent Juvenile and Repeat Offender Act of 1997.

24. *Ibid.*

25. Carolyn Skorneck, "Tougher Test for Young Defendants," Associated Press (May 9, 1997).

26. Jerry Gray, "Bill to Combat Juvenile Crime Passes House," *New York Times* (May 9, 1997), p. A1.

27. Gerald B. Lefcourt, "President's Column: Congress Confronts the Baby Boomerang: Bad Ideas from People Old Enough to Know Better," *Champion* (January/February 1998), p. 7.

28. Fox Butterfield, "Republicans Challenge Separate Jails for Juveniles," *New York Times* (June 24, 1996).

29. Fox Butterfield, "With Juvenile Courts in Chaos, Some Propose Scrapping Them," *New York Times* (July 21, 1997), p. 1.

30. Fox Butterfield, "States Revamping Youth Crime Laws," *New York Times* (May 12, 1996), p. 1.

31. Melissa Sickmund, Howard N. Snyder and Eileen Poe-Yamagata, *Juvenile Offenders and Victims: 1997 Update on Violence* (Washington, D.C.: National Center for Juvenile Justice, August 1997), p. 33.

32. Fox Butterfield, "Republicans Challenge Separate Jails for Juveniles," *New York Times* (June 24, 1996).

33. Fox Butterfield, "States Revamping Youth Crime Laws," *New York Times* (May 12, 1996), p. 1.

34. Fox Butterfield, "With Juvenile Courts in Chaos, Some Propose Scrapping Them," *New York Times* (July 21, 1997), p. A16.

35. Joyce Purnick, "Should Youth Crime Laws Be Tougher?," *New York Times* (May 9, 1996), p. B1.

36. "Pair Held in Slaying of Pizza Deliverers," Associated Press (April 22, 1997); Marc Peyser and T. Trent Gegax, "A Deadly Late-Night Delivery," *Newsweek* (May 5, 1997), p. 65.

37. Donna M. Bishop *et al.* "The Transfer of Juveniles to Criminal Court: Does It Make a Difference," *Crime and Delinquency* 171 (1996), p. 183; Jeffrey Fagan, "Separating the Men from the Boys: The Comparative Advantage of Juvenile Versus Criminal Court Sanctions on Recidivism Among Adolescent Felony Offenders," *A Sourcebook: Serious, Violent and Chronic Juvenile Offenders* Edited by James C. Sowell, *et al.* (Thousand Oaks, CA: Sage Publications, 1995). Marcy Rasmussen Podkopacz and Barry C. Feld, "The End of the Line: An Empirical Study of Judicial Waiver," *Journal of Criminal Law and Criminology* (1996), pp. 490–491; Eric L. Jensen and Linda K. Metsger, *Idaho Law Review* (1994), p. 174; Coalition for Juvenile Justice, "Few Juveniles Should Be Tried as Adults," *Juvenile Crime: Opposing Viewpoints* (San Diego: Greenhaven Press, 1997), p. 185.

38. Fox Butterfield, "With Juvenile Courts in Chaos, Some Propose Scrapping Them," *New York Times* (July 21, 1997), p. A16.
39. Lisa Stansky, "Age of Innocence," *ABA Journal* (November 1996), p. 61.
40. "Violent Juvenile Crime on Rise," *NACDL Legislative Policies* (Washington, D.C.: National Association of Criminal Defense Lawyers, off Internet May 23, 1997).
41. "Offenders Under Age 18 in State Adult Correctional Facilities: A National Picture," *Special Issues in Corrections No. 1* (1995).
42. Melissa Sickmund, Howard N. Snyder and Eileen Poe-Yamagata, *Juvenile Offenders and Victims: 1997 Update on Violence* (Washington, D.C.: National Center for Juvenile Justice, August 1997), pp. 36–37.
43. "Violent Juvenile Crime on the Rise," *NACDL Legislative Policies* (Washington, D.C.: National Association of Criminal Defense Lawyers; taken off Internet May 23, 1997), p. 5.
44. Lisa Stansky, "Age of Innocence," *ABA Journal* (November 1996), p. 62.
45. David Broder, "Funding Prevention Still Fights Crime Best," syndicated column (July 28, 1996).
46. Richard A. Mendel, "Prevention or Pork?," *Handsnet Headline* (Washington, D.C.: American Youth Policy Forum; posted on Internet January 24, 1996), p. 3.
47. Eric D. Jensen and Linda K. Metsger, "A Test of the Deterrent Effects of Legislative Waiver on Violent Juvenile Crime," *Crime and Delinquency* Vol. 40, No. 96 (1994).
48. "No Easy Answers: Juvenile Justice in a Climate of Fear," *1994 Annual Report* (Washington, D.C.: Coalition for Juvenile Justice, 1994), p. 29.
49. Timothy Egan, "Oregon Student Held in 3 Killings; One Dead, 23 Hurt at His School," *New York Times* (May 22, 1998), p. A1.
50. Fox Butterfield, "Republicans Challenge Separate Jails for Juveniles," *New York Times* (June 24, 1996).
51. "Jail Tops Campus in '95 U.S. Outlays," Reuters (February 25, 1997); David Nyhan, "Weld's Penny-Wise Texas Shuttle," *Boston Globe* (March 12, 1997), p. A19; *1995 State Expenditures Report* (Washington, D.C.: National Association of State Budget Officers, April 1996), pp. 77, 98; Fox Butterfield, "Crime Keeps On Falling, But Prisons Keep On Filling," *New York Times* (September 28, 1997), p. 4.

52. Steven Donziger, "The Hard Cell," *New York* magazine (June 9, 1997), p. 28.

53. "No Easy Answers: Juvenile Justice in a Climate of Fear," *1994 Annual Report* (Washington, D.C.: Coalition for Juvenile Justice, 1994); Jeffrey Fagan, *The Comparative Impacts of Juvenile and Criminal Court Sanctions on Adolescent Felony Offenders* (Washington, D.C.: National Institute of Justice, 1991).

54. Lisa Stansky, "Age of Innocence," *ABA Journal* (November 1996), p. 61.

55. Coalition for Juvenile Justice, "Few Juveniles Should Be Tried As Adults," *Juvenile Crime: Opposing Viewpoints* (San Diego: Greenhaven Press, 1997), p. 183.

56. Garry Cantrell, *ABC World News Tonight* (June 17, 1998).

57. "Four Year Old Drowns in Pool Game; No Charges," Associated Press (August 16, 1998).

58. Dan Bagdade, *ABC World News Tonight* (June 17, 1998).

59. Alan Colmes, *Hannity and Colmes*, Fox News (November 21, 1997).

60. "Little Criminals," *Frontline* Series (PBS December 2, 1997).

61. Jerry Adler and Peter Annin, "Murder at an Early Age," *Newsweek* (August 24, 1998), p. 28.

62. *Privacy and Juvenile Justice Records: A Mid-Decade Status Report* (Washington, D.C.: Bureau of Justice Statistics, May 1997); Neal Miller, "State Laws on Prosecutors' and Judges' Use of Juvenile Records," *Research In Brief* (November, 1995); Vincent Schiraldi and Mark Soler, *The Will of the People? The Public's Opinion of the Violent and Repeat Juvenile Offender Act of 1997* (Washington, D.C.: Justice Policy Institute and Youth Law Center, March 1998), pp. 7–8.

63. T. Markus Funk, "The Young and the Arrestless: The Case Against Expunging Juvenile Arrest Records," *Reason* (Reproduced on World Wide Legal Information Association web site, February 8, 1997).

64. David B. Kopel, *Guns: Who Should Have Them?* (New York: Prometheus Books, 1995), p. 354.

65. John Gibeault, "Who's Raising the Kids," *ABA Journal* (August 1997), p. 64; Robert E. Shepherd Jr., "Juvenile Justice: The Proliferation of Juvenile Curfews," *ABA Criminal Justice* (Spring 1997), p. 43.

66. Howard N. Snyder, Melissa Sickmund and Eileen Poe-Yamagata, *Juvenile Offenders and Victims: 1996 Update on Violence* (Washington, D.C.: Office of Juvenile Justice and Delinquency Prevention, February 1996), p. 27

67. *Ibid.;* Vincent Schiraldi, "Curfew Laws—No Panacea for Juvenile Crime," *JINN* (February 1, 1996), p. 2.
68. *Ibid.*, pp. 1–2; Mike Males and Dan Macallair, *The Impact of Juvenile Curfew Laws in California* (San Francisco: Center on Juvenile and Criminal Justice, June 1998).
69. E. Choi *et al.*, "Deaths Due to Firearm Injuries in Children," *Journal of Forensic Sciences* (1994); *Child's Play: A Study of 266 Unintentional Handgun Shootings of Children* (Washington, D.C.: Center to Prevent Handgun Violence, July 2 1988).
70. *Hutchins v. District of Columbia* 942 F. Supp. 665 (1996).
71. K.H. Chung, "Kids Behind Bars. The Legality of Incarcerating Juveniles in Adult Jails," *Indiana Law Journal* Vol. 69 (1991), pp. 999–1029; Eisikovits, Zvi and Michael Baizerman, "Doin' Time: Violent Youth in a Juvenile Facility and in an Adult Prison," *Journal of Offender Counseling Services and Rehabilitation* Vol. 6, No. 5 (1983); Martin Forst, Jeffrey Fagan and T. Scott Vivona, "Youth in Prisons and Training Schools: Perceptions and Consequences of the Treatment-Custody Dichotomy," *Juvenile and Family Court Journal* Vol. 40 (1989), p. 1.
72. Dale Parent, Terence Dunworth, Douglas McDonald and William Rhodes, "Transferring Serious Juvenile Offenders to Adult Courts," *Research in Action* (Washington, D.C.: National Institute of Justice, January 1997), p. 5.
73. Bruce Shapiro, "The Adolescent Lockup," *The Nation* (July 7, 1997), p. 7.
74. Testimony of Mark I. Soler before the Youth Violence Subcommittee of the Judiciary Committee of the United States Senate on the Core Requirements of the Juvenile Justice Act and the Violent Juvenile and Repeat Offender Act of 1997.
75. Fredricka Whitfield, *NBC Nightly News* (December 2, 1997); Christopher John Farley and James Willwerth, "Dead Teen Walking," *Time* (January 19, 1998), p. 50; Melissa Sickmund, Howard N. Snyder and Eileen Poe-Yamagata, *Juvenile Offenders and Victims: 1997 Update on Violence* (Washington, D.C.: National Center for Juvenile Justice, August 1997), pp. 44–45.
76. *Eddings v. Oklahoma* 455 U.S. 104 (1982); *Thompson v. Oklahoma* 487 U.S. 815 (1988).
77. Christopher John Farley amd James Willwerth, "Dead Teen Walking," *Time* (January 19, 1998), p. 50; Fredricka Whitfield, *NBC Nightly News* (December 2, 1997).

78. Jim Pitts, *Today* Show (April 20, 1998).

79. "Tougher Juvenile Sentencing Sought," Associated Press (December 29, 1998).

80. David B. Kopel, *Guns: Who Should Have Them?* (New York: Prometheus Books, 1995), p. 358.

81. Patrick F. Fagan, "The Breakdown of Families Causes Violence," *Violence: Opposing Viewpoints*. (San Diego: Greenhaven Press, 1996), p. 88.

82. David B. Kopel, *Guns: Who Should Have Them?* (New York: Prometheus Books, 1995), p. 359.

83. Lisa Stansky, "Age of Innocence," *ABA Journal* (November 1996), p. 63

84. Testimony of Mark I. Soler before the Youth Violence Subcommittee of the Judiciary Committee of the United States Senate on the Core Requirements of the Juvenile Justice Act and the Violent Juvenile and Repeat Offender Act of 1997.

Chapter 5
Shame: The Little-Known Secret of Crime

1. Joe Heaney, "Dirty Look Blamed in Stabbing at T Station," *Boston Herald* (January 24, 1996), p. 10.

2. John A. Rich and David A. Stone, *The Experience of Violent Injury for Young African-American Men: The Meaning of Being a "Sucker"* (Paper presented at the Society of General Internal Medicine Annual Meeting, Washington, D.C., April 1994). James Gilligan, *Violence: Our Deadly Epidemic and its Causes* (New York: Grosset/Putnam, 1996), p. 65.

3. *Ibid.*

4. James Wilson, "Television and Violence," Speech given at Claremont–McKenna College, California (aired on C-SPAN November 27, 1997).

5. Mark Starr and Allison Samuels, "Hoop Nightmare," *Newsweek* (December 15, 1997), p. 28.

6. Ron Borges, "Tyson's Fighting a Personal Battle," *Boston Globe* (June 25, 1998), p. F8.

7. *Brown v. Board of Education* 347 U.S. 483 (1954).

8. Frantz Fanon, *Black Skin, White Masks* (New York: Grove Press, 1967), p. 116.

9. Elijah Anderson, "The Code of the Streets," *Atlantic Monthly* (May 1994) p. 80.
10. John Lahr, "Sinatra's Song," *The New Yorker* (November 3, 1997), p. 84.
11. Carolyn Chute, *The Beans of Egypt, Maine* (New York: Ticknor and Fields, 1985).
12. Daniel Klaidman and Evan Thomas, "The Victim of His Virtues," *Newsweek* (April 14, 1997), p. 42; Joseph Contreras, "The Neighborhood Bully," *Newsweek* (April 14, 1997), p. 47; Daniel McGinn, "Deadbeat Nation," *Newsweek* (April 14, 1997), p. 50; "Letters: The Sultan Responds," *Newsweek* (April 14, 1997), p. 9.
13. Rod Steiger, on *Larry King Live*, CNN (April 5, 1997).
14. Garry Trudeau, "Doonesbury," syndicated comic strip (April 2 and 3, 1997).
15. Daniel Pedersen, "A Lonely Death in Texas," *Newsweek* (March 31, 1997), p. 53.
16. Melissa Sickmund, Howard N. Snyder and Eileen Poe-Yamagata, *Juvenile Offenders and Victims: 1997 Update on Violence* (Washington, D.C.: National Center for Juvenile Justice, August 1997), pp. 36–37.
17. David Lockwood, "Violence Among Middle and High School Students: Analysis and Implications for Prevention," *Research in Brief* (Washington, D.C.: National Institute of Justice, October 1997),pp. 1–2.
18. James Gilligan, *Violence: Our Deadly Epidemic and Its Causes* (New York: G.P. Putnam's Sons, 1996) pp. 45–46.
19. "Juveniles Could Face Chain Gangs," Associated Press (August 31, 1998).
20. Jeffrey Rosen, "The Social Police," *The New Yorker* (October 20 and 27, 1997), p. 175.
21. Debra Rosenberg, "Raising a Moral Child," *Newsweek* (Spring/Summer 1997), p. 93.
22. W.B. Miller, "American Youth Gangs. Past and Present," *Current Perspectives on Criminal Behavior* (New York: Alfred A. Knopf, 1974), p. 112.

Chapter 6
The Solution: Intervention, Families, Role Models, the Media and Rehabilitation

1. Wray Herbert, "Politics of Biology," *U.S. News and World Report* (April 21, 1997).

2. Colin Powell, "Why Service Matters," *Newsweek* (February 3, 1997), p. 36.
3. Joseph P. Shapiro with Dorian Friedman, Michele Meyer and Margaret Loftus, "Invincible Kids," *U.S. News and World Report* (November 11, 1996).
4. *Ibid.*
5. "On Volunteerism," *Boston Globe* (April 29, 1997), p. A3.
6. Ralph C. Martin speaking at the Boston Presidential Roundtable on Fighting Juvenile Crime at the University of Massachusetts (February 19, 1997).
7. Charles A. Radin, "Anti-Gang Group Faces Growing Problems," *Boston Globe* (May 26, 1998), p. A8.
8. Ralph C. Martin II, "Franklin Hill Turnaround," *Boston Globe* (March 8, 1998).
9. Jennifer Babson, "Bridging the Gap," *CommonWealth* (Summer 1996), p. 31.
10. Charles A. Radin, "Partnerships, Awareness Behind Boston's Success," Boston *Globe* (February 19, 1997), p. B7.
11. Jennifer Babson, "Community Policing," *CommonWealth* (Summer, 1996), p. 34.
12. Boston Police Captain Robert Dunford speaking at the Boston Presidential Roundtable on Fighting Juvenile Crime at the University of Massachusetts (February 19, 1997).
13. Jeffrey Brown speaking at the Boston Presidential Roundtable on Fighting Juvenile Crime at the University of Massachusetts (February 19, 1997).
14. John J. DiIulio Jr., Statement Before the United States Senate Subcommittee on Youth Violence (February 28, 1996).
15. Joe Klein, "In God They Trust," *New Yorker* (June 16, 1997), p. 48.
16. Michael Grunwald, "Looking to Boston for Homicide Solutions: Beset by Violent Street Crime, Minneapolis Copies an Intervention Plan," *Boston Globe* (August 3, 1997), p. A1.
17. Jean Baldwin Grossman and Eileen M. Garry, "Mentoring—A Proven Delinquency Prevention Strategy," *Juvenile Justice Bulletin* (April 1997).
18. Remarks of Christine Todd Whitman at the National Council on Crime and Delinquency Awards, Washington, D.C. (July 19, 1995).
19. Peter W. Greenwood, Karyn E. Model, C. Peter Rydell and James Chiesa, *Diverting Children from a Life of Crime: Measuring Costs and Benefits* (Santa Monica, CA: RAND Corp., 1996).

20. President Clinton speaking at the United States Justice Department Symposium on Youth Violence, Boston (June 11, 1997).
21. "The Cycle of Violence Revisited," *Research Preview* (Washington, D.C.: National Institute of Justice, February 1996).
22. Dolores Kong, "School Officials Didn't Order Boy into Counseling Because of Cuts," *Boston Globe* (May 23, 1998), p. A9.

Chapter 7
Conclusion: A 15-Point Plan

1. Barry Lopez in a speech before the American Bookseller's Expo, Chicago, aired on C-SPAN June 6, 1998.
2. "U.S. Prison Population Increased Nearly 6 Percent Last Year," Associated Press (January 19, 1998).
3. Jean Johnson, "Americans' Views on Crime and Law Enforcement," *National Institute of Justice Journal* (September 1997), p. 11.
4. *Criminal Justice in Massachusetts: The Public's View* (Boston: Mass INC, May 1997), p. 17.
5. "Police Leaders, Prosecutors, Crime Survivors Call for Greater Public Investments in Kids as Key to Fighting Crime," press release (Washington, D.C.: Fight Crime: Invest in Kids, July 26, 1996).
6. *Ibid.*
7. Remarks by Janet Reno at the National Forum on Youth Violence, Chantilly, Virginia (May 31, 1995).
8. Lori Montgomery, "A Divide on What's Fueling Youth Crime: Teens Raised for Violence or Just Well Armed," *Philadelphia Inquirer* (July 28, 1996), p. 1.
9. Dolores Kong, "Study Shows Cohesiveness Curbs Neighborhood Violence," *Boston Globe* (August 15, 1997), p. A9.
10. Darrell K. Gilliard and Allen J. Beck, *Prisoners in 1997* (Washington, D.C.: Bureau of Justice Statistics, August 1998), p. 3.
11. Neal Peirce, "Juvenile Crime Dip: Can We Build On It?," *Washington Post* (August 18, 1996).
12. Ted Gest with Victoria Pope, "Crime Time Bomb," *U.S. News and World Report* (March 25, 1996), p. 36.

Index

Abrahams, Nathaniel, 138
Acceptance, need for, 68
ADAPT, 199
African-Americans
    segregation, 171–172
    tried and punished as adults, 114–115
Alternatives to Incarceration program, 198
"America's Delinquent Daughters Have
        Nowhere to Run," 118
Amnesty International, 149–150, 152
Anderson, Elijah, 172
Anderson, Kerby, 64
Angotti, Joseph, 55
Arpaio, Joe, 41, 179
Arrests of young children, 39–41, 113, 135–
        142
Automatic transfer, 111

Bagdade, Dan, 138
Baird, Margaret, 65
Baker, Susan P., 95
Baldwin, Molly, 130, 132–133, 157, 183–
        185
Barkley, Charles, 203
Belton, Jayla, 138–139
Bennett, William, 4
Bergman, Roberta, 48–49
Big Brother/Big Sister program, 198
Biological predisposition to criminal be-
        havior, 44
Black Skin, White Masks (Fanon), 172
Blakey, G. Robert, 100
Blaming children, 66–69
Blitzman, Jay, 14
Blumstein, Alfred, 26, 43, 86–87, 89, 115
Bonding, maternal
    lack of, 34
Boston, 13, 189–194, 210

Boston Gun Project, 103, 209
Boston's Ten Point Coalition, 195–197
Brady Bill, 104
Breed, Allen, 127, 128
Brown, Jeffrey, 195–196
Buel, Sarah, 14

Caiazzo, Vito, III, 154–155
Callousness, 23
Cambodians, 115–116
Canada, crime and imprisonment in, 127
Cantrell, Garry, 135
Capital punishment: see Death penalty
Capone, Jerry, 32
Carcione, Louise, 194
Carneal, Michael, 79, 92
Carroll, James, 65–66
Child abuse and neglect, 52, 70, 72, 74, 75
    and fear of the death of one's soul, 178–
        179
Child care, 48–50, 208–209
Child care workers, requiring licenses for,
        49
Childrearing: see Parents
Children: see specific topics
Clark, Joe, 116
Clinton, Hillary Rodham, 63, 64
Clinton, President Bill, 188, 189, 197, 200
Cocaine, crack, 87
"The Code of the Streets," 172
Coles, Robert, xv, 16, 77, 78, 180
Colmes, Alan, 140
Colorado's Youth Offender System (YOS),
        157
Community, lack of, 60–66
Community disorganization effect, 87
Community policing, 193–197, 210
Competency: see Incompetency

Computer games, 58
Connolly, Thomas E., 23
Conscience, 180–181
    development of, 16
    lack of, 75, 161
Cooks, Voy, 115, 170, 176
Corrective facilities, juvenile, 7
Corriero, Michael, 124
Courts, juvenile, *see also* Juvenile offenders
    getting tougher, 134–135
Cousin, Shareef, 152–154
Crack cocaine, 87
Crime, *see also* Violent crime; *specific topics and crimes*
    before parents come home from work, 15, 47
    demographics, 75–76, 86
    drifting into world of, 17–18
    trends in and rates of, 5–6, 8–9, 23–25, 42, 56, 70–71, 75, 117–118
"Crime gene," 44
Crimes of the Heart, 95
Criminal identity, development of, 126
Culture, popular, 70
Curfews, 145–148
Curtis, John E., 176
"The Cycle of Violence Revisited," 201

Davely, Paul, 90
Day care: *see* Child care
Death, *see also* Life
    fascination with, 33
    viewed as game, 43–44, 90–92
Death penalty, 151–154, 208
Deterrence, xiv, 19
    myth of, 130–134, 154, 204
Dexter, Penna, 64
Dignity: *see* Respect
DiIulio, John J., Jr., 4, 6, 196
Disrespect: *see* Respect
Diverting Children from a Life of Crime, 200
Dole, Bob, 63–64
Domestic violence, children arrested for, 40–41
Drug offenses, 19
Drug selling, 176
Drugs
    guns and, 88–89
    war on, 38, 39, 114–115
Dunford, Bob, 194, 195
Dwyer, Kevin, 90

Eappen, Matthew, 28–29
Earls, Felton, 210–211
Elikann, Peter, xii, 161
Ellis, Bret Easton, 25
Empathy, youth lacking, 4, 23
Ethics: *see* Morality
Evans, Paul, 190, 191, 196

Fagan, Jeffrey, 126
Fairy tales, 59
Faith-based programs, 193–197, 209
Family
    disintegration of the, xiv, 44–50, 52
    lack of extended, 61
Family members shooting each other, 96–97
Family structure, importance of, 116, 187, 207
Fanon, Frantz, 172
Female juveniles
    increased crime among, 117–119
    leniency of legal system with, 120
Firearms: *see* Guns
Fleisher, Mark S., 74
Foster care, 70, 72
Fox, James Alan, 25, 43, 47
Frazier, Charles, 126
Frazier, Thomas, 48
French, Gary, 190
Friends shooting each other, 96–97

Gangs, 64–65, 67–69, 87–88, 163, 181
    guns and, 97–102
    prison, 129
Garcetti, Gil, 19, 124
Gay persons, violence against, 162–163
Gekas, George, 112
Gender differences, 116–119
Gerbner, George, 53, 56
Germany, crime and imprisonment in, 128
Gibson, John, 56
Gilligan, James, 73–74, 162, 164–166, 168, 178
Girls: *see* Female juveniles
Golden, Andrew, 81, 83–84, 91–93
Gonzalez, Rudy, 188
Goodman, Ellen, 49
Government: *see* Politicians; Social programs
Graham, David, 173–174
Greenfield, Meg, 11–12

Greer, Jane, 173–174
Grossberg/Peterson act of neonaticide, 34
Guggenheim, Benjamin, 77
Gun control, 10
Gun crime prevention, effectiveness of, 102–106
Gun laws, 103–104, 209
Gun projects, 102–106
Guns, 43
    access to, 81
        locking up guns, 92–94, 209
    background checks, 104
    deaths from, 43, 85, 86, 105, 106; see also Homicide
        accidental shootings, 91–92, 94
        suicides, 43, 86, 94–96
        victim-perpetrator relationship, 96–97
    "don't kill people," 91, 95
    drugs and, 88–89
    gangs and, 97–102
    make killing easier, 89
    prevalence, 82
    safety locks, 104
    in schools, 85–86, 89
    stolen, 92–93, 209
    as way of life, 80–89

Hannity, Sean, 112
Harris, Ryan, 135–137
Hatch, Orrin, 123–124
Hate crimes, perpetrators of, 116
Hawkins, Steven, 152
Hibbler, William, 124
Homicide, 9, 24, 27; see also Violent crime
    gun vs. nongun, 86; see also Guns, deaths from
Homosexuals, violence against, 162–163
Honor: see Respect
Hoover, Larry, 101
Howard, Ray, 141
Hulin, Rodney, Jr., 149–150
Humes, Edward, 25

Incompetency, juvenile, 135–142
Intervention, xii, 7, 183–185, 189–193, 197–201, 203–207, 210; see also specific interventions
    faith-based programs, 193–197, 209
    15-point plan, 207–211
"It's a Wonderful Life," 38

Jackson, Derrick Z., 57
Jealousy, 173–174
Jewett, Harold, 36
Johnson, Jean, 205
Johnson, Mitchell, 80–81, 83
Jordan, Roger, 152–154
Judicial waiver, 111
Juvenile offenders tried and punished as adults, xiii, xiv, 6, 13, 14, 19, 27, 35, 41, 56, 107–108, 208
    abandoning the old juvenile system, 122–125
    "blended sentences," 111–112
    doesn't necessarily result in longer sentences, 134–135
    endangers the public, 6–8, 19, 125–132, 149
    legislation by anecdote and, 108–109
    minorities, 114–116
    for nonviolent offenses, 120–122
    transfers to adult courts and prisons, 110–114, 125–127, 131, 208
Juvenile records, 142–145
    sealing, 143–145

Kagan, Sharon Lynn: see Child care
Kahan, Dan, 180
Kamin, Leon, 185
Kansas City Gun Experiment, 102
Kappelhoff, Mark, 10, 133
Kassel, Phillip, 41–42, 74–75, 107–108, 132, 151
Kennedy, David, 210
Kerlikowske, Gil, 128, 206
Keystone Kids, 72
Killing: see Homicide
Kinkel, Kipland, 69, 201
Kirn, Walter, 5
Kirwin, Barbara, 34
Kitzhaber, John, 69, 132
Klaas, Marc, 15
Klaas, Polly, 15
KlaasKids Foundation, xii
Knopf, Thomas, 130
Kopel, David, 144, 155
Krisberg, Barry, 10
Kupec, Bob, 186

Labeling, 179
Lamansky, Chad, 34–35

Latchkey kids, 17; *see also* Parents, being at home
Laws, juvenile crime, 10–11, 13, 121, 157
    anecdotally based, 14
    federal, impact on state courts, 122
    "get-tough," 13, 14, 161, 200
"Lean on Me," 116
LeBoeuf, Denise, 152
Lebowitz, Fran, 61
Lefcourt, Gerald, 122, 127, 132
Leggett, Levar, 23
Legislative exclusion, 111
Levin, Jack, 43, 48
Life, diminished value of human, 70, 90
Lin Chorn, 16
Liston, Sonny, 171
"Little Criminal," 141
Lockwood, Daniel, 177
Loners, 33
Louv, Richard, 40, 41
Lubow, Bart, 123

Mafia, 100
Males, Mike, 96
Malinga, Carl, 39
Martin, Ralph, 190
Massachusetts, 13, 14; *see also* Boston
    community-based programs in, 107
Massachusetts Department of Youth Services, 108
Massachusetts juvenile law, 108–109, 119
Mathieu, Marc, 104–105
McCarthy, Carolyn, 93
McCollum, Bill, 10–11
McNamara, Joseph, 8
Media, 56, 60, 207–208
Media violence, 52–55, 57–59, 79
Mendel, Richard, 131
Mentoring programs, 198, 210
Michaud, Donald L., 206
Miller, Arthur, 174
Miller, W. B., 181
Mitchum, Robert, 12
Moral Intelligence of Children (Coles), xv, 16
Morality, sense of, xv–xvi
    crisis in values and, 5
    lack of, 4
    teaching, 77
Mothers
    unfit, 71–72
    unmarried, 45–46

Motiveless crimes, myth of, 161–164
Moyers, Bill, xv–xvi
Murder rate, xiv; *see also* Homicide
Murphy, Patrick, 206
Murray, Lacresha, 138–139
Music industry, 57–58, 70
Myers, Daniel, 34–35
Myers, Tom, 97–98, 181
Myrick, Sue, 112

Neighborhoods, 61–63
    lack of community in, 61
    reclaiming, 62
Neonaticide, 34
New, Kenneth E., 101
New York City, 27
Nyhan, David, 133

O'Brien, Eddie, 13–14, 33–34, 109
Operation Night Light, 191, 198
Ortega, Ruben, 206

Parachini, Allan, 102
Parenting
    children having to raise themselves, xv
    poverty and, 71–72
Parents, *see also* Child abuse and neglect; Family
    being at home *vs.* at work, 15–17, 46, 48, 61, 208–209
Perry, Bruce, 73
Peters, Rebecca, 82
Phoung, Saroeum, 99, 163
Pine, Jeff R., 138
Pintard, John, 123
Pitts, Jim, 152, 154
Police chiefs, 13, 206
Politicians, blaming and vilifying children, 13, 41–42, 66, 70, 73, 148
Poverty
    growing, 50–52, 60, 75
    parenting and, 71–72
Powell, Colin, 61, 187
Prevention, xiii–xiv, 10, 203–207
    15 solutions to eradicate crime, 207–211
Prevention strategies, xii, 13, 15–16, 18, 20, 62, 107, 128; *see also specific programs*
    failure to enact, 25
Pride, positive aspects of, 180–181; *see also* Self-esteem

Prison(s)
    abuse of children in, 148–151
    adult, 6–8; *see also* Juvenile offenders
        crime rate and, 154–159
    alternatives to, 198, 208
    children denied protective custody, 150
    gangs in, 129
    intensify violent behavior, 126–127
    money spent on, 133
    staff, 149
    suicide in, 149–151
Promiscuity, 123
Property offenses, 120–121
Prosecuting Gangs: A National Assessment, 102
Prosecution, criminal, *see also* Juvenile offenders
    for misbehavior, 11–12
    of young children, 39–41, 135–142
Prosecutor discretion, 109, 111, 127, 155
"The Public's View," 205
Punishment(s), *see also* Death penalty; Deterrence
    corporal, 123
    shaming, 178–179

Racism, *see also* Hate crimes
    arrests and, 115–116
Racketeer Influenced and Corrupt Organization Act (RICO), 100, 101
Recidivism, 210
    sending youth to adult prison increases, 6–8, 19, 125–130
Rehabilitation, 7, 122–123, 183–186
Rehabilitation centers, community-based, 208
Reinharz, Peter, 25
Reno, Janet, 8, 106, 189, 207
"Resilient kids," 185–189
Respect, 119, 163–164, 181; *see also* Shame
    being a "sucker," 166–168
    being "dissed," 164–166, 172, 181
    "honor culture," 168–172
    pervasive need for, 172–176
Revenge, crime motivated by, 32
Rich, John A., 167–168
Richardson, Elliot, 20
Ridge, Tom, 110
Rights, voting, 13, 41–42
Rivers, Eugene, 197
Roberts, Steve, 95

ROCA, 183, 184
Rodriguez, Eric, 17–18, 98, 177, 183–185
Rodriguez, Richard, 62
Role models, lack of, 60–66
Ross L., 165–166
Rowan, Lynda, 53–54
Runaways, 118

Sampson, Robert J., 62
Sanders, Robert, 62–63
Scapegoat Generation (Males), 96
Scapegoating of children, 10, 66
    reasons for, 13, 41–42, 66
"Scarlet letter," 179
Scheidegger, Kent, 6
Schiraldi, Vincent, 10, 134
Schools
    afterschool programs and activities, 47–48, 208
    danger in suspending and expelling students, 209
    violence in, 26, 75–76, 79, 80, 85, 131–132, 162
    weapons in, 85–86, 89, 209–210
Schwartz, Michael, 39
Schwartz, Robert G., 13, 128
Segregation, racial, 171–172
Self-esteem, 163, 175, 178–181; *see also* Respect; Shame
Selfishness, 23
"Sending a message": *see* Deterrence
Sex, premarital, 47
    negative consequences, 45
Sexual promiscuity, 123
Shame, 174–177, 179–181; *see also* Respect
Shapiro, Bruce, 41
Sherman, Nancy Ajemain, 41
Shock Juvenile Awareness Program, 181
Silva, John, 89
Sinatra, Frank, 173
Skogan, Wendy G., 76
Smith, Logan Pearsall, 22
Social programs: *see* Intervention; Prevention
Sociopaths, youth crime wave not made up of, 75–78
Soler, Mark I., 8, 121, 150, 157
Solitary confinement, 123
South Park, 54
Special Olympics, 199

Spivak, Howard, 201
Sprewell, Latrell, 170–171
Status offenses, 120–121
Stereotyped profile, offenders who do not fit, 28–35
Stern, Donald, 193–194
Stewart, James, 38
Stone, David A., 167–168
Stuessey, Joseph, 57
"Suckers", young, urban, violent, 166–168
Suicide, xiv, 36–37, 69–75, 176
    diminished value of human life and, 70
    guns used for, 43, 86, 94–96
    in prison, 149–151
"Superpredators," xii, 4, 10, 11, 112, 121

Teen births, "out-of-wedlock," 45–46
Television violence: see Media violence
Three-strikes-and-you're-out program, 200
The Tough on Crime Myth: Real Solutions to Cut Crime (Elikann), 161
Traffic offenses, 120
Trauma, 73
Trinidad, Luis Omar, 137–138
Trudeau, Garry, 175
Tyson, Mike, 171

Unlocking Juvenile Corrections, 108

Values; see also Morality
    disturbed, 5, 43
    shared, 62
Victims of violence, young, 70–71
Video games, 58
Violence: Our Epidemic and Its Causes (Gilligan), 165

Violent crime, 3, 26; see also Crime; specific topics and crimes
    predictors of, 32–33
    rate of and trends in, 8–9, 75
        gender differences, 116–117
Violent Crime Control Act, 11
Violent Juvenile and Repeat Offender Act, 121, 157
Violent Youth Predator Act, 10–11
Voting rights, children's lack of, 13, 41–42

War on children, 40–44
Waters, John P., 4
Weapons, see also Guns
    in schools, 85–86, 89, 209–210
Webster, Daniel, 88–89
Weimholt, Vicky, 157
Wells, Ruth H., 118
Werner, Emmy, 187
West, Patricia L., 123
Weymouth, Steven, 75, 97, 109, 111, 156
Whiting, Darryl, 101
Whitman, Christine Todd, 199
Will, George, 50
Wilson, James, 52, 60, 65, 168, 169
Wilson, Pete, 152
Wilson, Suzette, 93
Wolfgang, Marvin, 211
Woodward, Louise, 28–29
Wynn, Jennifer, 66

Young, Rebecca, 11, 42, 129, 149, 155–156
Youth: see specific topics

Zamora, Diane, 173–174
Zamora, Ronny, 54–55